34 NEW Electronic Projects for Model Railroaders

MODEL RAILROAD HANDBOOK NO. 17

BY PETER J. THORNE

1 Introduction — page 2
2 Throttles — page 12
3 Simple projects — page 28
4 Intermediate and advanced projects — page 34
5 Sound circuits — page 45
6 Signaling systems — page 55
7 Command control — page 64
8 Radio control and computers — page 72

Editor: Burr Angle   Art Director: Lawrence Luser
Editorial Assistant: Marcia Stern   Artist: Bill Scholz

Color photo on front cover by Barney Bayliss, Toronto, Canada

Distributed by:
Airlife Publishing Ltd.
101 Longden Road, Shrewsbury SY3 9EB, England

FIRST EDITION, 1982. Second printing, 1986. Third printing, 1988. SECOND EDITION, 1990. Second printing, 1993.

© 1982 and 1990 by Peter J. Thorne. All rights reserved. This book may not be reproduced in part or in whole without written permission from the publisher, except in the case of brief quotations used in reviews. Published by Kalmbach Publishing Co., 21027 Crossroads Circle, P. O. Box 1612, Waukesha, WI 53187. Printed in the U. S. A. Library of Congress Catalog Card Number: 82-81375. ISBN: 0-89024-039-6.

Printed in United States

1 Introduction

THE ELECTRONIC projects in this book can be assembled by anyone who has had a little experience working with components, soldering irons, and, for some projects, printed circuit boards. If the concept of a printed circuit board is new to you the following sources provide information in detail.

The making of a "PCB," though not covered here, is explained in detail in a Radio Shack kit, part number 276-1576. Rub-on transfers for making the tracks are included in the kit or are available separately (276-1577). These numbers are from the 1933 catalog. Another source for these electronic transfers and printed circuit making materials is Datak Corporation, 3117 Paterson Plank Road, North Bergen, NJ 07047. Datak offers a kit to transfer the PCB layout directly from the printed page (as in this book) to a copper plated board for etching. This is probably the easiest method for the hobbyist. One of Datak's distributors is Jameco Electronic Components (address on the table, this page).

Components

The "where to buy" situation for electronic components has changed since this book was first printed. Some of the Radio Shack part numbers quoted have become obsolete because the mix of their catalog has changed and been reduced. There are, however, at least three major electronics components distributors that not only have large ranges of components but will also ship mail orders with a reasonable minimum order value. (See table, this page.)

They have free (at the time of writing) catalogs. Digi-Key and Mouser both have generic descriptions of the components that will enable you to convert easily the component description in this book to their part number. For example, Digi-Key has a wide range of electrolytic capacitors under the manufacturer's name of Panasonic. Mouser has a similar range under Xicon. The descriptions in their catalogs cover dimensions, shapes, values and voltages. This is more than adequate for you to achieve a cross reference. Similarly, film capacitors, resistors, relays, potentiometers, transistors, and integrated circuits are all cataloged. The Jameco catalog is less detailed, so it requires a general knowledge of components.

Industrial electronic distributors

If Radio Shack fails you as a component source, and you live in an area of electronics manufacturers, chances are there is a branch of one of the larger equipment maker distributors within striking range. These are listed in most Yellow Pages directories under the category of industrial electronics distributors. Most have several branches across the country. If the local branch as a walk-in sales counter, you will have a source of components at very reasonable prices together with (sometimes!) some technical help in cross referencing. Obviously you should phone first to verify they will sell direct. My favorite source is Electro Sonic, in Toronto, Canada. Their service is excellent and fast; somewhat akin to a new car dealer's parts department. A smart distributor knows that service is a way to combat competition in today's tough environment. Today's small customer (you) may well be tomorrow's major account.

Ideally there should be a catalog for reference, though the industrial distributors have large catalogs and will not donate these to individuals, only to corporations. Here are some electronic distributors that have catalogs: Newark Electronics; Active Components (a division of Future Electronics); and Allied Electronics Inc.(a subsidiary of Hall-Mark Electronics Corporation). Active and Newark also have Canadian locations. Three other distributors are Arrow Electronics Inc.; Hamilton/Avnet; and Kent Components Distribution.

Magazine advertisers

Suppliers of electronics components advertise in the hobby magazines, such as MODEL RAILROADER and *Model Railroad Craftsman*. The components are mostly throttle parts or lamps, light emitting diodes, and switches.

A much wider range of components, sometimes manufacturers' surplus at low prices, can be found advertised in the magazine *Electronics Now*, formerly known as *Radio Electronics*. This is available at many newsstands, and is a good source for relays, switches, transistors, diodes, and integrated circuits.

Difficult components

In the past, readers had some difficulty in sourcing CdS (cadmium sulfide) photocells as used for track detection in some circuits. These, when listed as a five-pack from Radio Shack (276-1657), are not always suitable as their values are not defined. Digi-Key now has a range. Its 338-54C348 is suitable.

Reed switches have also proved difficult. A manufacturer is Hasco Components International Corp., 247-40 Jericho Turnpike, Floral Park, N.Y. 11001. Phone (516) 328-9292. Their ORD-221 part suits all applications in this book. Another maker is Hamlin Inc., 612 East Lake St., Lake Mills, WI 53551. Phone (414) 648-3000. Newark Electronics is a Hamlin distributor.

Small, but powerful magnets for triggering reed switches are available from Edmund Scientific, 101 E. Gloucester Pike, Barrington, NJ 08007-1380, phone 6099-573-6350. A suitable (25 pack) is their D38,685. A catalog is available.

Let's move on to descriptions of the components themselves. The information presented here is in response to inquiries received about my construction articles in MODEL RAILROADER magazine. Figure 1-1 shows the symbols used for the most common components used in the projects: refer to this drawing as you read the description of each part.

Resistors, Fig. 1-2, are used to restrict the flow of current or reduce voltage. They are rated in ohms, kilohms (ohms x 1.000), or megohms (ohms x 1,000,000). The symbols are Ω, $k\Omega$, and $M\Omega$. Resistors are also rated in terms of the power they can dissi-

---

Black	0	0	X1	
Brown	1	1	X10	
Red	2	2	X100	
Orange	3	3	X1,000	
Yellow	4	4	X10,000	
Green	5	5	X100,000	
Blue	6	6	X1,000,000	
Violet	7	7		
Gray	8	8		
White	9	9		

Multiplier — Tolerance

Tolerance	Color
1%	Brown
2%	Red
5%	Gold
10%	Silver
20%	No color

RESISTOR COLOR CODE

Component catalog suppliers (mail order)

The following electronic component distributors offer free catalogs and will supply individuals by mail order. Note they have very reasonable minimum billing and shipping charges, but as they are primarily component suppliers to industry, please try to order all your requirements at one time.

Digi-Key Corporation, 701 Brooks Avenue, South, P.O. Box 677, Thief River Falls, MN 56701-0677. Phone 1-800-992-9943 for catalog; 1-800-346-6873 for orders, customer service and assistance in USA, Canada and Puerto Rico.

Mouser Electronics, (four locations in the U.S.). Phone 1-800-992-9943 for catalog; 1-800-346-6873 for orders, customer service and assistance in USA, Canada and Puerto Rico.

Jameco Electronic Components, 1355 Shoreway Road, Belmont, CA 94002. Phone 1-800-831-4142, fax 1-800-237-6848. The Jameco catalog lists also an extensive range of computers and peripheral equipment.

Fig. 1-1 SYMBOLS

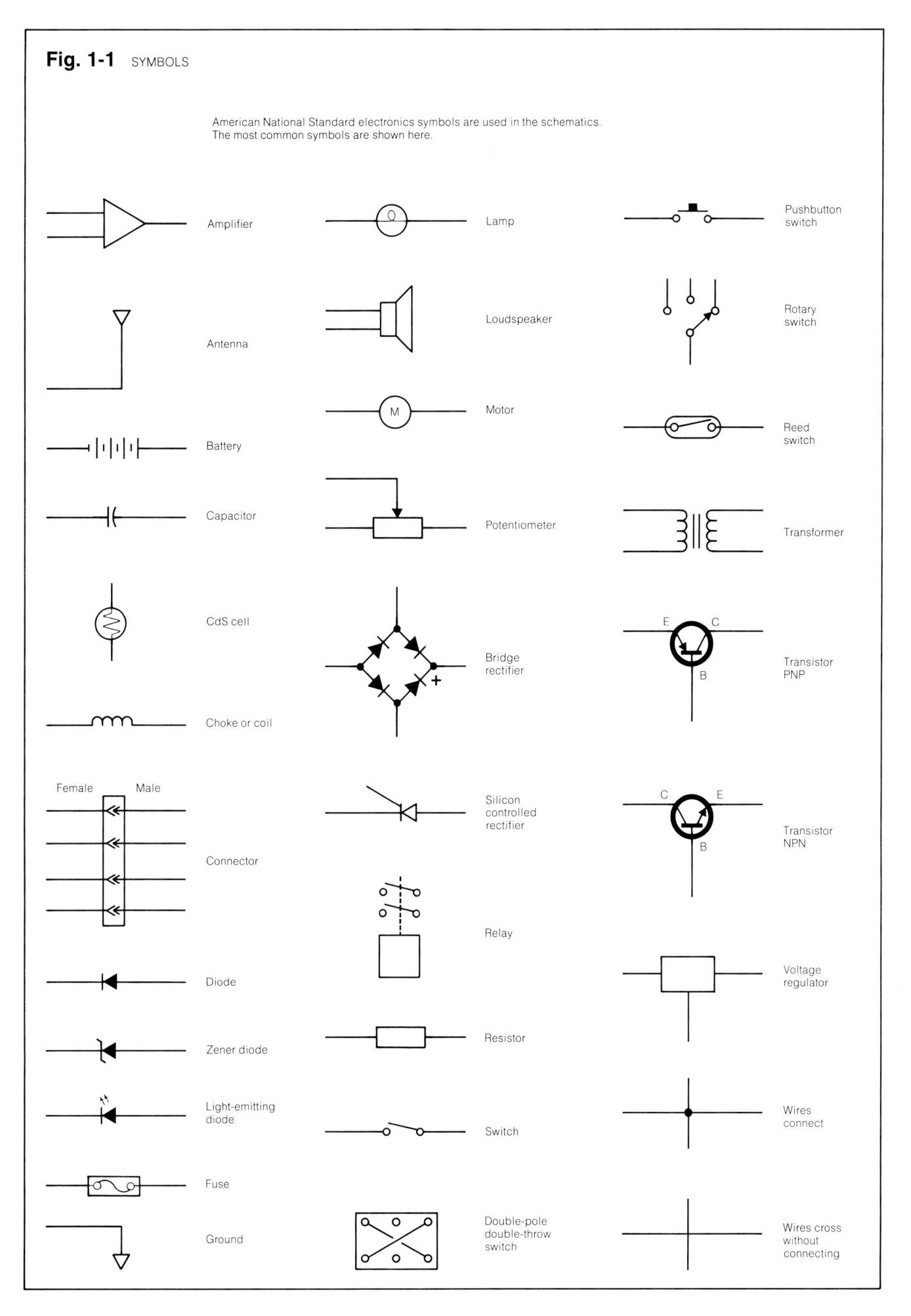

American National Standard electronics symbols are used in the schematics. The most common symbols are shown here.

Symbol	Name
—	Amplifier
—	Antenna
—	Battery
—	Capacitor
—	CdS cell
—	Choke or coil
—	Connector (Female / Male)
—	Diode
—	Zener diode
—	Light-emitting diode
—	Fuse
—	Ground
—	Lamp
—	Loudspeaker
—	Motor
—	Potentiometer
—	Bridge rectifier
—	Silicon controlled rectifier
—	Relay
—	Resistor
—	Switch
—	Double-pole double-throw switch
—	Pushbutton switch
—	Rotary switch
—	Reed switch
—	Transformer
—	Transistor PNP
—	Transistor NPN
—	Voltage regulator
—	Wires connect
—	Wires cross without connecting

3

FIG. 1-2. Physical size is a good indicator of a resistor's power rating. These range from 0.25 W (far left) to 4 W (far right).

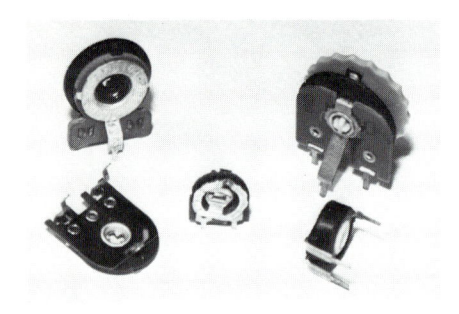

FIG. 1-3. These small trim potentiometers mount on printed circuit boards. Many of the projects use similar low-wattage potentiometers to control integrated circuit timing devices.

pate as heat. This heat-dissipating rating is stated in watts (W). Most resistors used in the projects in this book are 0.25 W, but if your supplier can only provide 0.5-W resistors, use them. They're only slightly larger than 0.25-W resistors, so will usually fit on the printed circuit board. Avoid 2-W and 5-W resistors, though, unless they're specifically called for, because they take up too much room.

You should have no difficulty obtaining the resistors called for in the parts lists. Although the ratings sound odd, e.g. 33 Ω or 47 Ω or 560 Ω or 68 kΩ, these are standard international values.

Resistors usually come in 5-percent or 10-percent tolerances (plus or minus percentages of the nominal value). Either tolerance is acceptable for the circuits in this book. Precision resistors with a tighter tolerance (1 or 2 percent) are not required for these projects, but may be used if you have some on hand. You may save money if you buy a resistor package containing 100 to 500 assorted pieces. Carefully check color-coded values with the color code on page 2, or if you're color-blind, check values with an ohmmeter. For the projects in this book it doesn't matter whether the resistors are composition, carbon film, or metal film: Any of these types can be used.

Potentiometers. These, Fig. 1-3, are variable resistors with a sliding contact which acts as a third connection to tap voltage from the resistor body. None exceeds 0.5 W in these circuits.

Capacitors

Capacitors are defined by their capacitance value, voltage rating, and physical type.

Electrolytic capacitors. These have large capacitance values, most often from 2 to more than 5000 microfarads (μF) and they have coarse tolerances (usually minus 20 percent to plus 50 percent of nominal value). They come in both axial-leaded and radial-leaded packages, Figs. 1-4 and 1-5. Use either. If you can't find an electrolytic capacitor with the exact value specified in the parts list, substitute one with a similar value. For example, if I've specified a 2200-μF capacitor, a 2000-μF or even a 3000-μF capacitor is perfectly acceptable.

COMPONENT MANUFACTURERS

Capacitors
Mepco/Electra, Inc.
Columbia Road
Morristown, NJ 07096
(201) 539-2000

Mallory Capacitor/Distributor Co.
4760 Kentucky Avenue
Indianapolis, IN 46241
(317) 856-3731

Integrated circuits
National Semiconductor
2900 Semiconductor Drive
Santa Clara, CA 95051
(408) 737-5000

Motors
The Pittman Corporation
Harleysville, PA 19438
(215) 256-6601

Optoelectronics
Litronix, Inc.
19000 Homestead Road
Cupertino, CA 95014
(408) 257-7910

Clairex Electronics
560 South 3rd Avenue
Mount Vernon, NY 10550
(914) 664-6602

Relays
Deltrol Controls
2745 South 19th Street
Milwaukee, WI 53215
(414) 671-6800

Potter and Brumfield
200 Richland Creek Drive
P. O. Box 322
Princeton, IN 47671
(812) 386-1000

Resistors
R. Ohm
16931 Milliken Avenue
P. O. Box 19515
Irvine, CA 92713
(714) 546-7750 (East Coast [312] 843-0404)

Allen-Bradley
1201 South 2nd Street
Milwaukee, WI 53204
(414) 671-2000

Switches
Alco Electronic Products, Inc.
1551 Osgood Street
North Andover, MA 01845
(617) 685-4371

Cutler-Hammer, Specialty Products Div.
4201 North 27th Street
Milwaukee, WI 53216
(414) 442-7800

Transformers
Essex/Stancor Products
3501 West Addison Street
Chicago, IL 60618
(312) 463-7400

Hammond Manufacturing Company
1690 Walden Avenue
Buffalo, NY 14225
(716) 894-5710

Transistors, SCRs
Motorola Semiconductor
P. O. Box 20912
Phoenix, AZ 85036
(602) 244-6900

Voltage regulators
Lambda Electronics Division of VEECO Instruments Inc.
515 Broad Hollow Road
Melville, NY 11746
(516) 694-4200

(Above) FIG. 1-4. An electrolytic capacitor may have radial leads for easy horizontal mounting. (Right) FIG. 1-5. Electrolytic capacitors with axial leads are easy to mount vertically, saving space.

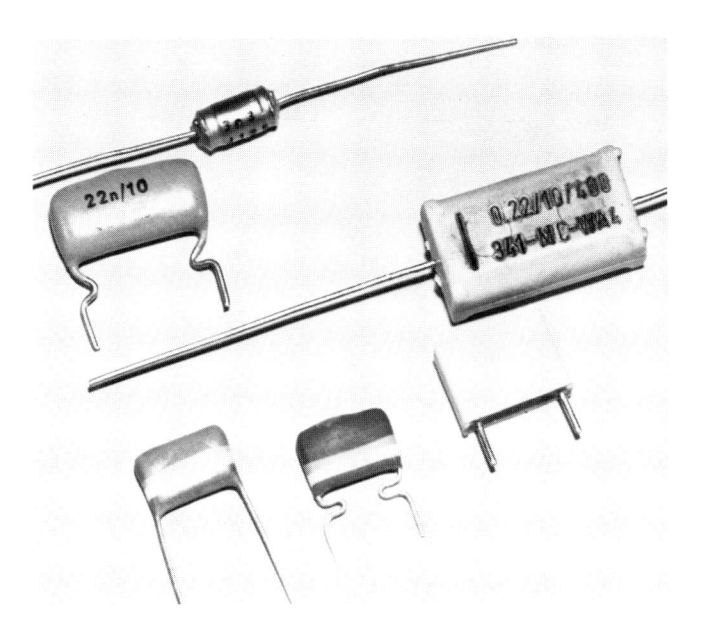

FIG. 1-7. Film capacitors come in many sizes and shapes.

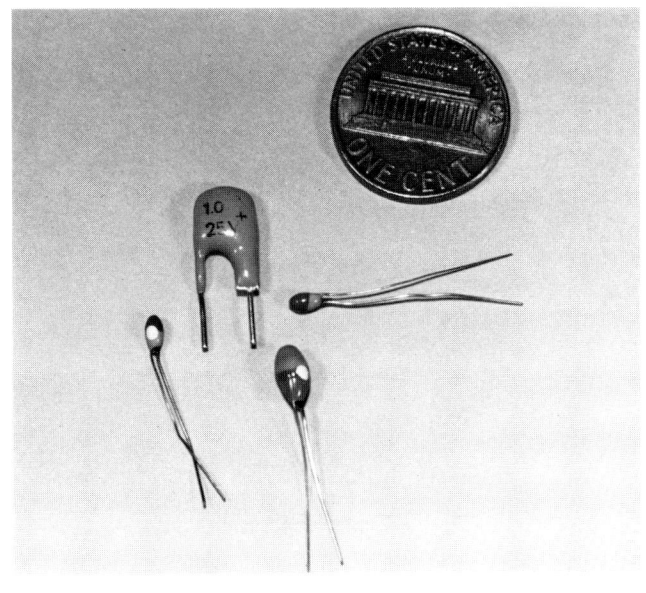

FIG. 1-6. Use solid aluminum (larger device) and tantalum capacitors whenever specified.

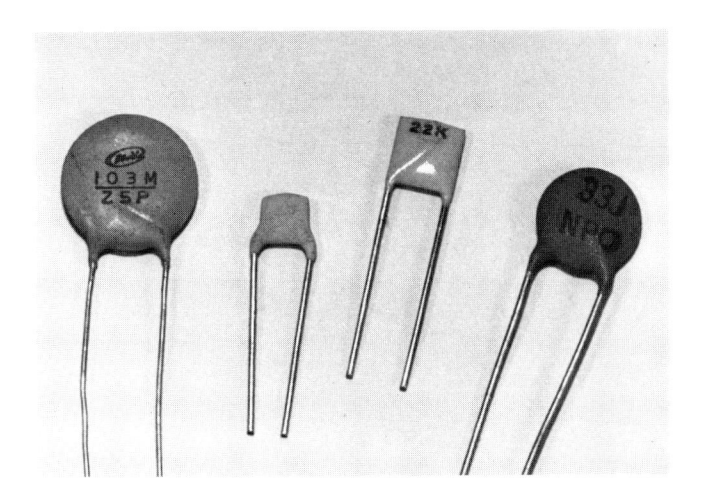

FIG. 1-8. The capacitance and voltage rating of ceramic, or disk, capacitors is usually printed on the device, but may be color-coded with the same code used for resistors.

FIG. 1-9. Many of the projects use medium power transistors (left) and small signal transistors (right). Always use the type and part numbers specified.

Electrolytic capacitors are most often available in voltages from 2.5 to 100. If you have to consider a substitute, always take the next higher voltage rating, never a lower one. Most electrolytic capacitors are sensitive to electrical polarity and the leads are marked + and −. They must always be wired as shown in the figures.

Tantalum or solid aluminum capacitors. These have closer tolerances and are more expensive than other electrolytic capacitors, Fig. 1-6. Don't use them unless they are called for in the parts list. Never reverse + and − on a tantalum capacitor.

Film capacitors. These, Fig. 1-7, have lower capacitance values than electrolytic types. They are called film capacitors because an insulating, or dielectric, film is used between the two capacitor connections or plates. For the circuits in this book, it doesn't matter if the film is paper, polycarbonate, polyester, PETP, or Mylar. For these projects, choose film capacitors rated for at least 100 V — those with even higher voltage ratings can be used, but there's no point in doing so.

Catalog listings of the capacitance values of film capacitors may be confusing to read. Until recently the value was uniformly stated in microfarads, just as with electrolytic capacitors. Common values ranged from 0.005 µF to 4.7 µF. Several manufacturers are now stating capacitance in "nanofarads" (nF). A nanofarad is one-thousandth of a microfarad. Thus, 10 nF = 0.01 µF, and 100 nF = 0.1 µF. This book uses "µF" throughout, but some catalogs may require you to convert the values. If a film capacitor is color-coded, the units are picofarads (pF) and the color code is the same as that used for resistors. (A picofarad is one-millionth of a microfarad.)

Film capacitors usually have a tolerance of 10 or 20 percent. A 20-percent 0.1-µF capacitor can have an actual value from 0.8 µF to 0.12 µF. There is usually no problem using a 5-percent or 10-percent film capacitor to replace one with a 20-percent tolerance — or vice versa. Further, unless the film capacitor specified is a high-precision type, you may substitute a tantalum capacitor to save space.

The physical form of film capacitors varies widely: They can be tubular or rectangular, and may have radial or axial leads. Film capacitors are not polarity sensitive, so are not marked + and −.

Ceramic capacitors. Also known as disk capacitors, Fig. 1-8, these have the smallest capacitance values, from less than 1 pF to about 0.1 µF. Not all ceramic capacitors are disk-shaped; some are rectangular and are usually called "plate" capacitors. So far as we are concerned, all styles are interchangeable. Use care in selecting voltage ratings: Choose ceramic capacitors rated for at least 50 V; 100 V is even better.

For most model railroad applications the coarsest tolerance is acceptable. This is indicated "GMV," which stands for "guaranteed minimum value" and which indicates a tolerance of minus 20 percent, plus 50 percent of the nominal value. "Z5U" and "Z5F" are two other widely used codings indicating normal tolerance and temperature characteristics.

In rare cases where a close tolerance is required, a 2-percent tolerance and "NPO" might be applicable. The "NPO" means that the capacitor's characteristics are not affected by even major changes in the ambient temperature. Close tolerance is required when the capacitor is used in a tone- or frequency-controlled circuit, as in the bell sound circuit described in Chapter 5. Ceramic capacitors are physically small, only slightly larger than tantalum capacitors. Packages of assorted disk capacitors are often a good buy: Radio Shack's package of 100 (272-801) sells for less than $2.00.

There are many other types of capacitors, including those with polypropylene or mica dielectrics, but most are more expensive than the types I've described, and none is used in these projects.

Transistors

Many projects in this book use transistors as amplifiers or switches. Let's examine the types of transistors you'll be using.

NPN and PNP transistors. In an NPN transistor, the power supply +, or positive, voltage goes directly or indirectly to the collector, and the −, or negative, voltage ends up at the emitter. In a PNP transistor these connections are reversed. The two types must not be substituted: Never use a PNP in an NPN circuit or vice versa. I have usually specified NPN transistors because they are more common. Always wire a transistor into the circuit as shown in the figures.

Silicon and germanium transistors. Silicon transistors are better for our purposes than germanium transistors because they can operate at higher temperatures. Early model railroad transistor throttle designs used germanium transistors simply because they were the only types available. Silicon transistors have driven germanium transistors from the market: Only a few manufacturers make germanium types these days.

Darlington amplifiers. These are simple integrated circuits consisting of two transistors in one case. The collectors are connected together and the emitter of one is connected to the base of the other. Also included are a pair of resistors and a diode. Darlington amplifiers are convenient wherever a design requires that one transistor drive another. They're readily available, so I've used them in the throttles to simplify construction.

Small transistors. The physical size of a transistor is a fair indicator of how much current it can handle, Fig. 1-9. As a rule, small transistors can switch about 0.1 A, compared to 1 A for medium power transistors and 15 A for some large power transistors.

All of the small transistors specified in this book have 3 leads, most are NPN types, and you must be careful when choosing substitutes, because even though the case may be identical, the arrangement of the base, emitter, and collector leads may not be the same. If you use a substitute, always check the arrangement of the leads. In general, you can substitute transistors with higher gain, voltage, or current ratings than those I've specified. Of course, you should never substitute transistors with lower gain, voltage, and current ratings.

Power transistors. Power transistors come in a wide variety of packages, although the TO-220, TO-202, and TO-3 cases are most popular, Fig. 1-10. The cases allow these transistors to dissipate quite a bit of heat, but very large currents require external heat sinks. Heat sinks are available for all types of power transistor cases. Always use a heat sink if it is called for in the assembly instructions. The heat sink must be electrically insulated with a mica washer or plastic bushing, and thermally conductive silicone grease is used to ensure adequate heat transfer. Transistor sockets may be used whenever space permits. If space is limited, simply solder the transistor leads to the printed circuit board or to the appropriate wires or lugs, being careful, as always, that the emitter, base, and collector are correctly oriented.

Diodes

Germanium and selenium diodes were once common, but modern semiconductor diodes are made of silicon, Fig. 1-11. As the name implies, diodes have only two

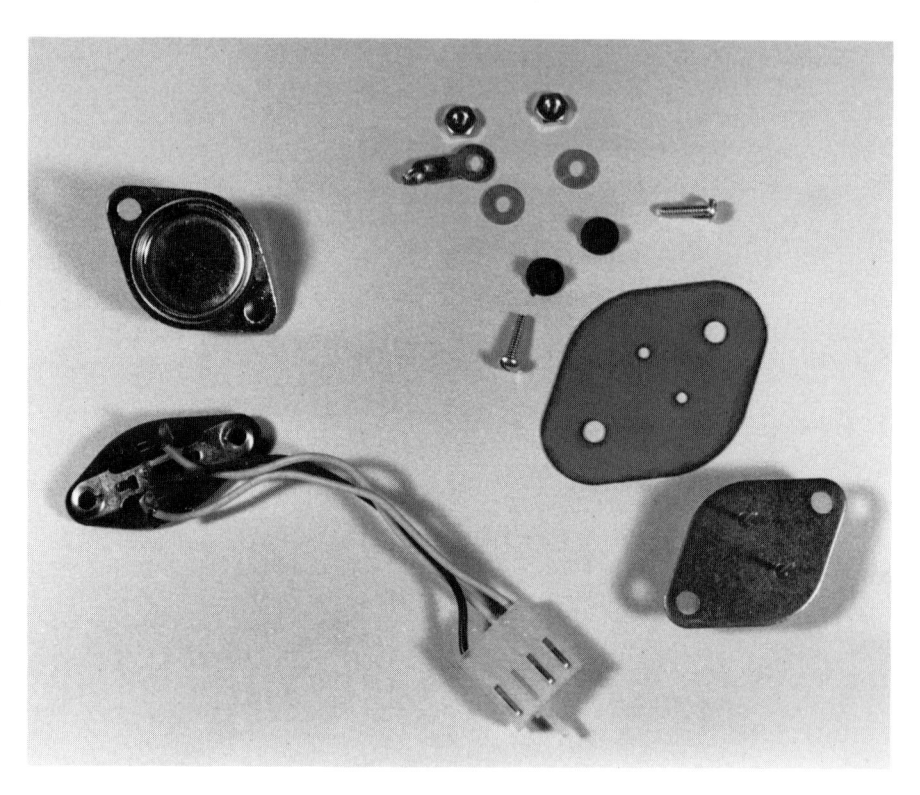

FIG. 1-10. This large power transistor is in a TO-3 case and will be mounted with the hardware to its right.

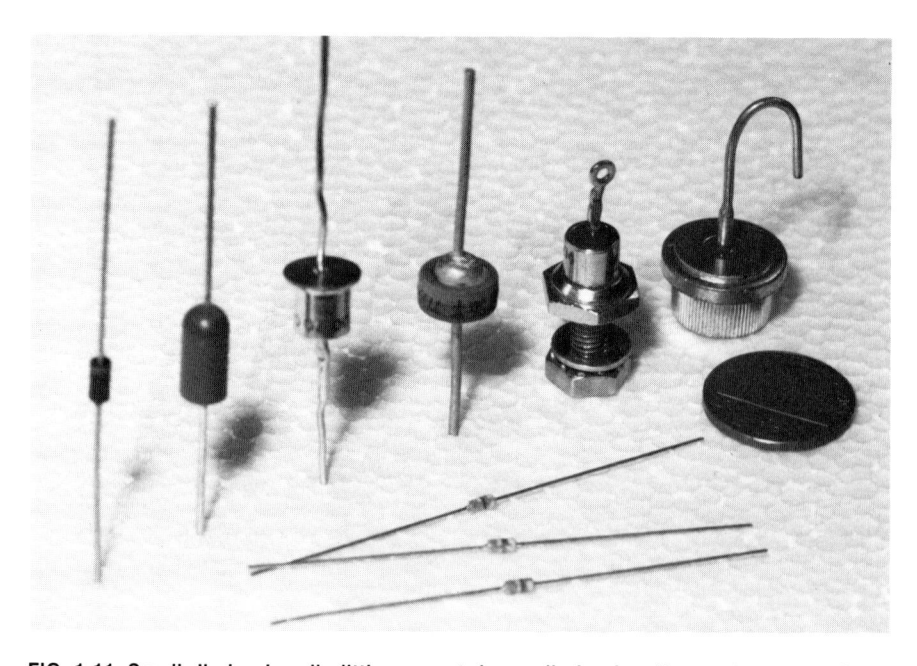

FIG. 1-11. Small diodes handle little current; large diodes handle much more and are packaged for maximum heat-dissipating ability.

FIG. 1-12. From left to right, bridge rectifiers rated at 1, 2, 3, and 4 amperes. Bridge rectifiers are used in many power supplies.

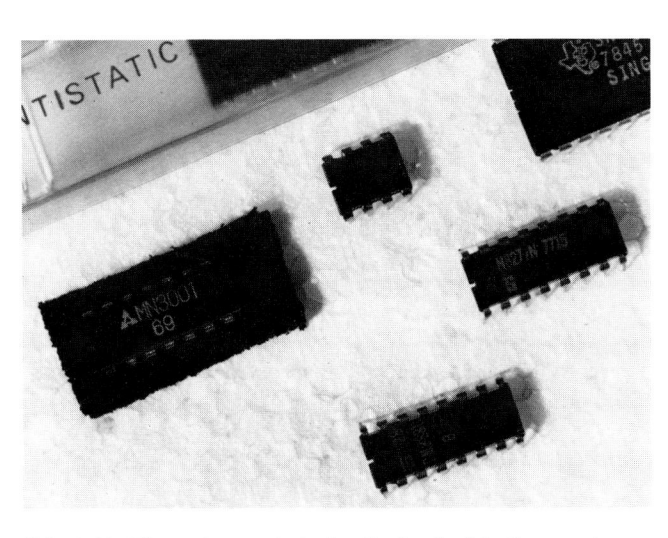

FIG. 1-13. These integrated circuits in dual in-line packages have from 8 to 40 pins. The 555 timer in an 8-pin DIP is the most frequently used IC in these projects.

leads, an anode and a cathode. The cathode terminal is indicated by a dot, a color band, a tapered section of the case, or in some other way. Diodes must always be wired into the circuit with the cathode lead oriented as shown in the figures. A bridge rectifier, Fig. 1-12, is simply four diodes in one case; I've used them in many power supplies because they are convenient and take up less space than four separate diodes.

If you must substitute diodes or bridge rectifiers, always choose those with higher-than-specified voltage and current ratings: This will provide extra reliability at only a small increase in cost. Never use a smaller rectifier or diode than I've specified; it simply won't be able to handle either the average or peak loads required by the circuit. A power supply rectifier designed for an average current of 3 A may have to handle capacitor-induced peak loads of 50 A. Therefore, choose diodes and rectifiers carefully and keep in mind the big difference between average and peak current ratings.

Special semiconductors

Special semiconductors used in the projects include Darlington amplifiers, silicon controlled rectifiers, triacs, and voltage regulators. I've already described Darlington amplifiers; now let's examine the other types.

Silicon controlled rectifiers. Most often called SCRs, these are three-terminal semiconductor devices that switch on when a voltage is applied to the "gate" electrode. They're often used in throttles and in controls for switch machine motors. As with diodes, substitute only devices with a higher current rating than specified.

Triacs. Another three-terminal device, triacs have two anodes and a gate. A triac does not rectify, instead it regulates the flow of alternating current. Triacs are found in incandescent light dimmers, and special versions can be used in AC throttles for Lionel and Märklin trains. In a throttle, the triac must be installed on the low-voltage side of the transformer.

Voltage regulators. These are small integrated circuits in transistor cases. They are used to provide a fixed DC output voltage from a filtered and slightly higher DC input voltage. In addition, voltage regulators turn off if overloaded and turn on again when the overload is removed. In this book, they're used in power supplies, throttles, and constant lighting circuits. Voltage regulators are designed to stabilize either positive or negative voltage: All the regulators in the projects are the positive type. Never substitute a negative for a positive regulator. Positive regulators from different manufacturers may be substituted as long as the type number and output voltage are the same. Always use a heat sink if it is specified in the assembly instructions.

Integrated circuits

Because they replace many discrete (individual) components, integrated circuits (ICs) greatly simplify construction projects. Integrated circuits can be broadly classified as analog or digital. Digital ICs act as switches or gates. They're the heart of computer chips; they count, divide, and memorize. Analog (or linear) ICs are amplifiers, oscillators, and timers. We use both types in model railroad electronics.

Integrated circuits may be packaged in transistor or other cases, but are most often available in a "dual in-line package" (DIP), Fig. 1-13. A DIP has two parallel rows of terminals (pins) at right angles to the body. The pins are inserted into a socket on the printed circuit board. Some DIPs have only 4 pins, but most have 8, 14, or 16 pins, and a few have many more.

Identifying ICs. Integrated circuits are usually identified by a code consisting of two letters followed by three or more digits. The digits may be followed by one or more letters. The digits identify the device (all manufacturers use the same digits for the same circuit). If present, the last letter or letters identify the type of package. For example, "NE555N" tells you that the device is a 555 timer and the package is an 8-pin DIP.

You should use the device and the package I've specified, because I've chosen ICs that are easily available and will do the best job for the least money. You'll notice that every project in this book which requires a 555 timer uses the 8-pin DIP version (Radio Shack 276-1723). If you have sufficient data, you could, of course, substitute other versions of this IC, but you would have to carefully check the pin connections and rearrange my printed circuit layouts, so why bother? However, as long as the circuit number and the package are the same as I've specified, don't worry about which firm built the IC — those from all manufacturers work well.

When you examine electronic part catalogs, you'll find acronyms like CMOS, NMOS, and PMOS. These words usually have no relevance to us; ignore them and just order the part I've specified.

Handling ICs. Many ICs can be ruined by static electricity if they are handled carelessly before being inserted in the circuit. If the device comes with its pins inserted into a plastic pad or is packaged in a conductive plastic bag, leave it there until you're ready to use it. Always use sockets with ICs, because the ICs are difficult to remove for troubleshooting or replacement if the pins are soldered directly to the board. Finally, always insert an IC into its socket with the pins correctly oriented. The pin 1 location on an IC is identified by a notch, dot, or other feature on the case, and the pin 1 location is shown in the figures in this book.

Optoelectronic devices

Electronic devices that react to changes in illumination or that produce light when electricity flows through them have many applications in model railroading, Fig. 1-14.

Photoconductive cells. A photoconductive cell is a simple two-terminal device whose resistance varies with the illumination on the cell. The device is also known as a light-dependent resistor (LDR), light-sensitive resistor, or photoresistor. Those containing cadmium sulfide wafers are frequently called cadmium sulfide (CdS) cells. A photoconductive cell's resistance may be

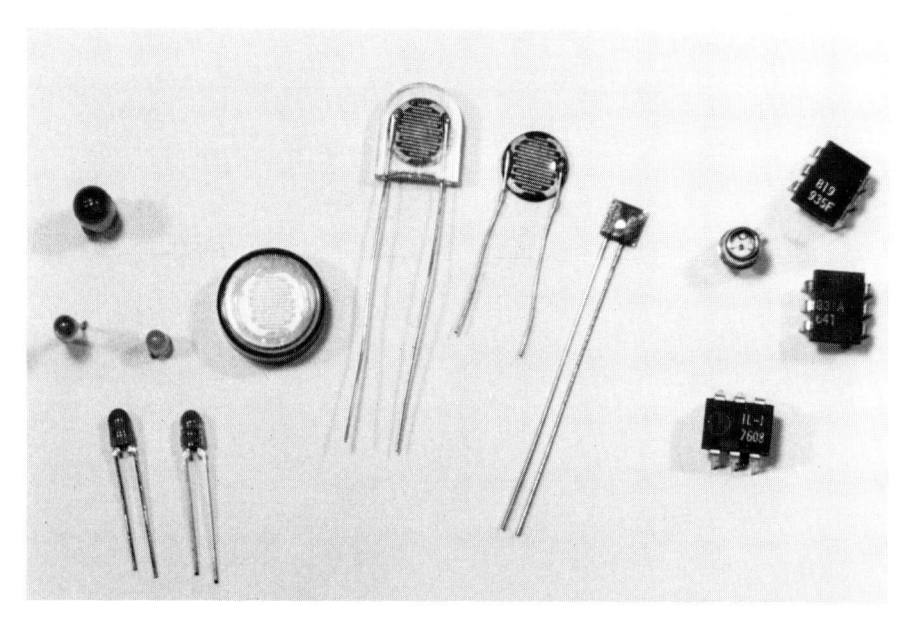

FIG. 1-14. Light-emitting diodes (left), photoconductive cells (center), and optoisolators (right) are among the optoelectronic devices used in several train detectors and throttles, including the radio-control throttles.

(Above) FIG. 1-15. Using relays, a small current can switch a much larger current. The DPDT relay at the far right mounts on a printed circuit board. (Below) FIG. 1-16. Here's a Potter and Brumfield DPDT latching relay that alternates contact positions each time its coil is energized.

10 MΩ in the dark but only 200 Ω in bright light. The cells are used in several throttles and train detectors in this book. Always test the cells before using them, because prolonged exposure to bright light (as on a store display rack) can damage them.

Light-emitting diodes. Usually called LEDs, these devices produce light when current flows through them. In the visible light spectrum, they're available in red, yellow, and green, and are ideal for signals. Radio Shack even sells an LED (276-035) that glows red on DC, green if the DC polarity is reversed, and yellow on AC. A red LED is available that contains its own flasher IC (276-036).

Infrared LEDs can be used to invisibly control other devices on your railroad. The receiver is often an infrared-sensitive photoconductive cell.

Optoisolators. Also known as optical couplers, optocouplers, photoisolators, and by several other names, these are devices in which an LED is optically coupled to a photodetector, providing perfect electrical isolation between input and output. The light-controlled device inside the package can be a transistor, Darlington amplifier, SCR, or triac. They're available in DIPs. In this book, I've used optoisolators and relays in several versions of an SCR throttle.

These optoisolators operate from 1.6 VDC and the current must not exceed 20 mA. If a circuit has a 12-VDC power supply, use a 560-Ω resistor in series with the LED to drop the voltage to 1.6 VDC. And never reverse the polarity of the LED in an optoisolator: The breakdown voltage is often as low as 3 V.

Relays

A relay is an electrically operated electromechanical or solid-state switch. It allows circuits to be switched from a distance and permits a small current to switch a much larger current.

Electromechanical relays. Electromechanical relays, Figs. 1-15 and 1-16, are far from obsolete. New relay designs provide us with a variety of types suitable for almost any switching operation. For example, there is now the bistable, impulse, or latching relay which can reverse contact direction every time its coil is energized. I have used a relatively new Potter and Brumfield latching relay to reverse motor direction in a couple of throttle designs in this book. Some 40 Hamilton/Avnet Electronics branches across the U. S. sell Potter and Brumfield relays, as do many other electronics distributors.

Model railroaders are already familiar with reed switches. The contacts on these are mounted on metallic reeds which are enclosed in a sealed glass tube containing a vacuum or inert gas. The contacts close in the presence of a correctly polarized magnetic field, which is usually produced by a small permanent magnet mounted on a piece of rolling stock. The reed switch is set between the rails and switches when the locomotive or car passes over it. Reed switches are used in Chapter 4 as train detectors for signals or other remote control operations. Some reed switches are bistable: Energize once and the contacts close, energize again and the contacts open. This is achieved with the aid of an internal polarizing magnet.

A reed relay contains a reed switch and one or more cores wound with wires that act as electromagnets and switch the contacts.

Unlike solid-state relays, the electromechanical types can have a multitude of contact arrangements. The simplest arrangement is "Type A," which is SPST NO (single-pole, single-throw, normally open). "Type C" is DPDT NO (double-pole, double-throw, normally open). The American National Standards Institute has defined 14 other contact arrangements.

Surplus relays are often available in electronics stores, and it's well worth keeping a handful of 6-VDC or 12-VDC relays on hand. Don't bother with AC relays; they're usually for 117 V and are buzzy, producing a 60-Hz hum.

Always use a 200-PIV, 1-A diode across a relay coil when the coil is energized by a

Courtesy North American Philips Controls Corp.

FIG. 1-17. Use only switches approved by the UL or CSA for 117-VAC circuits.

(Top) FIG. 1-18. This ironless-armature Airpax motor attains an amazing 70 percent efficiency. (Above) FIG. 1-19. An open-frame motor (circled) is cheaper but less efficient than the can motors beside it.

transistor or optoisolator. Connect the diode so it does not normally conduct; it will then short-circuit the reverse polarity voltage spike that occurs whenever the relay coil is switched off. This prevents damage to the transistor or optoisolator. If a coil buzzes or chatters, connect a 100-μF, 35-VDC electrolytic capacitor across the relay coil.

Other switches

The switches used in the projects have been carefully selected to ensure they can safely switch the loads they are required to handle, Fig. 1-17. Rotary and slide switches are used whenever the DC current is less than 0.5 A. (The AC rating of such a switch may be 1 to 3 A, but the DC rating is much less.) Pushbutton switches are used only for loads of 0.1 A or less. Toggle switches are used for DC loads up to 3 A. If you ever need to switch more than 3 A DC, use a large, conservatively rated, UL- or CSA-approved switch or a heavy-duty relay. Switch 117 VAC only with approved toggle or rocker switches.

Hall-effect solid-state switches are available in small transistor packages and can be used as train detectors. They operate when in a magnetic field, somewhat akin to reed switches. They're smaller and need a power supply, but can be used to switch many types of integrated circuits.

Locomotive motors

Three types of motors are used in model locomotives: open-frame, can, and ironless-armature, Figs. 1-18 and 1-19.

Open-frame motors. An open-frame motor has an alnico (aluminum, nickel, and cobalt) magnet and 3, 5, or 7 poles. The number of copper segments on the commutator tells you how many poles the motor has. Commutator, brushes, and bearings are easily accessible, so these motors can be serviced quickly. Stay away from 3-pole open-frame motors because they are subject to "cogging" at low speeds. Cogging means that the armature abruptly jerks in and out of the magnetic field as it rotates.

Can motors. In a can motor, a plastic or ceramic magnet lines the inside of the motor case (the can). Plastic magnets are used in inexpensive 3-pole can motors: These are common in N scale locomotives. Inexpensive can motors draw as much current as their open-frame competitors (200 mA to 500 mA), but often run smoother because the magnetic field can be skewed to reduce cogging. In Europe, this style of motor is known as "ring field."

Higher-quality can motors, such as some Sagami models, have a ceramic magnet and more armature poles for improved performance.

Ironless-armature motors. Ironless-armature motors, sometimes called micro motors, are advanced versions of can motors. They were originally designed for use in portable dictating machines and printing calculators and usually have a steel or ceramic magnet. The armature windings are skewed to eliminate cogging, and the entire armature (which is made of nonferrous alloys) is lightweight to allow rapid starts.

Ironless-armature motors can't be serviced, but to offset this, they are designed to be exceptionally reliable. Expensive versions even have gold-plated commutators and silver-plated brushes. A good ironless-armature motor draws far less current than an open frame motor but gives similar drawbar power. For example, an ironless-armature motor might draw only 50 mA at 5000 rpm, with a 50-percent efficiency.

When is the extra cost of an ironless-armature motor justified? That depends on the power supply and throttle you are using. Ironless-armature motors are best for train-mounted radio-control throttles, because the motor can be driven right from the receiver battery. Also, if you use moderate pulse transistor throttles and are keen on extra-slow running, the ironless-armature motor is your best choice.

On the other hand, if you are using a carrier control system in which the track power is 16 to 20 V and the motor is powered by narrow or half-wave pulses, there's no point in using an expensive motor. And don't use ironless-armature motors with a rheostat throttle: The rheostat doesn't have enough resistance to slow them down. Wiring a 12-V lamp across the track voltage terminals will solve the problem, but you really have no business operating $30 motors from a $10 pack!

Making printed circuit boards

Most of the projects in this book use printed circuit boards, and the drawings show both the foil and the component sides of each board full-size. Here's one way to make single boards. First, cut the board to size (usually 3" x 3"). Epoxy-fiberglass board is easier to drill than phenolic plastic board, but is slightly more expensive. Next, place the board under the hole-location drawing and, using a sharp pointed tool such as the tip of a school compass, mark the holes on the uncoated side of the board. Remove the board, and indent the hole locations with a center punch. Drill the holes with a motor tool and a No. 65 to No. 70 drill at low speed (1000 rpm gives longest drill life), Fig. 1-20. Carefully deburr the copper side of the board by rubbing it with a fine-grit whetstone, Fig. 1-21. Or, deburr the board with a grinder on a motor tool, Fig. 1-22.

9

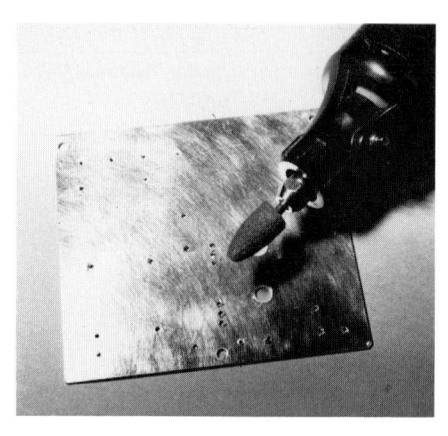

(Left) FIG. 1-20. The component location drawings and foil patterns in this book are accurate to 0.01″, so all parts should fit correctly. Drill the holes with a No. 65 or No. 70 drill turning at 1000 rpm. **(Center) FIG. 1-21.** Deburr the drilled board by rubbing it gently with a fine whetstone. **(Right) FIG. 1-22.** Alternately, deburr the board with a motor tool.

Now clean the copper side. Scour the copper side of the board with household cleanser (e.g. Ajax) and wash it with liquid detergent. Rinse under running water until the water flows off in sheets and allow the board to dry.

Obtain fine-tip (276-1530) and broad-tip photoresist pens at Radio Shack or some other electronics store. Lay the board copper side up, being careful not to touch the copper, and copy the copper outline in the drawing onto the copper, linking up the appropriate holes. Use the fine-tip pen to draw IC leads, the broad-tip pen to fill out larger areas. If you want, you can also use dry-transfer photoresist materials. These are tough rub-on sheets cut to the shape of transistor and IC sockets and other components. They are sold by Radio Shack (276-1577). A set (R407DP) is also available from Vector Electronic Company, 12460 Gladstone Avenue, Sylmar, CA 91342, Fig. 1-23.

You'll notice that my board designs leave much of the copper unetched. This helps to maintain the strength of the etchant. Cure the photoresist by baking the board in an oven for 20 minutes at 200 degrees F.

The next step is to etch away the uncoated parts of the copper. Ammonium persulfate can be used, but ferric chloride solution is the best etchant. Place the container of etchant (276-1535) in a pan of hot water and let it warm to about 120 or 130 degrees F. Ferric chloride is a powerful oxidizing agent, so be careful! Wear eye protection and rubber gloves. Chlorine gas is produced during the etching process, so work in a well-ventilated area and don't breathe the fumes. Place the board in a shallow glass or plastic container. Pour on the etchant, covering the board at least $1/2''$. Gently agitate the board at least once a minute, and leave it in the solution for 15 or 20 minutes until the copper has been etched away and converted to copper chloride. You must agitate the board or the etchant will undercut the photoresist.

Rinse the board thoroughly under running water, then remove the photoresist. Although it is highly flammable, acetone is a good photoresist solvent. Examine the board with a magnifying glass to make sure there are no unwanted copper bridges. If you find any, scrape them off.

That's it, your board is ready to use. If you remember to use only a fine-tipped low-wattage soldering iron when attaching components and are careful not to overheat the board, you should have no difficulty using the completed printed circuit board.

Safety

You must be extremely careful when working with any equipment connected to 117 VAC: The standard 15-A circuit breaker or fuse in your home electrical system will not protect you from a lethal electric shock. The plain fact is that a current of 10 mA can kill. Ideally, your layout and workshop should be protected by a ground-fault circuit interrupter (GFCI). This device replaces the standard wall socket with an electronic sensor that disconnects all power when a 5-mA leakage from the hot AC line to ground (a "ground fault") occurs.

Always ground metal chassis containing power transformers, and wire all 117-VAC connections as indicated in Fig. 1-24. If possible, use UL- or CSA-approved model train power packs for low-voltage AC power sources. Otherwise, use only UL- or CSA-approved transformers, switches, fuse holders, and cords in the 117-VAC circuit.

Troubleshooting

I've built and tested all of the projects in this book, so you can be certain they'll perform as described. However, even the most careful workers sometimes encounter faulty components or make mistakes in assembly, so you should have a good digital or analog multimeter to conduct voltage, amperage, and resistance checks on the projects. An oscilloscope is convenient, but not required. Here's a list of symptoms and cures for the most common problems.

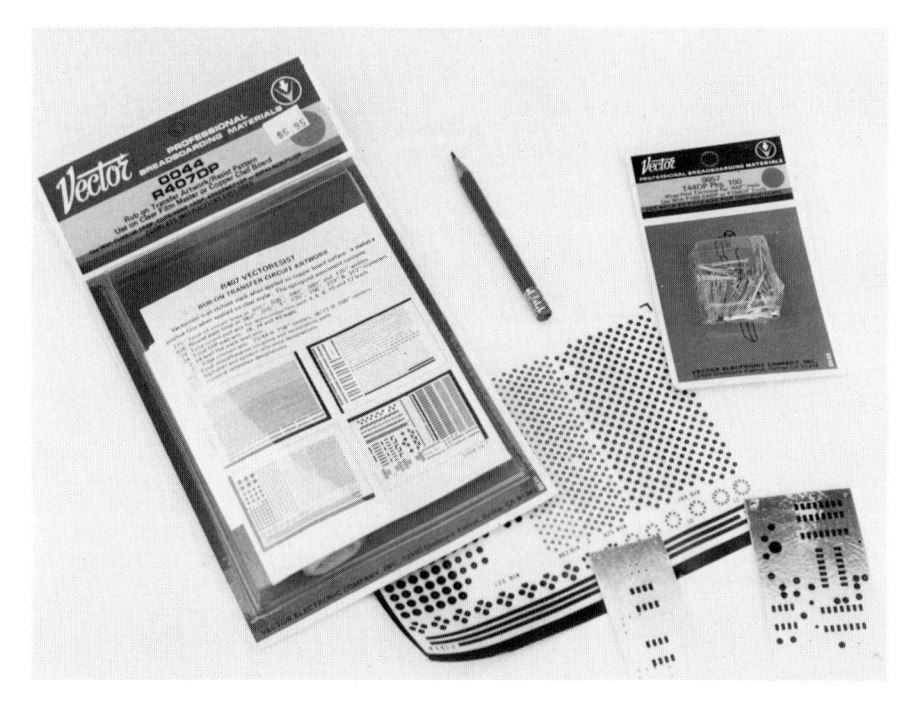

FIG. 1-23. Vectoresist dry-transfer circuit artwork makes quick work of preparing printed circuit board patterns. The bubble pack on the right contains wire-wrap pins that can be used with printed circuits made with the Vector artwork.

Symptom: Power transformer produces loud hum.
Cure: Unplug the transformer. Check for short-circuits. Check all component values. Check that rectifier diodes are oriented correctly. Check that SCR is oriented correctly.

Symptom: No output from throttle.
Cure: Unplug the throttle. (You did plug it into a live outlet, didn't you?) Check transistors or SCR for correct polarity or opens.

Symptom: Throttle runs flat out all the time.
Cure: Unplug the throttle. Check power transistor for correct polarity. Check for short-circuited transistor.

Symptom: Throttle output too low or no momentum effect.
Cure: Check momentum capacitor for correct polarity. Replace capacitor if polarity is wrong — it's probably ruined.

Symptom: LEDs are on continuously.
Cure: Check timing capacitor; replace if incorrect value.

Symptom: LED doesn't light.
Cure: Check for correct polarity. Check value of voltage-dropping resistor.

Symptom: Blown or otherwise inoperative IC.
Cure: Check for correct orientation. Check for bent pins. Note: Handle ICs carefully, especially when inserting them into tight-fitting sockets.

Symptom: Blown or otherwise inoperative transistor.
Cure: Check for correct orientation of emitter, base, and collector. Check for correct part number and type (never use a PNP transistor if an NPN is specified).

Symptom: Wrong tone in a sound circuit or too-fast sequence in a timing circuit.
Cure: Check timing capacitor for correct type, value, and polarity. Never use an electrolytic capacitor if a foil or film capacitor is specified in the project. If a tantalum or low-leakage electrolytic capacitor is specified, use it.

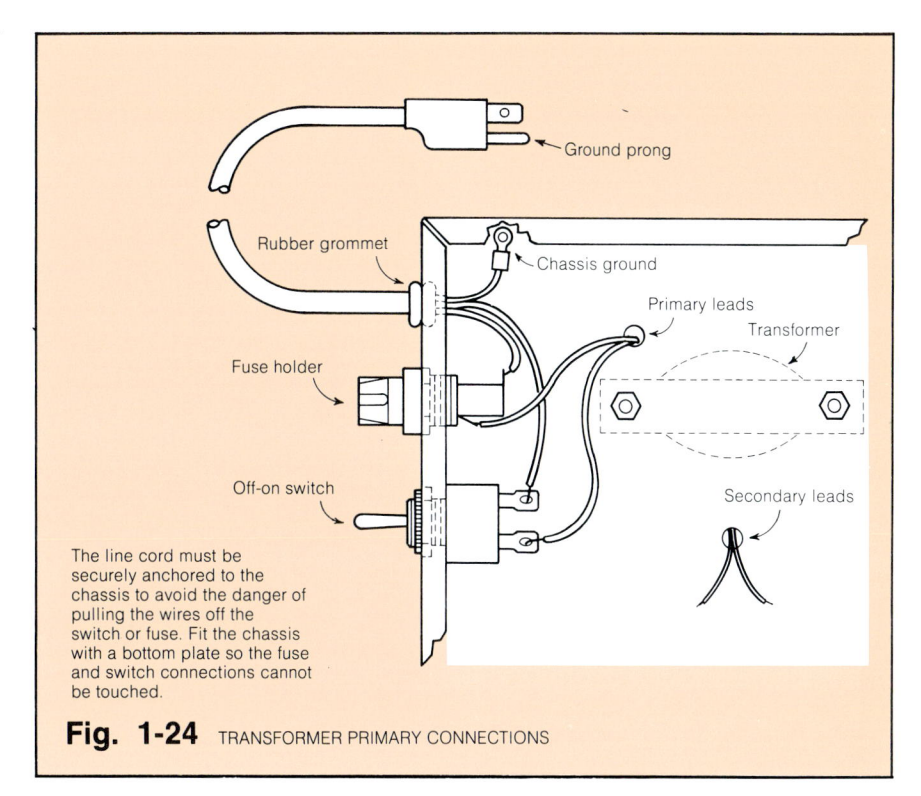

Symptom: Mysterious glitches.
Cure: Using a magnifying glass, check printed circuit board for hairline cracks in foil leads and for unwanted solder bridges. Ask a friend to inspect the board. Check for cold solder joints and resolder any that you find. Check the values of resistors. For example, R8 in the SCR throttle of Chapter 2 should be 56 Ω. The third color band of this resistor is black: It's possible to misread a brown or a dull red as a black and insert a 560-Ω or a 5.6-kΩ resistor. At 560 Ω, the throttle output is low; at 5.6 kΩ, output is nonexistent. Check logic ICs for correct output.

Symptom: Corrosion at solder joints.
Cure: You used acid-core solder! Throw away the project and build it over, using resin-core solder.

The line cord must be securely anchored to the chassis to avoid the danger of pulling the wires off the switch or fuse. Fit the chassis with a bottom plate so the fuse and switch connections cannot be touched.

Fig. 1-24 TRANSFORMER PRIMARY CONNECTIONS

If all else fails. If you've conducted all of the above tests and have exhausted the expertise of friends, write to me in care of Kalmbach Publishing Co. at the address on the first page of this book. Describe the project in this book that you're having trouble with and state the symptoms as clearly as possible: I'll try to help. Notice that I said "project in this book" — I don't have time to become an all-purpose consulting service!

Commercial rights. One final note: The projects in this book are designed to be built by hobbyists for their own personal use and enjoyment. The circuits are not suited for mass-production (many of the component values are very conservatively rated) and purchasers of this book do not have my permission to manufacture any of them commercially.

2) Throttles

THE THROTTLE PROJECTS in this chapter range from basic to complex. All have been thoroughly tested, so you can be confident each will work well. The projects present three types of throttles: a simple transistor throttle, an advanced transistor throttle, and an SCR throttle. I will describe the basic design of each of the three types, then tell how you can add refinements that increase operating flexibility.

A word of caution: If you're a novice, try one of the first two designs before attempting something as ambitious as the radio-control throttle.

A simple transistor throttle

This throttle, Fig. 2-1, can be built and used just like any conventional throttle, or you can use one throttle for each block on your layout. This arrangement eliminates block switching and gives great flexibility of control. It becomes easy to control two trains in four, five, or six blocks, using calibrated speed controls and direction switches for each block.

Note that "calibration" is the key word. With conventional power packs, when a train runs from one block to another, the train lurches as the motor reacts to a change in track voltage. Through calibration, this throttle provides each block with identical voltages, eliminating lurching. The throttle also features a 6-position or 12-position switch to simulate the throttle notches on full-size locomotives.

How it works. The power-supply transformer is a 16-V to 20-V unit rated for 1 A or 12 voltamperes to 20 voltamperes. You may use a doorbell transformer or the uncontrolled AC output of any good HO power pack. Each block throttle has its own transformer and all transformers must be identical in order to minimize differences in block voltages.

The AC input is first converted to DC by bridge rectifier D1. Notch switch S2 controls the voltage to the input of the three-transistor current amplifier (Q1, plus Darlington amplifier Q2 which contains two transistors). Track voltage is half-wave DC at 120 Hz; maximum output is 1 A. The limited output capacity of the transformer provides a form of overload protection.

Resistors wired in a daisy chain around S2 permit this 12-position switch to select the track voltage in 12 discrete steps. Thus, if "6" is dialed on two adjacent blocks, a loco can run across the block boundary with no change in speed — provided the direction switches are correctly set! S2 should be a "shorting" type; that is, adjacent contacts are shorted in the brief interval when switching from one setting to the next. If you don't use a shorting switch, protect Q1 with a 100-kΩ resistor between its base (B) and the minus line. If you prefer larger speed steps, S2 can be a 6-position rotary switch: Simply double the values of the speed resistors and use half as many. (This type of rotary switch is commonly available as a 2-pole, 6-position type, so one pole-and-contact set is not used.)

You can build several throttles on one panel (use aluminum for the panel, to keep Q2 cool), provided each Q2 is installed with an insulated mounting kit. Thus, throttles and direction switches can be grouped for one-hand control, if you find that convenient.

Wiring the simple throttle. Layout is not critical. A photo in Fig. 2-1 shows Q2 mounted on the front of the throttle case, a good location. Note that some components are attached to the case with standard mounting hardware; others, such as D1, are held with silicone sealant.

Then connect:
- R2 through R13 to S2. Note that R3 through R12 are 150 Ω but R13 is 390 Ω.
- D1 + to solder lug at C of Q2.
- C of Q1 and R2 to solder lug at C of Q2.
- A from S2 to solder lug at C of Q2.
- B of Q1 to B of S2 via R1.
- E of Q1 to B of Q2.
- Other lead of R2 to LED +.
- E of Q2 to lug 6 of S1 via lug 3 of S1.
- LED – to D1 –.
- C of S2 to D1 –.
- D1 – to lug 1 of S1 via lug 4 of S1.

The AC input goes to the two AC contacts on D1 and the block wiring goes to lugs 2 and 5 of S1.

An improved transistor throttle

The basic transistor throttle works well, particularly with simple 3-pole motors. My improved version uses the same notch switch as the preceding version, but adds a pulse generator and a voltage regulator. The pulse generator, controlled by a 555 timer IC, produces a mechanically quiet but effective 150-Hz pulse for good slow-running performance. The pulse disappears at stop and at maximum speed, so there's no danger of creep or overheating the motor in the locomotive.

The voltage regulator ensures even closer tracking of the dialed speed between blocks because it fixes the input voltage regardless of motor load. The voltage regulator also provides short-circuit and overload protection. If either occurs, the device automatically cuts out until the cause is corrected. The AC input for the improved transistor throttle can be as low as 12 V. It must not exceed 16 V because the DC input (after rectification and filtering) is 1.4 times the AC input.

The improved transistor throttle can be uprated to 3 A maximum load if a larger voltage regulator is installed, as explained on page 20.

The pulse generator. The pulse generator, Fig. 2-2, is built on a small printed circuit board. Rectangular pulses are produced at the output of the 555 IC, pin 3, which is connected as an oscillator. Pulse duration ranges from narrow (2 percent) to square wave (50 percent), and is adjusted by potentiometer VR. You may want to mount VR on a front panel to allow fine speed adjustments for a variety of motors. Use narrow pulses for high-quality motors and wide pulses for cheaper motors. If you use a separate throttle for each block, the VR settings should be approximately equal.

The pulse is reduced from 14 V to 5 V, converted to positive-going only, and pulses the base of Q1 (now mounted on the pulse generator printed circuit board), which passes the current to the base of Q2. Transistors Q1 and Q2 serve as current amplifiers. The same pulse generator is used in the improved Pacematic throttle described later in this chapter, so the schematic and the component location drawing in Fig. 2-2 show resistors R6 and R7 and connections BR1 and BR2: These are used only in the Pacematic throttle. Ignore them and connect R5 directly to the base of Q1.

Wiring the simple throttle with pulse generator. Consult Fig. 2-2 and prepare the pulse generator printed circuit board.

Figure 2-3 contains the schematic for the improved simple throttle with pulse generator. Use the drilling pattern in Fig. 2-3 to prepare a 3" × 7" aluminum plate. Obtain the components used for the simple transistor throttle (except Q1 and R1), as well as those listed in Fig. 2-3. Mount the voltage regulator and Q2 with TO-3 hardware, being certain to install solder lugs under the mounting nuts for the voltage regulator – (common) and C of Q2.

Then connect:
- D1 – to the solder lug at – of voltage regulator.
- D1 – to lug 2 of S1 via lug 5 of S1.
- C of S2 to solder lug at – of voltage regulator.
- LED – to solder lug at – of voltage regulator.
- – of C1 and – of C2 to solder lug at – of voltage regulator.
- D1 + to IN of voltage regulator.
- C1 + to IN of voltage regulator.
- Emitter (E) of Q2 to lug 4 of S1 via lug 1 of S1.
- E of Q2 to one lead of R2.
- Other lead of R2 to LED +.
- A of S2 to solder lug at C of Q2, to OUT of voltage regulator, and to + of C2.

Mount the circuit board with silicone sealant, and connect:
- + to voltage regulator OUT.
- – to solder lug at voltage regulator –.
- B to base (B) of Q2.
- S to B of S2.

CIRCUIT FOR SIMPLE THROTTLE

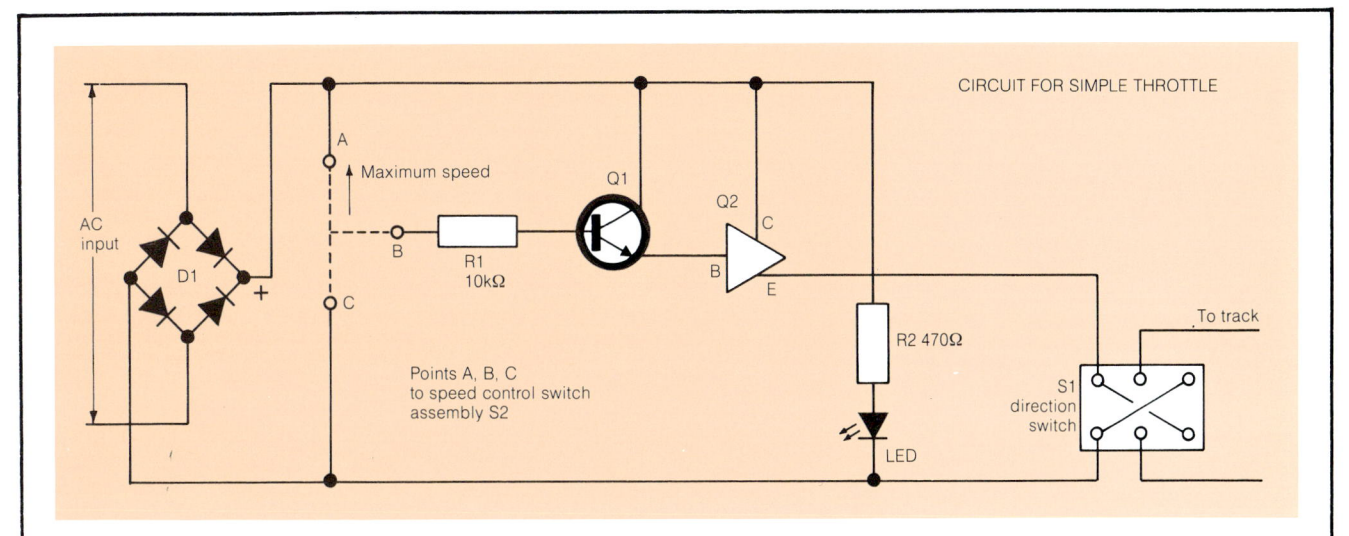

D1	100-PIV, 10-A bridge rectifier (276-1185)
LED	any light-emitting diode (276-026)
Q1	0.3-A, 40-V NPN transistor (276-2030)
Q2	8-A, 40-V NPN Darlington amplifier in TO-3 case (276-2042, or Motorola 2N6055 or 2N6056, or Lambda PMD-12K-60)
R1	10-kΩ resistor (271-1335)
R2	470-Ω resistor (271-019)
R3-R12	150-Ω resistors (271-1312)
R13	390-Ω resistor (271-018) Higher resistance gives higher starting voltage.
S1	DPDT toggle switch, center off (275-1533)
S2	single-pole, 12-position rotary switch (275-1385)
Miscellaneous	3" × 7" (approximate dimensions) aluminum plate or chassis (serves as heat sink, so must be metal), barrier terminals (e.g. 274-658), TO-3 mounting hardware (276-1371), solder lugs, spaghetti tubing, silicone sealant, silicone grease (276-1372), control knob for ¼" shaft.

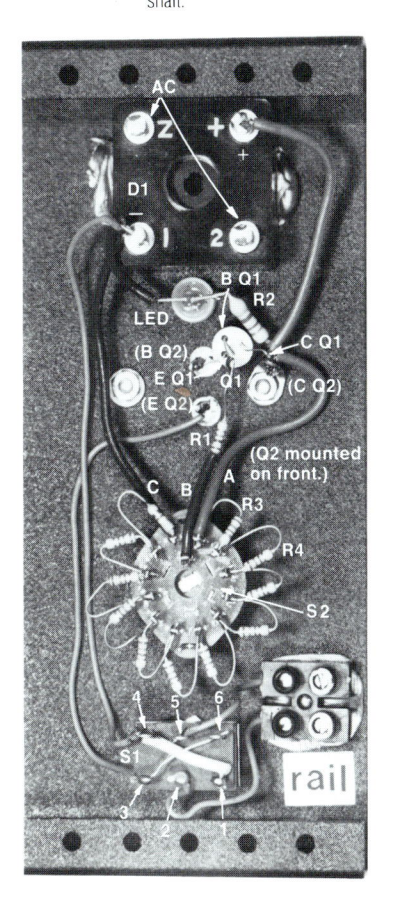

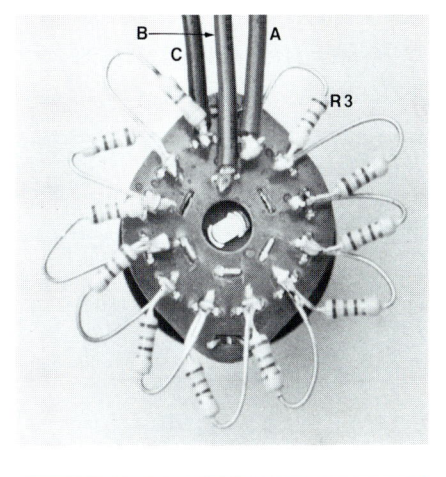

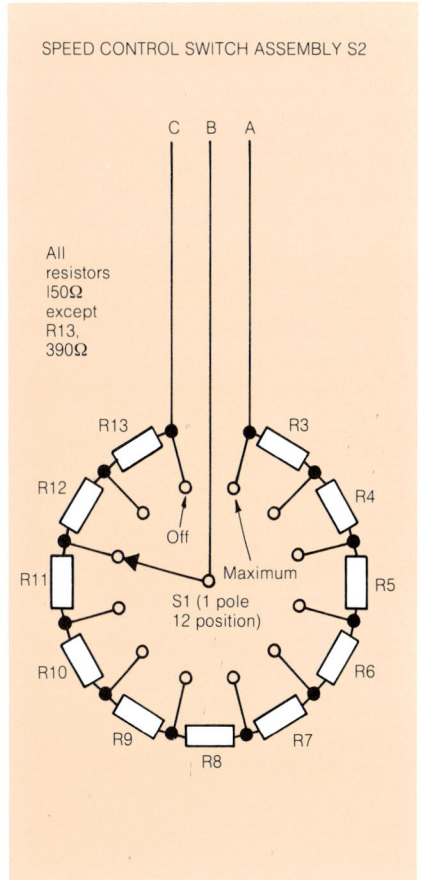

SPEED CONTROL SWITCH ASSEMBLY S2

All resistors 150Ω except R13, 390Ω

S1 (1 pole 12 position)

Insulate long leads and jumpers with spaghetti tubing.

Fig. 2-1 SIMPLE TRANSISTOR THROTTLE

13

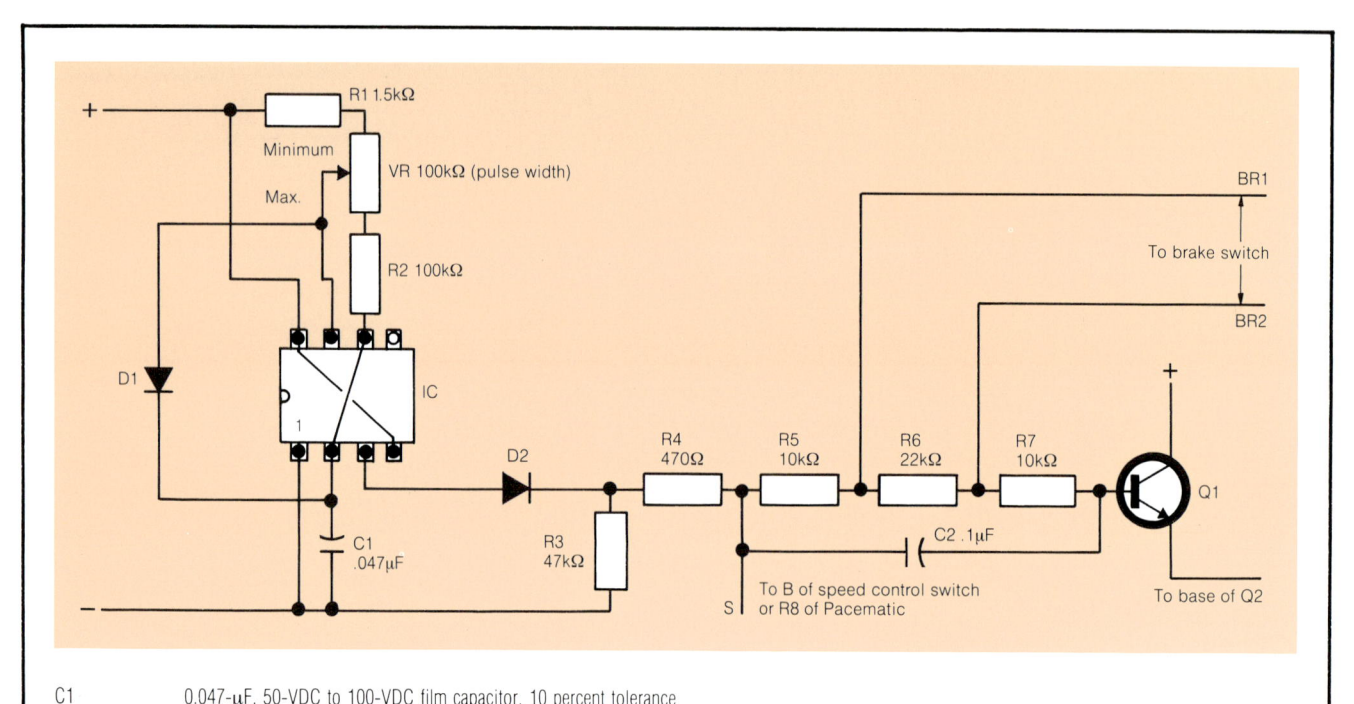

C1	0.047-μF, 50-VDC to 100-VDC film capacitor, 10 percent tolerance
C2	0.1-μF, 50-VDC to 100-VDC film capacitor, 10 percent tolerance
D1, D2	50-PIV, 1-A silicon diode, 1N4148 (276-1122)
IC	NE555N (8 pin) (276-1723)
Q1	0.5-A, 40-V NPN transistor (276-2030)
R1	1.5-kΩ resistor
R2	100-kΩ resistor
R3	47-kΩ resistor
R4	470-Ω resistor
R5, R7*	10-kΩ resistor
R6*	22-kΩ resistor
VR	100-kΩ potentiometer (271-220 or 271-338)
Miscellaneous	Printed circuit board, 8-pin DIP IC socket (276-1995), insulated hookup wire, soldering pins

*R6 and R7 used only with the Pacematic throttle.

Note: R6, R7 and connections BR1, BR2 are omitted on simple throttle and R5 is connected directly to B of Q.

PULSE GENERATOR BOARD (component side). Shown full size 2¾" × 2".

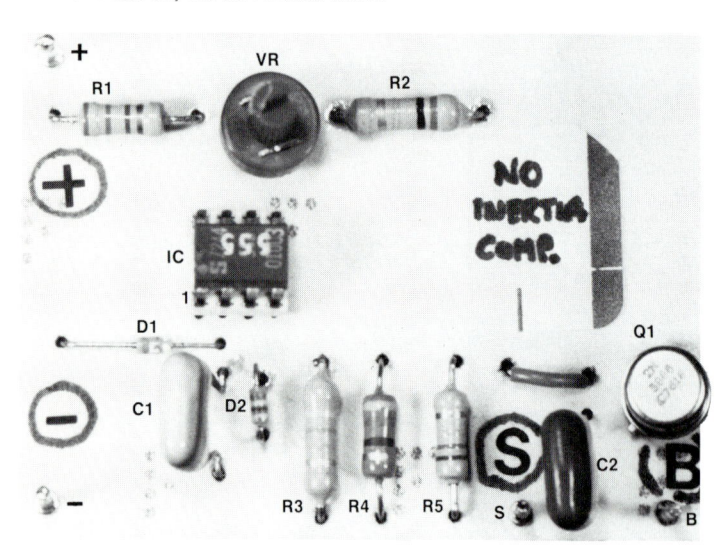

Pulse generator board.

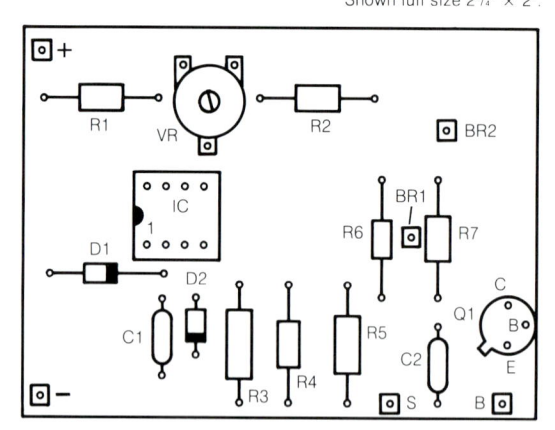

PULSE GENERATOR BOARD (foil side). Shown full size 2¾" × 2".

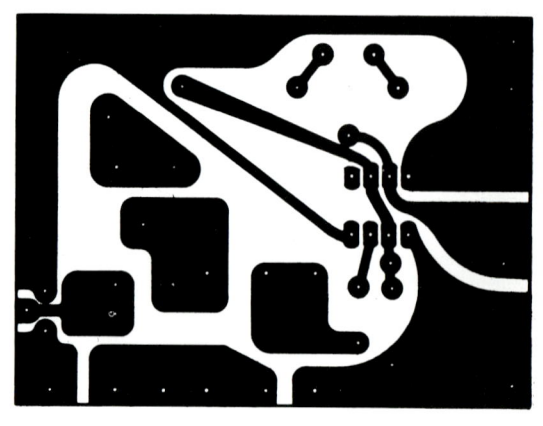

Fig. 2-2 PULSE GENERATOR FOR IMPROVED TRANSISTOR THROTTLE AND PACEMATIC THROTTLE

14

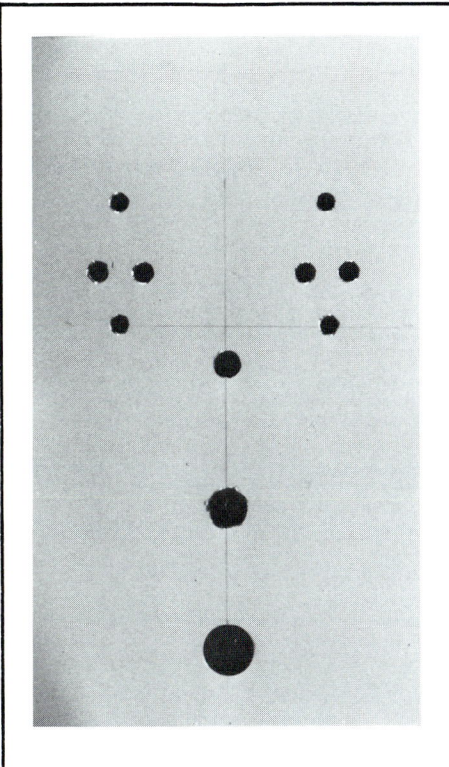

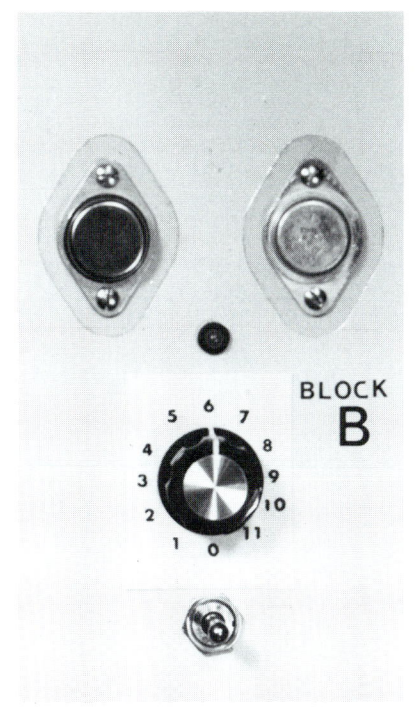

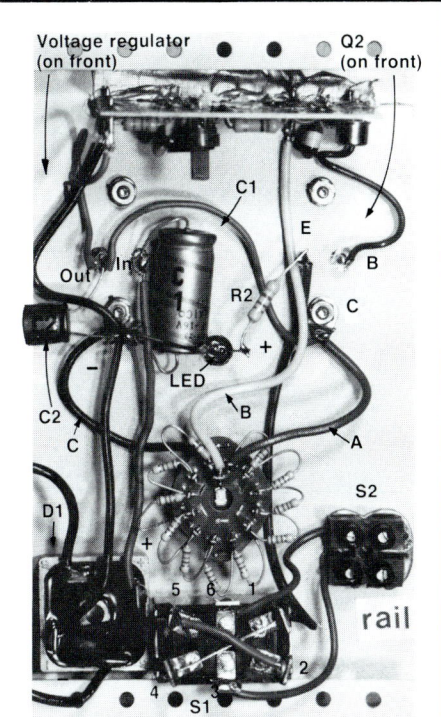

Drilling pattern for the aluminum plate (shown approximately ²/₃ full size).

The voltage regulator and Q2 mount on the front of the aluminum plate.

PARTS LIST FOR IMPROVED TRANSISTOR THROTTLE

Use parts listed in Fig. 2-1, except delete Q1 and R1. Also obtain C1, a 1000-μF, 35-VDC electrolytic capacitor (272-1019); C2, a 100-μF, 25-VDC electrolytic capacitor (272-1016); and a 1-A, 15-V voltage regulator in a TO-3 case (National Semiconductor LM340K-15 or Motorola MC7815KC). Also obtain an extra set of TO-3 mounting hardware.

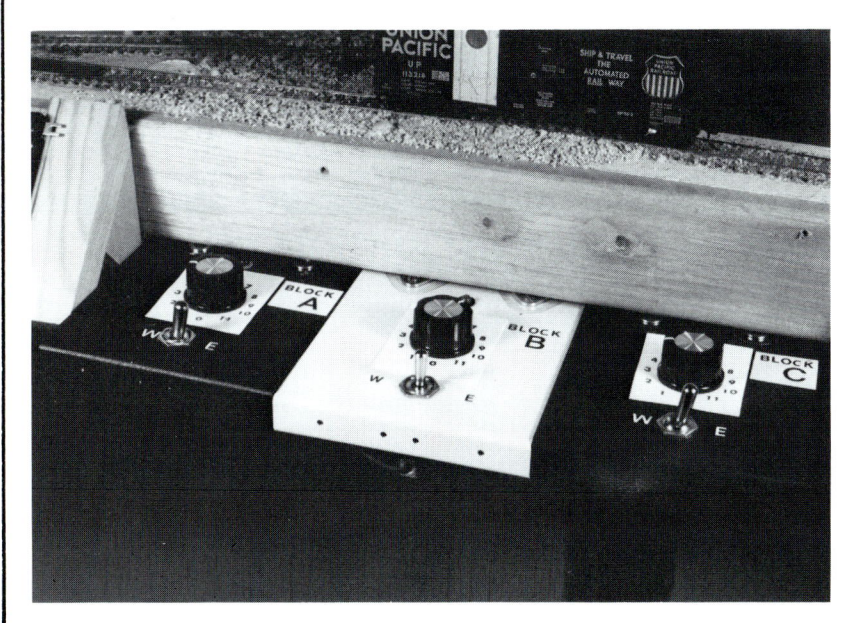

Several improved transistor throttles may be mounted side by side to allow convenient control of as many blocks.

Fig. 2-3 IMPROVED TRANSISTOR THROTTLE WITH PULSE GENERATOR

15

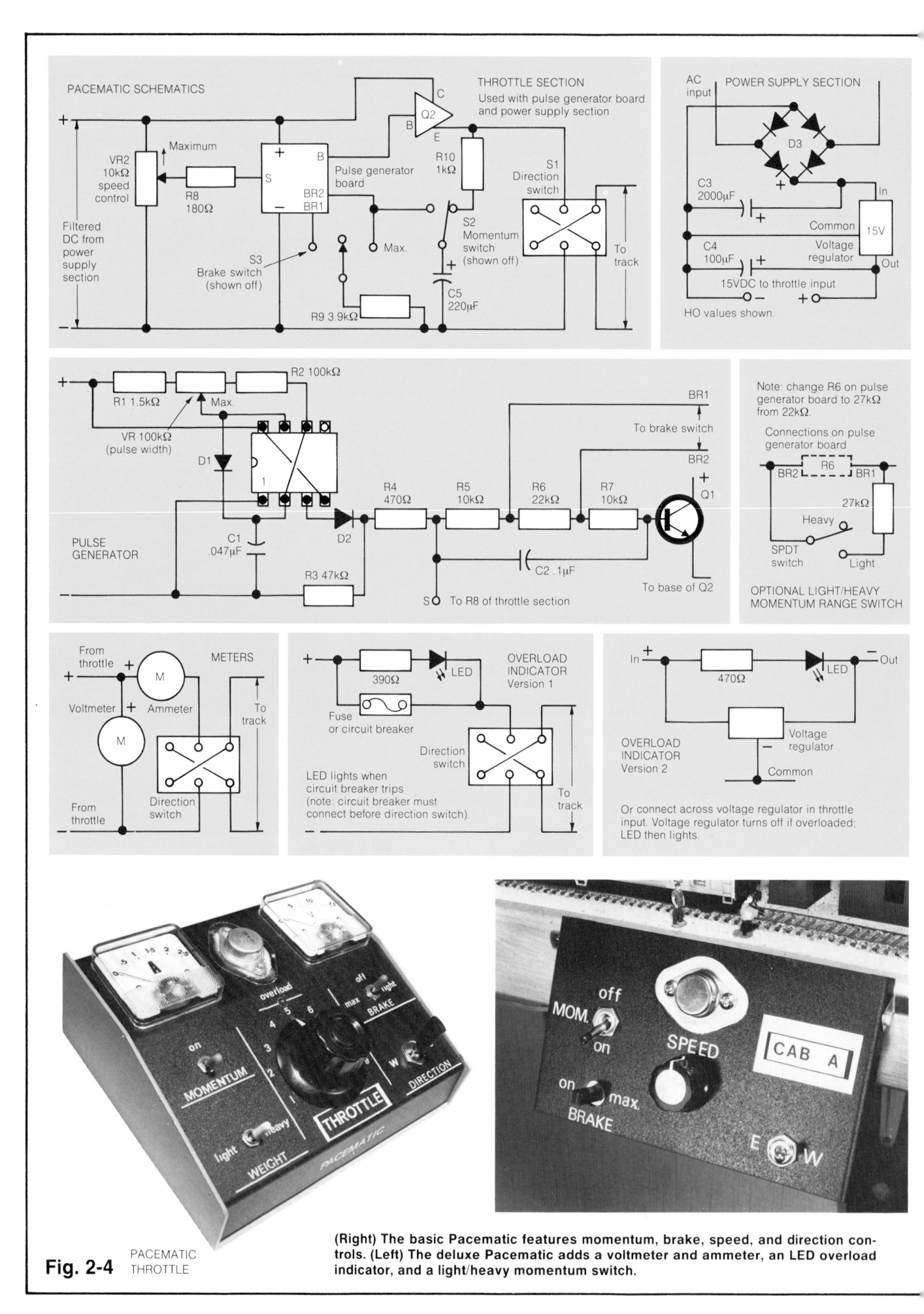

Fig. 2-4 PACEMATIC THROTTLE

(Right) The basic Pacematic features momentum, brake, speed, and direction controls. (Left) The deluxe Pacematic adds a voltmeter and ammeter, an LED overload indicator, and a light/heavy momentum switch.

16

Throttle section

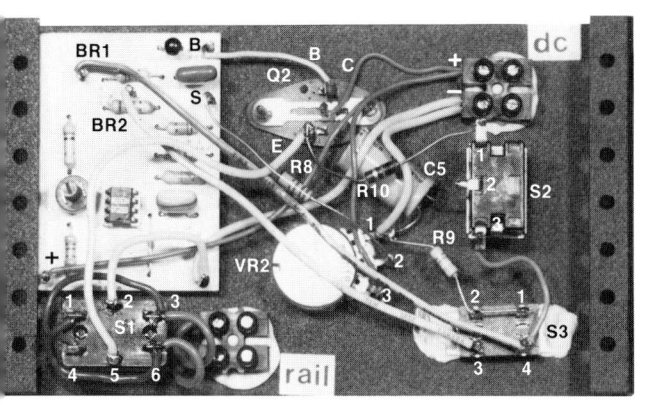

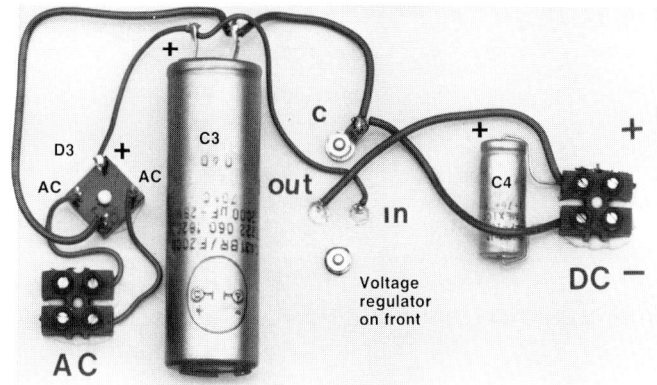

DC power supply

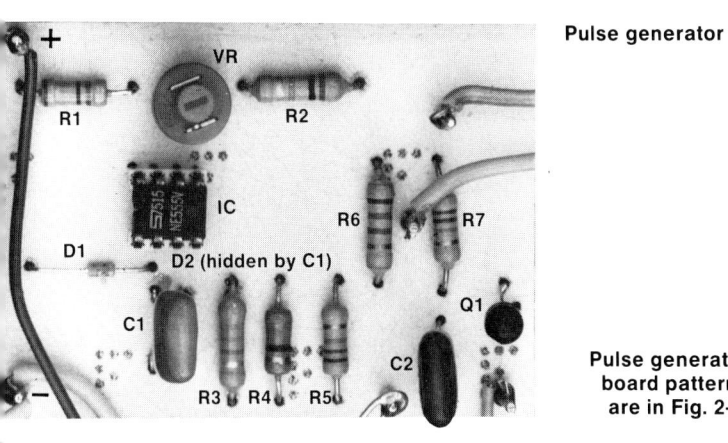

Pulse generator

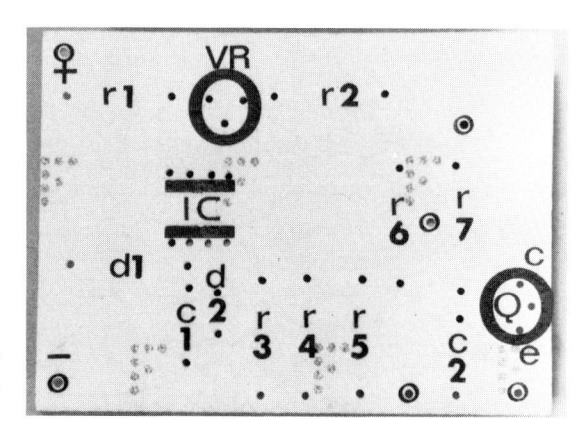

Pulse generator board patterns are in Fig. 2-2.

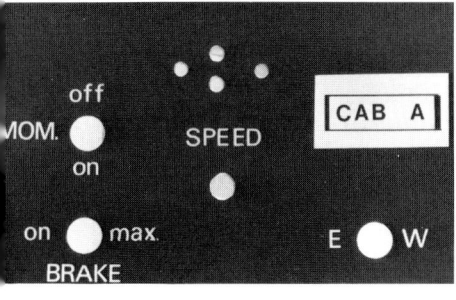

Drilling pattern for aluminum plate (shown approximately ⅓ size).

Mount Q2 on a large heat sink for the O scale version of the Pacematic throttle. Do the same with the voltage regulator.

PARTS LIST FOR PACEMATIC THROTTLE

DC POWER SUPPLY

C3	electrolytic capacitor. Use 1000 µF, 25 VDC for each A of output; e.g. 1000 µF for Z or N, 2000 µF for HO, 5000 µF for O.
C4	100-µF, 25-VDC electrolytic capacitor
D3	bridge rectifier. Use 100 PIV, 2 A for Z or N; 100 PIV, 4 A for HO; 100 PIV, 25 A for O.
voltage regulator	Use a 12-V, 1-A regulator (National Semiconductor LM340K-12 or Motorola MC7812KC) for Z. Use a 15-V, 1-A regulator (National Semiconductor LM340K-15 or Motorola MC7815KC) for N. Use a 15-V, 3-A regulator (Lambda Electronics LAS-1415) for HO. Use a 15-V, 5-A regulator (Lambda Electronics LAS-1915) for O. For 3-A or 5-A regulators, add a 3.3-µF, 25-VDC or 4.7-µF, 25-VDC tantalum electrolytic capacitor between IN and COMMON on the regulator. Mount the regulator on a separate heat sink for the O version.
Miscellaneous	3" × 7" aluminum plate, barrier terminals, TO-3 mounting hardware, silicone grease, silicone sealant

THROTTLE SECTION

C5	220-µF, 25-VDC electrolytic capacitor
Q2	NPN Darlington amplifier in TO-3 case. Use 8 A (or higher) for Z or N (Motorola 2N6055 or 2N6056, or Lambda PMD-12K-40, or Radio Shack 276-2042). Use 12 A for HO (Motorola 2N6282, Lambda PMD-10K-40, or Radio Shack 276-2042). Use 16 A to 20 A for O (Lambda PMD-16K-40). For O, Q2 must be mounted on a separate heat sink (276-1361).
R8	180-Ω resistor (lower value gives lower starting pulse)
R9	3.9-kΩ resistor (higher value gives slower brake rate)
R10	1-kΩ resistor
S1	DPDT toggle switch, center off. Must be rated at 5 A DC for the O version.
S2	Any type of SPDT switch
S3	Any type of SPDT center-off switch. Or use 2 NO pushbuttons.
VR2	10-kΩ linear taper potentiometer. Radio Shack 271-1721 can be used, but may give poor speed control because it does not have a linear taper.
Miscellaneous	See DC POWER SUPPLY list

PULSE GENERATOR

See Fig. 2-2.

17

The AC leads go to the AC connections of D1. The block wiring goes to lugs 3 and 6 of S1.

Voltage checks in the simple throttles. The simple throttles use half-wave pulses throughout, so most voltmeters will read the average voltage, corresponding to what the motor thinks it receives. That is, a 22-VAC input will read only 11 V after the bridge rectifier, and this voltage should appear across the speed control. In the basic throttle, the voltage difference from B of Q1 to minus should range from 0 V (notch 0) to 11 V (notch 11). In the improved version, this should range from 0 V to 15 V.

The E of Q1 should track this range of voltages, less about 0.7 V, and E of Q2 should also track, less a further 1.4 V. All voltages drop when a load is applied, although the improved throttle is "stiffer" and drops less. Unless you have an oscilloscope the only way to detect the pulse generator operation is to listen to motor buzz at low speeds.

The Pacematic transistor throttle

I described an earlier version of the Pacematic transistor momentum throttle in the December 1977 issue of MODEL RAILROADER magazine. That design was suitable for all scales from Z to O: Components with lower current ratings were used for the smaller scales, higher-rated components were used for O scale. This version retains that feature and includes two major improvements and several options. The improvements are an integrated-circuit pulse generator for excellent slow-running performance and a voltage regulator for stable output and overload protection.

The options are a light/heavy momentum switch, ammeter and voltmeter, and an LED overload indicator. Figure 2-4 shows the schematic for the throttle, a DC power supply, and the optional features. Figure 2-4 also contains the schematic for the pulse generator board; although the same circuit is shown in Fig. 2-2, I've repeated it here for your convenience. Figure 2-4 even contains photos of two versions of the assembled throttle and wiring photos. You've already seen the pulse generator in Fig. 2-2; photos of the board used in the Pacematic and the mounted components are in Fig. 2-4, also for your convenience.

Momentum effect. Momentum, or inertia, effect allows us to simulate slow acceleration and braking. The action of the speed control is electrically delayed: Even if you crank the throttle from closed to maximum, the track voltage rises slowly. The action is much like a flywheel, but has two advantages over a mechanical flywheel: Electronic momentum, unlike a flywheel, can be switched off when switching or working in close quarters, and its effect is adjustable.

Examine Fig. 2-4: The momentum-producing components are R6 (on the pulse generator board) and C5. Switch S2 turns the momentum effect on and off. C5 is charged via R10 even when C5 is switched out of the circuit. This reduces motor hiccuping, a common problem with many mo-

Fig. 2-5 AN SCR THROTTLE

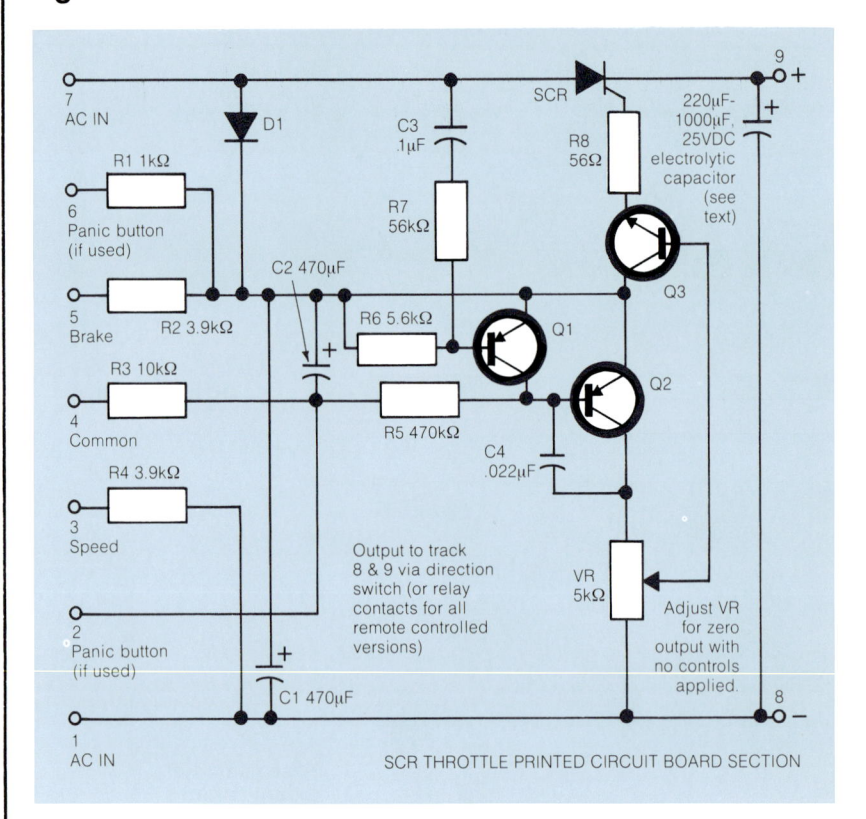

PARTS LIST FOR SCR THROTTLE

C1, C2	470-µF, 35-VDC electrolytic capacitor
C3	0.1-µF, 100-VDC film capacitor
C4	0.022-µF, 100-VDC film capacitor
D1	100-PIV, 1-A rectifier diode, 1N4148 (276-1122)
Q1, Q2	0.2-A, 40-V PNP high-gain transistors, 2N2905A or 2N2907A (276-2034)
Q3	1-A, 40-V NPN medium-gain transistor (Motorola MJE 4921 or 2N4921, or Radio Shack 276-2030 or 276-2052)
R1	1-kΩ resistor
R2, R4	3.9-kΩ resistor (increasing the value of R2 slows braking, increasing R4 slows acceleration)
R3	10-kΩ resistor (increasing the value of R3 gives more momentum effect)
R5	470-kΩ resistor
R6	5.6-kΩ resistor
R7	56-kΩ resistor
R8	1-W, 56-Ω resistor
SCR	100-PIV, 25-A silicon controlled rectifier (Motorola 2N3896, 2N3897, 2N6171, or 2N6172)
VR	5-kΩ linear taper potentiometer (271-217)
Miscellaneous	3" × 3" printed circuit board, soldering pins
	RUN, BRAKE, and PANIC BUTTON use any SPST NO pushbutton switches.
	DIRECTION for manual control, use a DPDT center-off toggle switch between output and track. For remote control, use Potter and Brumfield DPDT latching relay S89R11DBD1-24 powered by a 3-A bridge rectifier. Always install a 3-A to 5-A circuit breaker between the switch or relay and the track.

SCR THROTTLE VOLTAGE CHECKS

	Pins 3 and 4 connected (run) 10 VDC output	Pins 4 and 5 connected (brake) 0 V output
Q3 C	29 VDC	29 VDC
B	9 VAC, 6 VDC	0 V
E	20 VAC, 13 VDC	0 V
Q2 C	18 VAC, 9 VDC	0 V
B	60 VAC, 29 VDC	60 VAC, 29 VDC
E	29 VDC	29 VDC
Q1 C	60 VAC, 29 VDC	60 VAC, 29 VDC
B	60 VAC, 29 VDC	60 VAC, 29 VDC
E	29 VDC	29 VDC

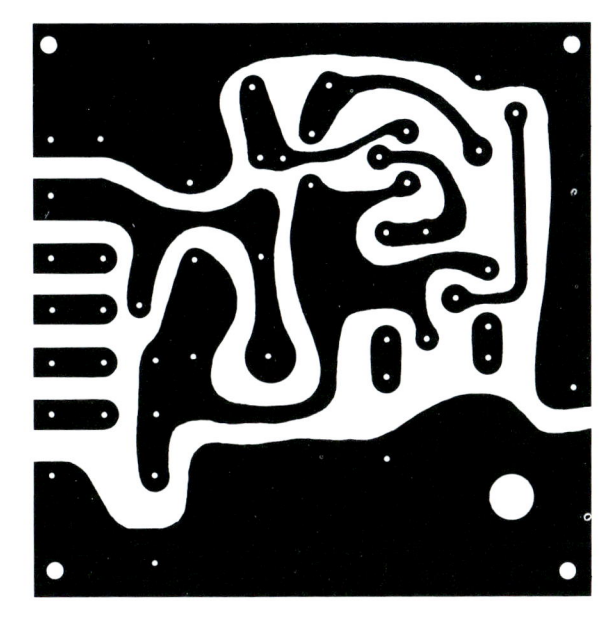

SCR THROTTLE BOARD (foil side). Shown full size 3" × 3".

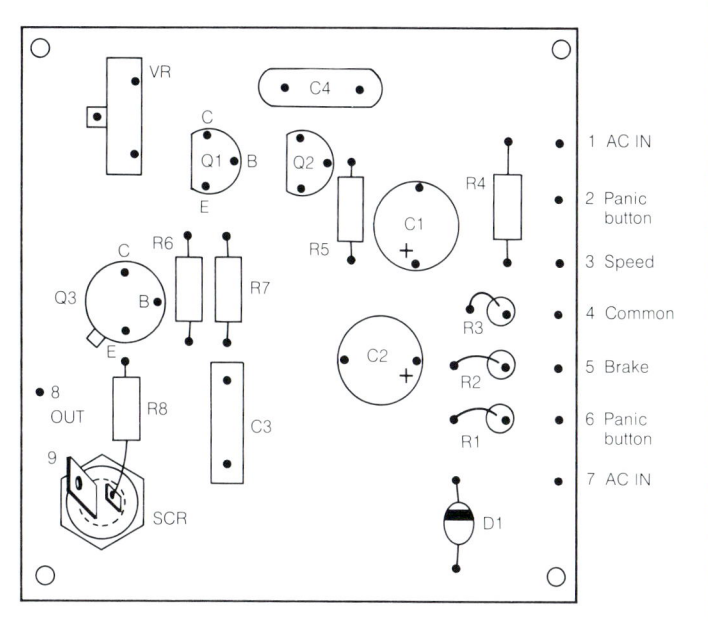

SCR THROTTLE BOARD (component side). Shown full size 3" × 3".

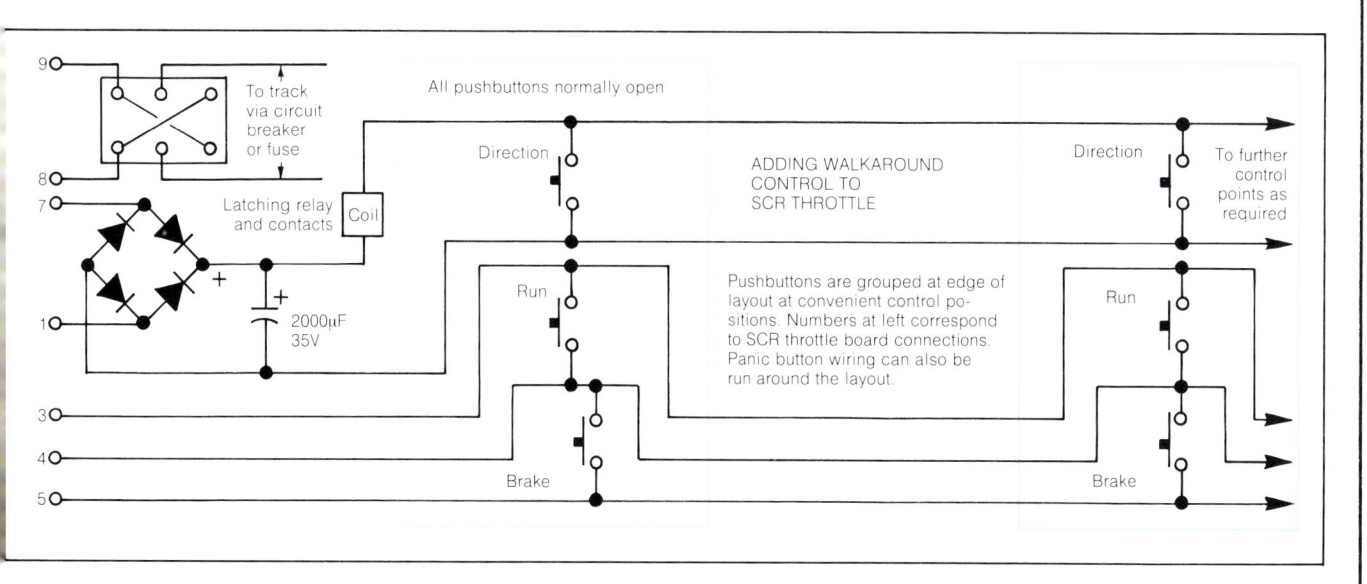

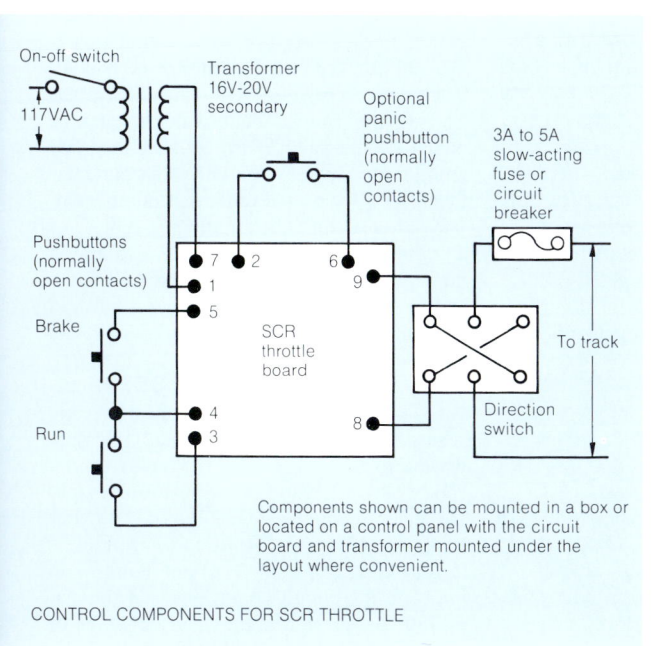

ADDING WALKAROUND CONTROL TO SCR THROTTLE

All pushbuttons normally open

Pushbuttons are grouped at edge of layout at convenient control positions. Numbers at left correspond to SCR throttle board connections. Panic button wiring can also be run around the layout.

To further control points as required

CONTROL COMPONENTS FOR SCR THROTTLE

Components shown can be mounted in a box or located on a control panel with the circuit board and transformer mounted under the layout where convenient.

SCR THROTTLE PRINTED CIRCUIT BOARD

19

mentum throttles when switching momentum on and off. Figure 2-4 shows the circuit for the optional momentum range switch.

Pacematic power supply. For Z, N, and HO, the AC input for the Pacematic power supply can be the uncontrolled AC output of any HO power pack. For O scale locos, use a 12.6-V to 16-V transformer capable of handling up to 5 A. A used tinplate throttle rated at 75 voltamperes to 100 voltamperes will also work well.

The schematic for a DC power supply for the Pacematic appears in Fig. 2-4. Bridge rectifier D3 converts the AC input to a DC output, which is filtered by C3. The voltage regulator stabilizes this output to 15 V. Use a 1-A voltage regulator for Z, N, and efficient HO motors; a 3-A or 5-A regulator for standard HO motors; and a 5-A regulator for O motors. The 1-A regulator can be mounted on the 3" x 7" piece of aluminum that holds the other power supply components, but larger regulators require a separate heat sink, such as that used with Q2. The value of capacitor C3 also changes as the current rating increases: Check the parts list and be certain to use the correct value.

The Pacematic's speed control is a potentiometer, VR2. At minimum setting the output voltage is 0, because the slider of the potentiometer shorts out the pulse. (Some throttles allow a minute flow of current even when the speed control is completely closed; this tiny current is enough to turn efficient can motors.)

The voltage selected by the potentiometer slider, between 0 V and 15 V, is transferred through isolation and momentum resistors to B of transistor Q1 (on the pulse generator board). The E of Q1 follows this voltage and transfers it to B of Q2, a power Darlington amplifier. The E of Q2 also tracks its B connection, so that the throttle output at E of Q2 follows the voltage selected by the speed potentiometer. Transistor Q1 loses about 0.7 V internally, Q2 loses 1.4 V, and there's also a small loss in the resistors connecting the potentiometer to B of Q1. As a result, 15-VDC input gives about 12-VDC maximum output.

You can pinpoint throttle problems by tracing the voltages I've described. Checking from the potentiometer slider on, and swinging the voltage up and down, makes it easy to locate a defective component. For example, if the base of Q1 tracks voltage, but its emitter remains more or less fixed, then Q1 is defective.

The power Darlington amplifier, Q2, dissipates as much heat on average as the voltage regulator. The 3" x 7" front plate provides adequate cooling up to 3 A; it must have a big heat sink for larger currents.

The DC power supply and control section can be mounted together or separately. As long as the control plate is easily accessible, the power pack or transformer and DC power supply can be hidden.

A deluxe Pacematic can be constructed as a complete package. The version shown has two ranges of momentum (light and heavy) as well as a momentum on/off switch. It also includes an ammeter, a voltmeter, and an LED overload indicator. The case is Hammond 1456-FE2; the transformer is mounted externally. The schematics show how to add the meters, overload indicator, and momentum selector switch to any version of the Pacematic.

Wiring the Pacematic DC power supply. The DC power supply panel holds bridge rectifier D3, the voltage regulator (mounted on the other side of the panel and fitted with a heat sink for the more powerful versions), filter capacitors C3 and C4, and terminals for the AC and DC leads. The parts list gives correct values for several versions of the power supply. Observe that if you use a 3-A or 5-A voltage regulator, you must add a 3.3-µF or 4.7-µF, 25-VDC tantalum electrolytic capacitor between IN and C (−) on the voltage regulator. Mount the voltage regulator, putting a solder lug under the nut that holds its − lead. Fasten D3 and the AC and DC terminals to the panel with silicone sealant.

Then connect:
- AC terminals to AC terminals on D3.
- D3 + to voltage regulator IN via C3 +.
- D3 − to solder lug on voltage regulator C (−) via C3 −.
- DC + terminal to voltage regulator OUT.
- DC − terminal to solder lug at voltage regulator C (−).
- C4 + to DC + terminal.
- C4 − to DC − terminal.

If appropriate, connect + of a 3.3-µF or 4.7-µF, 25-VDC tantalum electrolytic capacitor to IN of the voltage regulator, and − of this capacitor to the solder lug at voltage regulator C (−).

Pacematic pulse generator. I've already described the design and construction of the pulse generator used in the Pacematic: It's the same circuit that's used in the improved simple transistor throttle. Consult Fig. 2-2 and Fig. 2-4 and note that the Pacematic does use resistors R6 and R7 and leads BR1 and BR2 that were not used in the simple transistor throttle.

Wiring the Pacematic control section. Figure 2-4 shows mounting holes on a 3" x 7" aluminum plate such as you may use to mount the throttle components. Other components are mounted with silicone sealant. Prepare a suitable plate and install Q2 and the other hardware-mounted components. Use a separate heat sink for Q2 if you're building a high-capacity version. Glue the other components in place.

Then connect:
- DC − to S1 lug 2 via pulse generator −.
- DC − to lug 1 of VR2.
- DC + to C of Q2.
- DC + to pulse generator +.
- DC + to lug 3 of VR2.
- C5 + to lug 2 of S2.
- C5 − to lug 1 of VR2.
- Lug 2 of VR2 to pulse generator S via R8.
- Pulse generator B to B of Q2.
- E of Q2 to lug 5 of S1.
- E of Q2 to lug 1 of S2 via R10.
- Lugs 1, 2 of S3 to lug 1 of VR2 via R9.
- Lug 4 of S3 to pulse generator BR1.
- Lug 3 of S3 to pulse generator BR2.
- Lug 3 of S1 to lug 4 of S1.
- Lug 1 of S1 to lug 6 of S1.
- Lug 3 of S1 to track terminal.
- Lug 6 of S1 to track terminal.
- Lug 3 of S2 to lug 4 of S3.

Wire the power supply panel to the throttle panel as shown. Reversed polarity will destroy the 555 and Q1.

Pacematic voltage checks. Before conducting voltage measurements on the Pacematic throttle, make sure that the track is not shorted, because the voltage regulator switches off when it's shorted. You should find 15 VDC across VR2. The connection between the center lug of VR2 and pulse generator S should range from 0 V to 15 V as you rotate the knob of VR2. Slightly reduced, this range of voltages should track through R4, R5, R6, and R7 to B of Q1. If not, S3 or C5 may be defective. Pin E of Q1 and pin B of Q2 should track from 0 V to about 13.5 V. If they don't, Q1 is defective. Pin E of Q2 should track from 0 V to 12 V. If it doesn't, Q2 is defective. About 5-V to 6-V peak pulses should appear at the junction of R3 and R4. You need an oscilloscope to check this and other parts of the pulse generator. If the pulse is too fast, check the value of C1. Keep in mind that D1 and D2 must be correctly oriented — if you install them backwards you will blow the 555.

An SCR throttle

Silicon controlled rectifiers (SCRs) are suitable for model railroad throttles for two reasons. First, when driven by 60-Hz AC, an SCR switches on and off 60 times a second, providing a pulsed voltage that is desirable for smooth operation. Second, the duration of the pulses (and hence the power delivered to the motor) can be easily controlled, allowing a wide range of motor speeds.

My latest SCR throttle, Fig. 2-5, has momentum effect and uses pushbutton controls for speed and brake. Blip the appropriate button and the speed or brake action slowly takes effect; keep the button pressed and acceleration or braking is much more rapid. The throttle can be built with all controls mounted on a panel, with controls mounted around the layout, or with controls contained in a hand-held case. Yet another option is to use the SCR throttle as the heart of a radio-control system. Before examining these options, let's look over the AC power supply requirements and discuss how to build the printed circuit board that holds the SCR and other components.

AC power supply for the SCR throttle. The SCR throttle can be used for any scale except Z (the pulses may overheat these tiny motors) and the AC power supply can be any 12-V to 20-V transformer capable of supplying the current required by your trains. For N, wire a 220-µF to 1000-µF electrolytic capacitor with + to pin 9 and − to pin 8 on the circuit board, and add this capacitor for HO if a motor shows any sign of overheating. I use an old American Flyer 16-V transformer for N or HO trains. Some

Fig. 2-6 HAND-HELD CONTROL UNIT FOR SCR THROTTLE

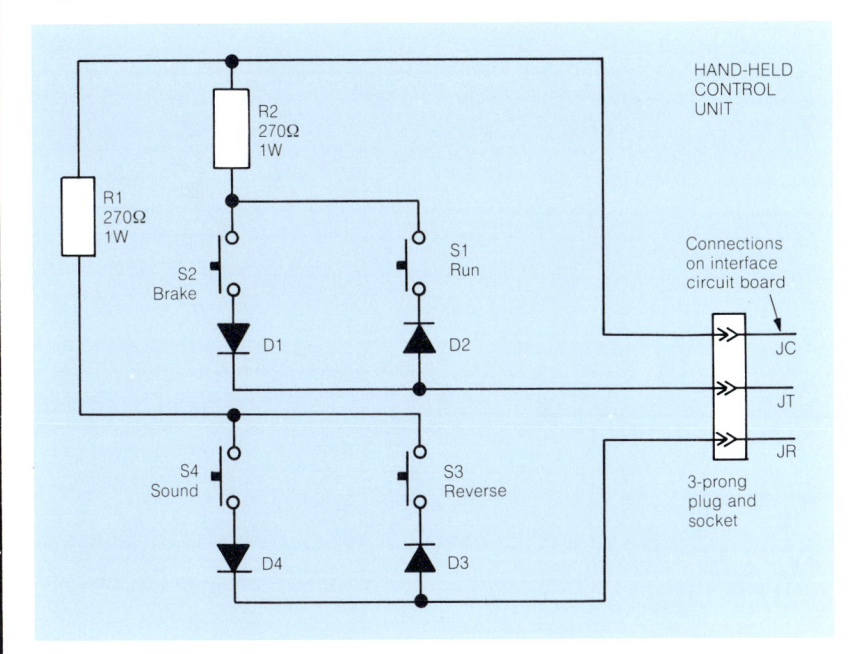

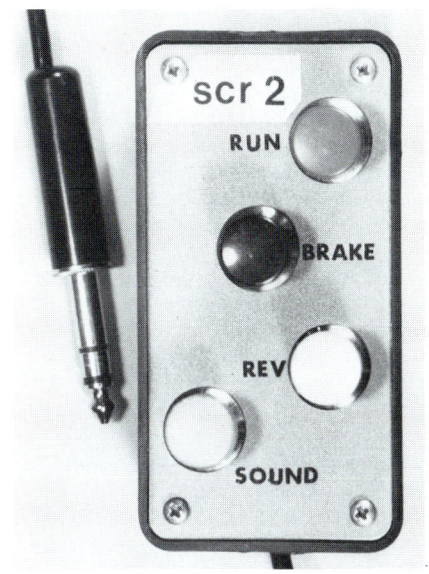

This control unit contains only 4 diodes, 2 resistors, and 4 pushbutton switches, so it's lightweight and easy to use.

PARTS LIST FOR HAND-HELD CONTROL UNIT

D1-D4	100-PIV, 100-mA diodes, 1N4148 or 1N914 (276-1122)
R1, R2	1-W, 270-Ω resistors
S1-S4	NO pushbutton switches (275-609)
Miscellaneous	Plastic box about 2″ × 2″ × 2″ (270-231), 3-conductor telephone cable (278-361), 3-conductor ¼″ phone plug (274-139), enclosed ¼″ stereo phone jack, double closed circuit (274-277 modified, see text, pages 22 and 24), terminal strip, silicone sealant (You may use an A3M 3-pin audio connector [274-010] with a D3F chassis mount socket [274-013] instead of the phone plug and jack.)

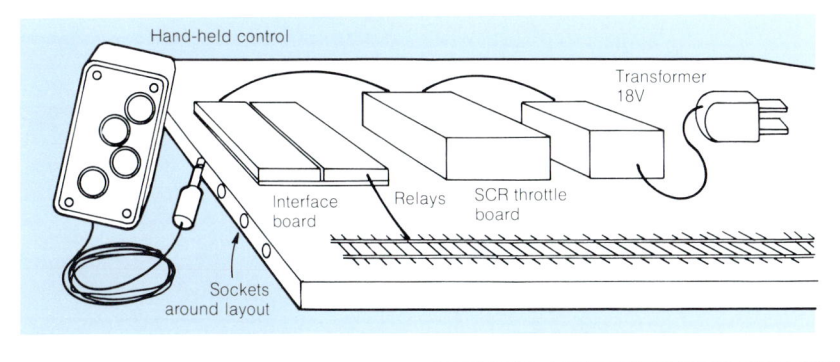

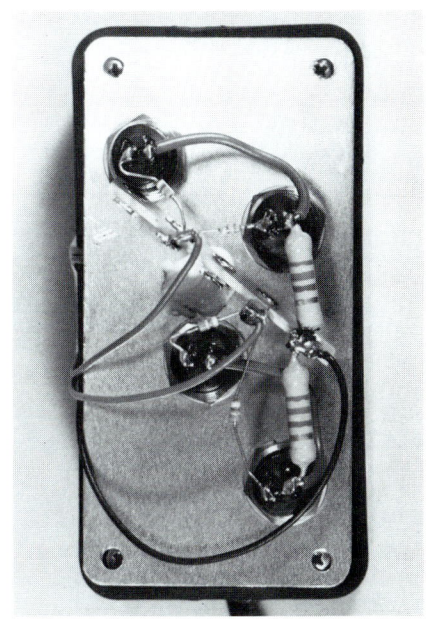

O scale motors might require a transformer rated for 5-A maximum output.

If you can't find a suitable transformer, you can wire the outputs of two transformers in series to obtain the needed voltage. For example, you can connect the output of a 12.6-V transformer (Radio Shack 273-1511) and the 6.3-V center tap of a second 273-1511 to obtain a nominal 19-V, 3-A maximum output. Install a 3-A to 5-A slow-blow fuse or circuit breaker (or an 1157 automotive lamp with both filaments connected in parallel) for short-circuit protection.

Printed circuit board for the SCR throttle. The 3″ x 3″ printed circuit board, Fig. 2-5, holds the SCR, capacitors, transistors, resistors, a diode, and a potentiometer. The potentiometer sets the throttle's maximum output: Turn its knob toward pin 8 for more output, toward pin 9 for less output.

Prepare the printed circuit board and install the components, being certain that the SCR, transistors, diodes, and capacitors are oriented correctly.

Self-contained SCR throttle. The circuit board and throttle controls can be mounted on a panel or case. See Fig. 2-5. The AC input is at pins 1 and 7. The output to the track is 8 and 9, via a DPDT, center-off direction switch. Use SPST NO pushbutton switches for brake, run, and panic buttons. The brake pins are 4 and 5, the run pins are 3 and 4, the panic button pins are 2 and 6. Run and brake both have momentum effect; the panic button switch overrides momentum, braking the train almost immediately. You can obtain more momentum effect by increasing the value of R3. Increasing R2 slows the braking action, while increasing R4 slows acceleration.

SCR throttle voltage checks. Many test points on the SCR throttle are pulsed voltages that can be accurately measured only with an oscilloscope. The values in Fig. 2-5 were obtained by using the AC and DC voltage scales of a high-impedance voltmeter. The SCR throttle has a feedback feature — if motor current draw increases, as when climbing a hill, the output voltage increases to maintain speed. Therefore, the tests should be done with a load connected to the output, either a motor or a 25-Ω to 50-Ω, 5-W resistor. The optional capacitor between pins 8 and 9 is also connected. Input is 18 VAC. Output is 10 VDC (left column) and 0 V (right column). Transistor Q3 is the most likely cause of failure; if it's defective, there will no output. Be certain to use one of the transistors given in the parts list for Q3.

Simple walkaround control: parallel pushbuttons for the SCR throttle. If you locate groups of three pushbuttons at convenient locations around the layout and wire them in parallel, you can obtain a simple form of walkaround control. Figure 2-5 shows the wiring; the numbers at left correspond to the SCR throttle printed circuit board connections. A double-pole, double-throw latching relay is required for the direction switch. I use a Potter and Brumfield S89R11DBD1-24 relay powered by a 3-A bridge rectifier.

Hand-held walkaround control for the SCR throttle. Many walkaround control units consist of a hand-held throttle connected to the layout by a cable made of four large-gauge wires: The direction switch requires two wires, the power input needs two more. The result is that the hand-held control is heavy and awkward to use. We need a lightweight control that requires little current and so can be connected to the layout with a light-gauge cable. Here's one solution: Use LEDs and cadmium sulfide cells in an interface unit with the throttle in place of pushbuttons for run and brake, and use optoisolators and Darlington amplifiers to operate a direction relay and an auxiliary relay for sound or lights. The LEDs and optoisolators draw only about 20 mA, so the cable connecting the hand-held control to the interface unit can be thin and flexible: I use 3-conductor telephone cord.

The hand-held control unit, Fig. 2-6, consists of four pushbutton switches with diodes and resistors, so it is compact and lightweight. One of the leads connects to one of the 18-VAC to 20-VAC throttle inputs. This voltage passes through two separate current-limiting resistors, R1 and R2, and each of the two branches is rectified into positive-going or negative-going pulses by diodes D1, D2, D3, and D4, depending on which of the pushbuttons is pressed.

One of the other two cable leads goes to the pairs of LEDs and CdS cells in the interface unit, the third goes to the optoisolators, Fig. 2-7. One of the pairs of LEDs and CdS cells is connected to operate from the positive pulses, the other from the negative pulses. The same is true of the optoisolators. In this way, two wires carry four separate messages. No harm is done if all switches are pushed simultaneously: The train stops and both relays operate.

Furthermore, the loco just keeps rolling along for a time when the hand-held unit is unplugged and carried to the next jack. One hand-held unit can control any number of cabs, just by plugging it into the socket for another cab. You can't beat that for convenience and versatility!

Wiring the hand-held control. Consult Fig. 2-6 and mount the pushbuttons, then attach the terminal strip to the plastic case with silicone sealant. After the sealant sets, install the resistors, diodes, jumpers, and connecting cable.

Use the right plug and socket! The AC connection must go to the tip of the plug or short-circuits will blow the optoelectronic devices in the interface unit whenever you

Fig. 2-7 INTERFACE FOR HAND-HELD CONTROL UNIT FOR SCR THROTTLE

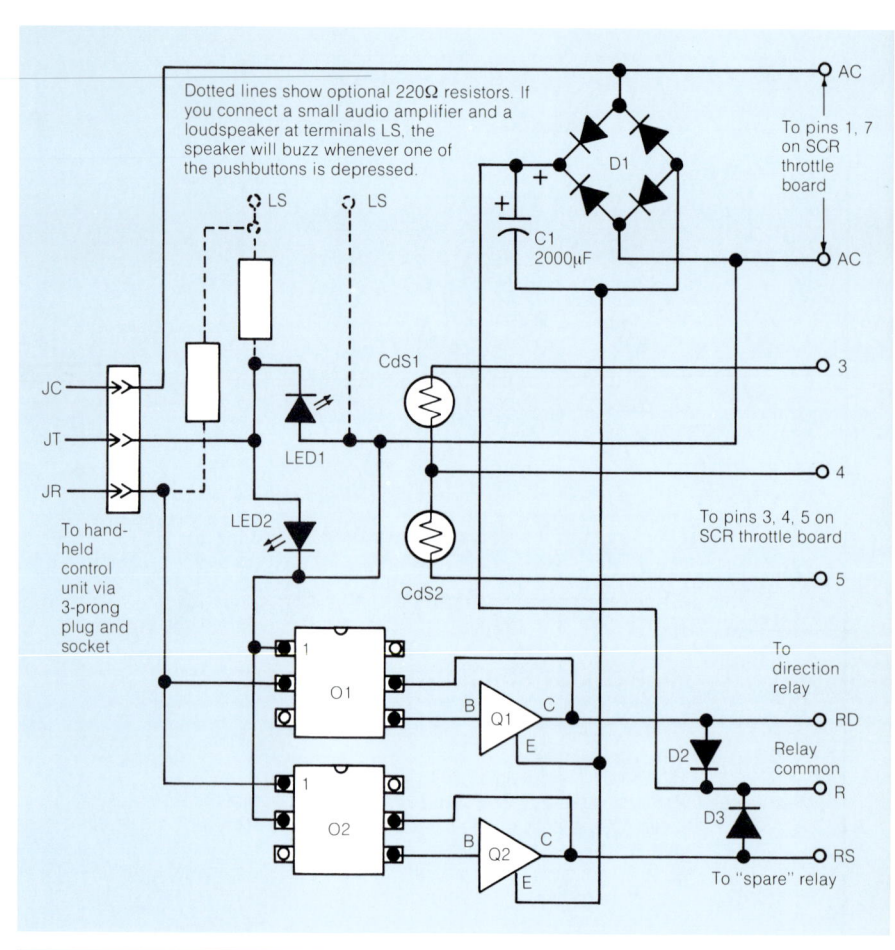

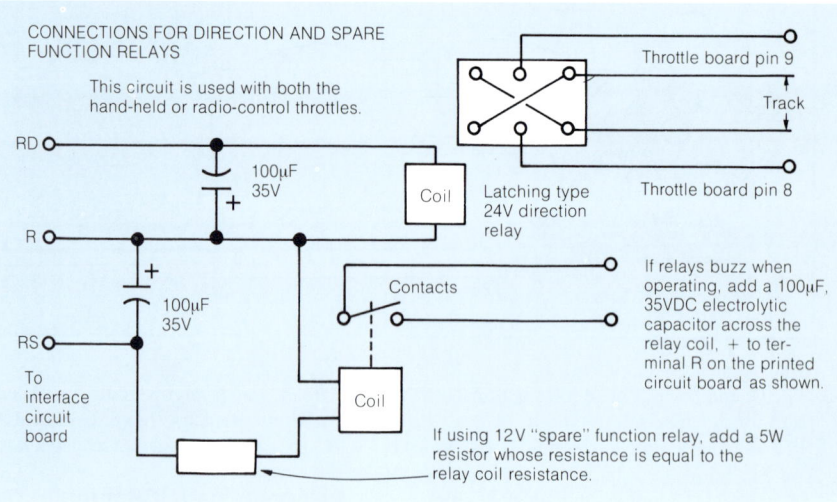

PARTS LIST FOR INTERFACE FOR HAND-HELD CONTROL UNIT

C1	2000-µF, 35-VDC electrolytic capacitor
D1	100-PIV, 1-A bridge rectifier (276-1152)
D2, D3	400-PIV, 1-A rectifier diodes, 1N4005 (276-1103)
LED1, LED2	red light-emitting diodes (276-041)
CdS1, CdS2	cadmium sulfide photoconductive cells (276-116)
O1, O2	optoisolators (Radio Shack 276-132 may be used, but a 30-V or higher type is better; e.g. 4N35 through 4N38.)
Q1, Q2	40-V, 3-A NPN Darlington amplifiers in TO-220 or TO-126 case (Suitable devices include TIP120, TIP121, TIP123, 2N6037 through 2N6039, 2N6043 through 2N6045, MJE800T, and MJE2090.) (276-2068)
Miscellaneous	3″ × 7″ aluminum plate, 3″ × 3″ printed circuit board, soldering pins, spacers, opaque plastic for light shield

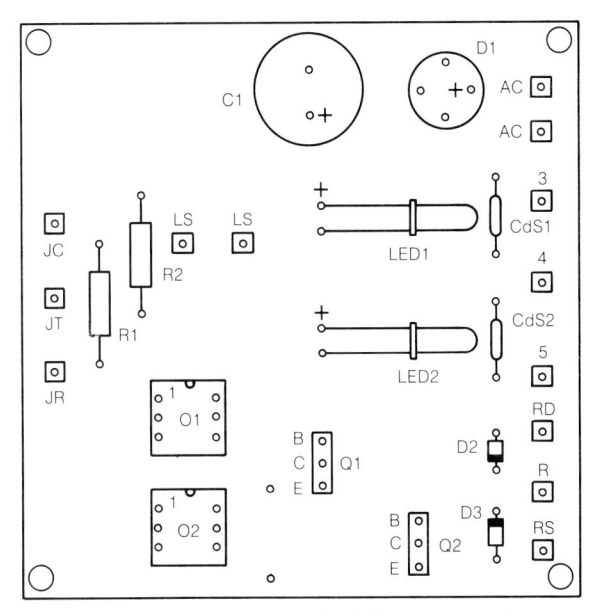

WALKAROUND CONTROL INTERFACE BOARD (component side).
Shown full size 3" × 3".

WALKAROUND CONTROL INTERFACE BOARD (foil side).
Shown full size 3" × 3".

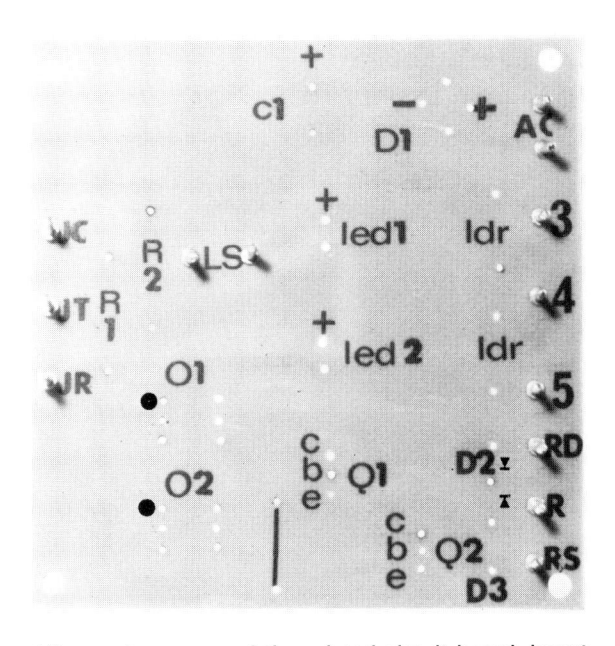

After you've prepared the printed circuit board, insert soldering pins as shown here.

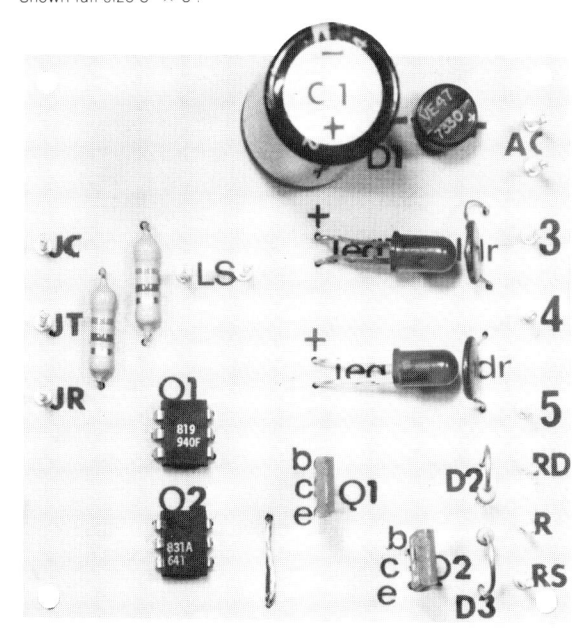

Then install the remaining components. A small dot at the upper left corner of each IC indicates pin 1.

Cover the LEDs and photoconductive cells with an opaque plastic light shield, then mount the interface board and the relays on an aluminum plate.

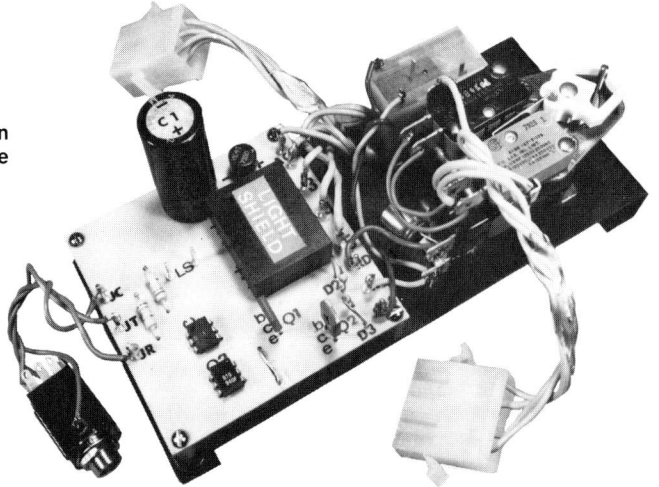

23

insert or withdraw the plug. Most jacks permit a short to occur between the tip of the plug and the ring of the jack, and the tip connection on the jack must be carefully reshaped to prevent this. I suggest you use a Radio Shack 3-conductor ¼" phone plug (274-323) and a 3-conductor enclosed ¼" stereo phone jack (274-277). This jack has a pair of switches which can be wired so that the AC doesn't connect to the tip of the plug until the plug has been pushed in all the way. Disassemble the jack and carefully file the insulated piece that operates the switch to further delay the switch action. Test your modification thoroughly with a meter to ensure there is no short on plugging in or out. If you use any other type of 3-conductor phone plug and jack, test carefully and make any necessary modifications to prevent shorting.

Alternately, you can use a somewhat less convenient (because you must check pin orientation when plugging in) 3-prong audio connector and a chassis mount socket. I recommend that you also use plugs and sockets to connect the interface boards to the track and throttle boards. The plugs and sockets simplify troubleshooting if you have several cabs and make it easier to isolate defective components.

Control interface for the hand-held SCR throttle. As I mentioned, the SCR throttle operates entirely by light signals for this hand-held conversion. Figure 2-7 shows the interface circuit board. Two LEDs illuminate a pair of CdS cells, CdS1 and CdS2. Each LED/CdS cell pair is shielded from the other pair and from ambient light. The CdS cells have a dark resistance of about 500 kΩ to 1 MΩ, but when one of the LEDs turns on, the resistance of the CdS cell facing it falls to about 100 Ω to 500 Ω. One pair of LED and CdS cell replaces the brake pushbutton switch; the other pair replaces the run pushbutton.

The direction switch is more complex because the relay requires about 250 mA. I've used two optoisolators (O1 and O2 in Fig. 2-7) switching power Darlington amplifiers (Q1 and Q2) to control the two relays — direction and spare function. The optoisolator is a small 6-pin integrated circuit that contains a miniature LED and a light-sensitive transistor which can only be illuminated by the LED. The light-sensitive transistor turns on when a 10-mA to 20-mA current lights the LED (though you can't see it through the package). This transistor then turns on a power Darlington amplifier that controls the direction relay. The same type of Potter and Brumfield latching relay is used as previously, Fig. 2-5, so each flash of light from the LED inside the optoisolator changes train direction.

The auxiliary signal (marked as "spare relay" and "RS" in the schematic and on the printed circuit board) is connected to operate another relay in the same fashion as the direction relay. This can be another latching type, which could be used to switch on tape-recorded sound, turning off at the next blip of the pushbutton. Or, it can be any standard relay, to operate a crossing

Fig. 2-8 RADIO-CONTROL INTERFACE FOR SCR THROTTLE

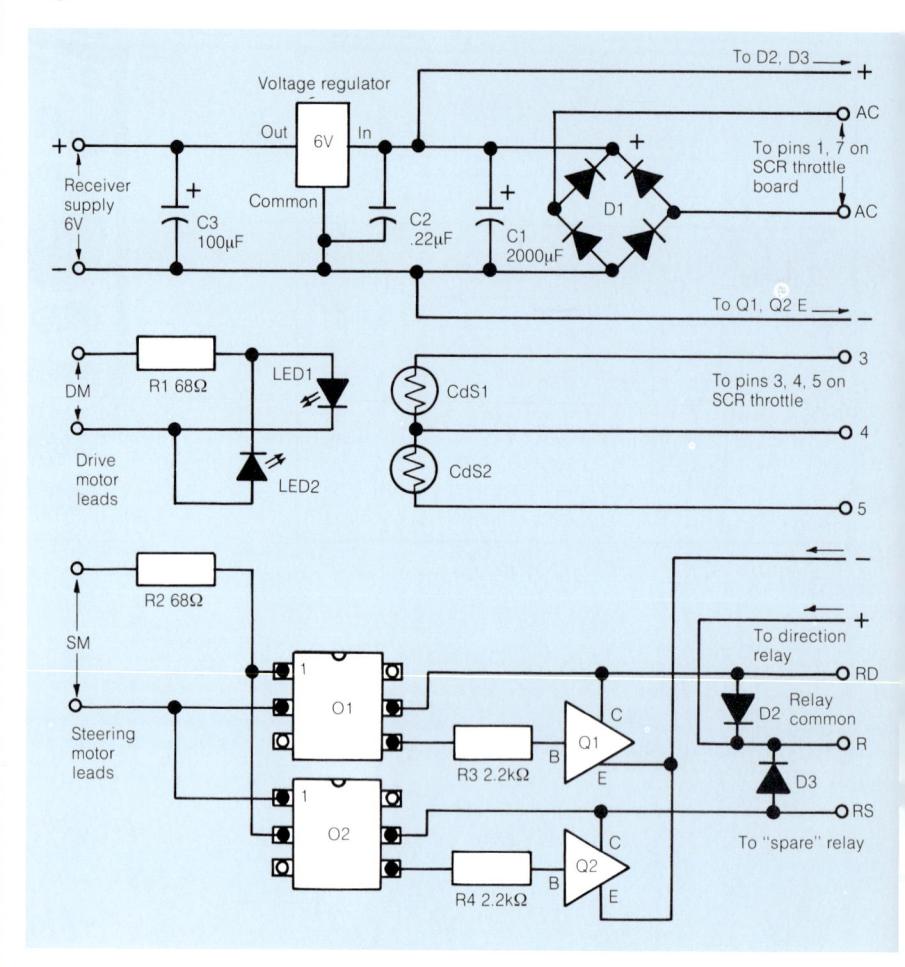

PARTS LIST FOR RADIO-CONTROL INTERFACE FOR SCR THROTTLE

C1	2000-µF, 35-VDC electrolytic capacitor
C2	0.22-µF, 100-VDC film capacitor
C3	100-µF, 16-VDC electrolytic capacitor
CdS1, CdS2	cadmium sulfide photoconductive cells (276-116)
D1	100-PIV, 1-A bridge rectifier (276-1152)
D2, D3	400-PIV, 1-A rectifier diodes, 1N4005 (276-1103)
LED1, LED2	red light-emitting diodes (276-041)
O1, O2	optoisolators, 4N35, 4N36, or 4N37 (276-132)
Q1, Q2	40-V, 3-A NPN Darlington amplifiers in TO-220 or TO-126 case (see parts list in Fig. 2-7 for suitable devices)
R1, R2	68-Ω resistors unless receiver uses a 9-V battery, in which case R1 and R2 should each be 270-Ω
R3, R4	2.2-kΩ resistors
voltage regulator	6-V, 1-A voltage regulator in TO-220 case such as National Semiconductor LM340T-6.0 or Motorola MC7806CP. The regulator must have a heat sink such as Radio Shack 273-1363. If receiver uses a 9-V battery, use an 8-V voltage regulator such as National Semiconductor LM340T-8.0 or Motorola MC7808CP.
Miscellaneous	4" × 7" aluminum plate, 2" × 4" printed circuit board, soldering pins, spacers, opaque plastic for light shield

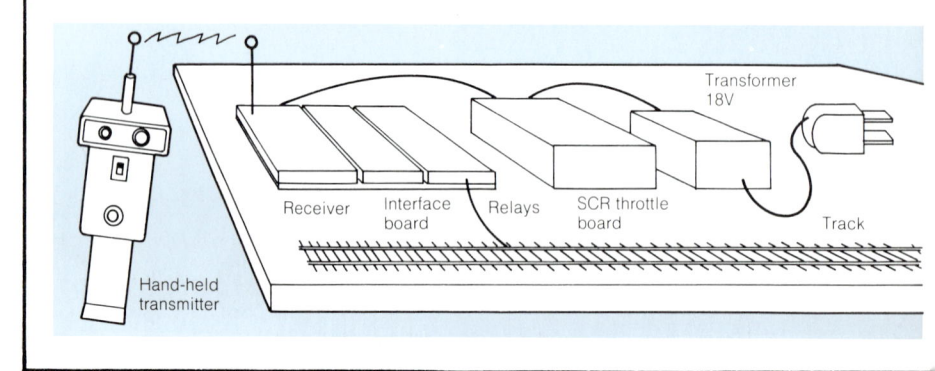

24

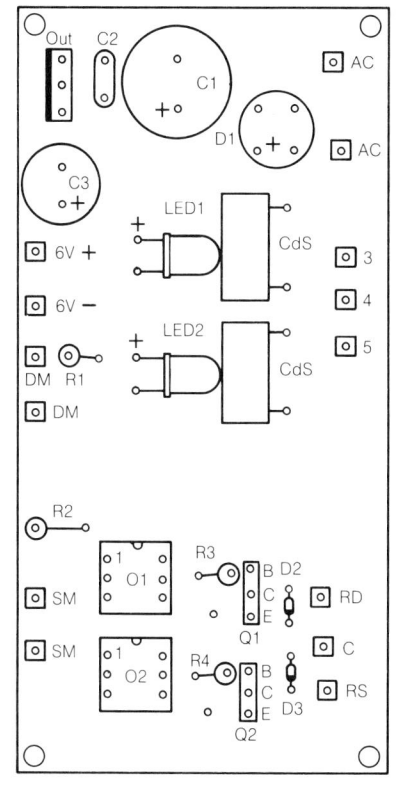

RADIO-CONTROL INTERFACE BOARD
(component side). Shown full size 2" × 4".

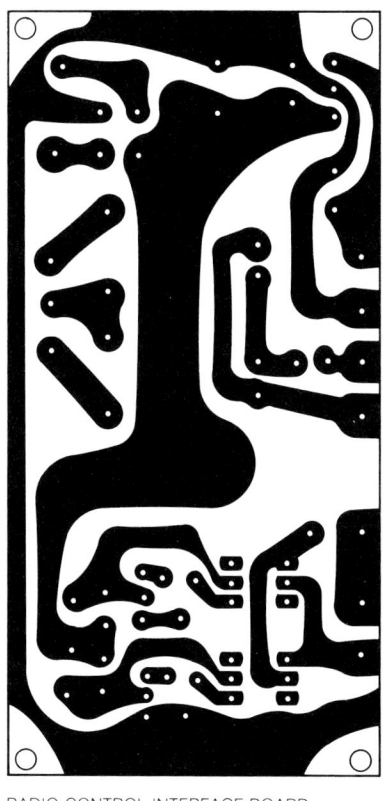

RADIO-CONTROL INTERFACE BOARD
(foil side). Shown full size 2" × 4".

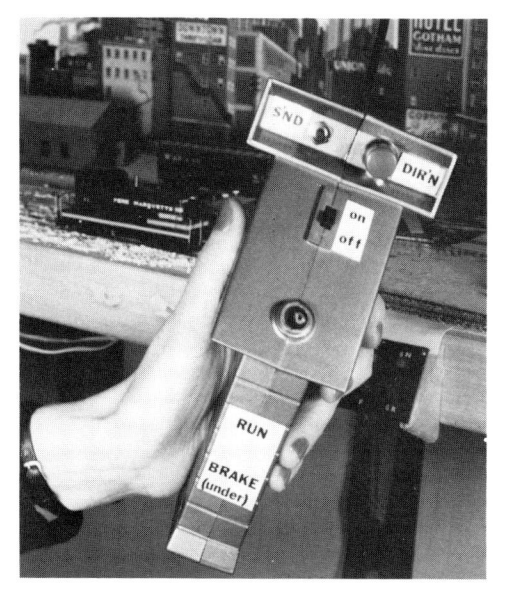

After modifying the transmitter, I painted its gaudy yellow case a more tasteful color.

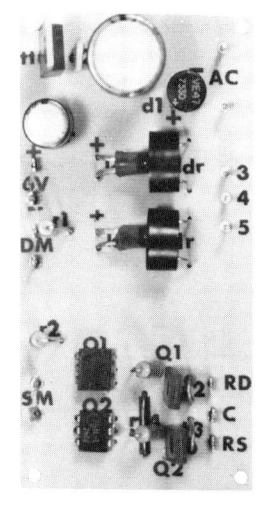

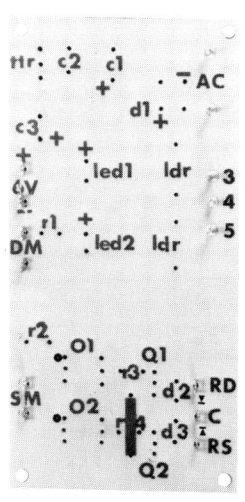

The radio-control interface uses the transmitter and receiver from a toy car such as the Mego Dune Machine.

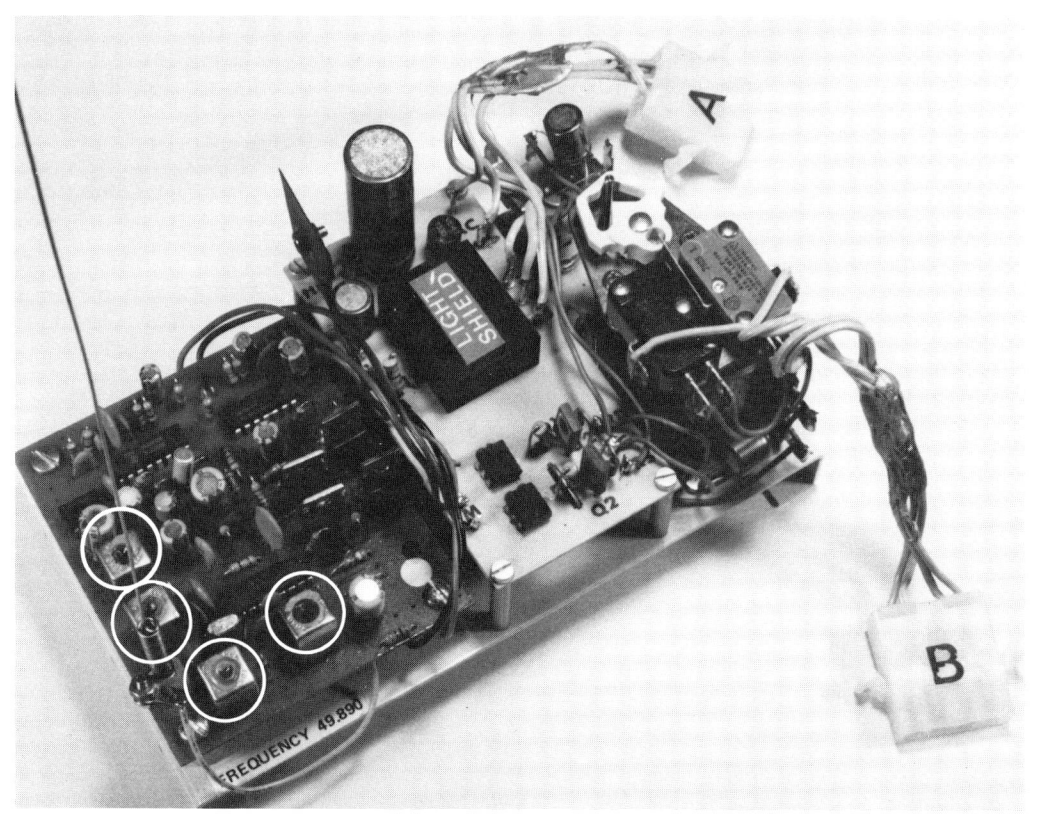

The intermediate frequency transformers (circled) identify this as a superheterodyne receiver.

25

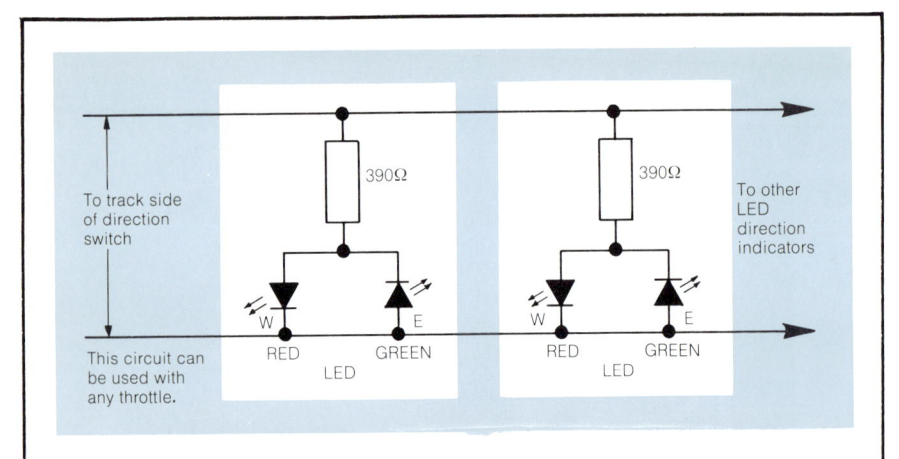

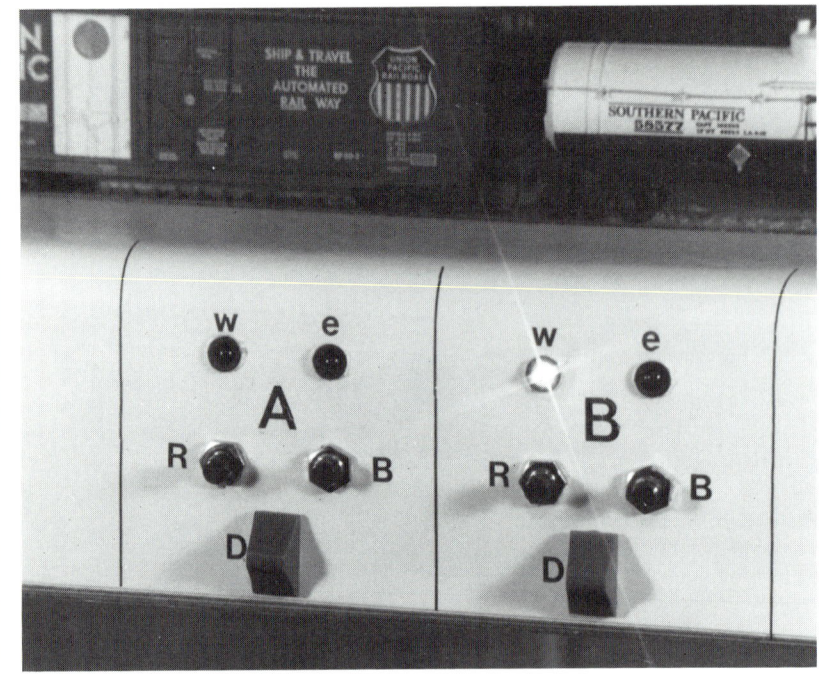

Fig. 2-9 LED DIRECTION INDICATORS

flasher, for example. As before, the DC to operate the relays comes from D1 and C1, rectified from the throttle AC input transformer. Be certain to install the protection diodes D2 and D3, Fig. 2-7.

Wiring the SCR interface. Figure 2-7 shows the interface printed circuit board. Prepare the board, mount the components as shown, and then fabricate a plastic light shield so that each pair of LED and CdS cell is isolated from the other pair and from ambient light. Consult Fig. 2-7 and assemble the direction and auxiliary relays. You'll probably want to mount the relays and the interface board on a single panel.

Radio-control SCR throttle

Commercial hobby radio-control systems consist of a hand-held transmitter with a battery power supply, a receiver/decoder, and one or more servos, each of which mechanically actuates a control in an airplane, boat, car, or other model. A single battery usually powers the receiver and servos. In some applications, as in electronic throttles for electric motors, the servo is dispensed with and the decoder electronically controls the throttle or other device. Several magazine articles have already described how to use hobby radio-control systems to mechanically actuate the potentiometer and switches on conventional throttles, and this approach is worth considering if you are a licensed radio-control hobbyist and have a radio-control system on hand.

You don't need a hobby radio-control system or a license to build my radio-control SCR throttle — the radio parts come from an inexpensive toy car. The hand-held transmitter sends very low power encoded radio waves to the receiver, mounted in an interface unit. The receiver detects, amplifies, and decodes the signals and operates optoelectronic devices (just as in the hand-held SCR throttle) that control run, brake, and direction.

You don't need a license because the transmitter operates on a frequency reserved for very low power radio-control toys. Never operate any other type of transmitter without an FCC or DOC license. Be aware, too, that unless you have an advanced amateur radio operator's license or have passed other FCC or DOC exams, you may not build a transmitter or change the frequency or power output of any radio transmitter, even the simple transmitters in toys.

The toy car and radio system I used is a "Dune Machine," Fig. 2-8, distributed in the US by Mego Corp., New York, NY 10010. In Canada, the model was distributed by Grand Toys, Montreal. The Dune Machine uses two integrated circuits, a National Semiconductor LM1871N in the transmitter, and an LM1872N in the receiver. (These are described on page 74.)

Toy cars come and go rapidly, so it's unlikely that you'll find this exact model. Here's what you want to look for when buying a similar toy:

● Operating frequency in the 49.69-MHz to 49.89-MHz band: The 27-MHz band is undesirable because of CB interference, especially in urban areas. In time, according to Murphy's law, 49 MHz may become just as congested, because cordless telephones also use this band. All other things being equal, shorter antennas suffice at 49 MHz. If you plan to use two or more radio-control throttles on your layout, be sure the toy is available in several frequencies, because you'll need a different frequency for each throttle.

● Steering that operates even when the model is stationary. On some models, the steering functions only when the drive motor is working: avoid these.

● A superheterodyne receiver. Superhets are more selective than other types (e.g. superregenerative), so the receiver will be less susceptible to interference and you'll be able to use several throttles controlled by transmitters separated by small differences in frequency.

How do you identify a superheterodyne receiver? First, check the printed circuit board for three or four small coils inside square aluminum cans (see Fig. 2-8). These are intermediate frequency transformers, found on all superhets, but not on other types. Second, check the crystal frequencies (there's one crystal each in the transmitter and receiver). If the receiver is a superhet, the crystal frequencies will differ by 455 kHz, whereas the frequencies will be the same in a superregenerative receiver.

Modifying the receiver. My Dune Machine was powered by 4 1.5-V C cells that ran the receiver, the steering motor, and the drive motor. The LM1872N in the receiver is rated for an absolute maximum of 7 V, so this voltage determined my choice of receiver power supply components. I chose 6 V as a safe maximum. I tapped the current from the SCR throttle via a bridge rectifier and a voltage regulator, Fig. 2-8. The same rectifier supplies 25 V to the direction and auxiliary relays.

I discarded the drive motor and connected its leads to the LEDs that form half of two pairs of LEDs and CdS cells (these are the same as in the interface unit for the hand-held walkaround version of the SCR throttle). One LED turns on when the polarity is positive, (the car's forward speed control), the other when it is negative (the car's reverse speed control). These LEDs illuminate the CdS cells that control throttle run and brake — just as in the walkaround control version. As before, each pair of LED and CdS cells is light shielded from the other pair and from ambient light so that each LED lights only its own CdS cell.

Similarly, I discarded the steering motor and used the two leads from the receiver to the steering motor to operate two optoisolators, one of which controls the direction relay and the other an auxiliary relay. This, again, is the same as the walkaround interface. Steer left at the transmitter and direction changes, steer right and the auxiliary relay operates. To change either of the commands, simply reverse a pair of motor leads.

Several parts of the receiver are not used in my conversion. These include a cam switch and two ICs that provided motor sound effects, and a feedback potentiometer for the steering system. I adjusted the potentiometer to its center position and left it there; you could replace it with a fixed resistor of equivalent value. By the way, I found that the transmitter must be switched on before the receiver or the relays chatter, which gives the train hysterics.

Modifying the transmitter. The transmitter draws only about 12 mA, and a 9-V heavy-duty carbon-zinc or alkaline battery lasts for a month of light operation, so I made no changes to the transmitter power supply.

The transmitter's output power is less than 50 mW, but this is enough to ensure reliable operation 25 feet or more from the receiver. You can overload the receiver if the transmitter is too close to the receiver antenna, so I mounted the receiver antenna at the back of the benchwork — there's no way I can get too close to it. I also covered both the receiver and transmitter antennas with plastic tubing to make them more visible, to prevent shorts, and to protect the ICs from damage by static electricity.

I replaced the steering wheel on the transmitter with one normally closed and one normally open pushbutton switch and set the steering wheel potentiometer in its center (null) position. The pushbutton switches activate the direction and auxiliary relays. As I mentioned, the original motor forward and reverse switch controls run and brake. The transmitter case was molded in gaudy yellow plastic; I painted this a more restful color.

Wiring the radio-control interface. Figure 2-8 shows the circuit for the interface between the receiver and the SCR throttle. Figure 2-8 also shows the printed circuit board patterns and the component locations. Be certain to mount polarity-sensitive components as shown. I mounted the receiver, interface board, and relays on a single metal panel.

If your receiver is powered by a 9-V battery, install an 8-V positive voltage regulator instead of the 6-V positive regulator I used. Also change the two 68-Ω resistors in series with the LED and optoisolator pairs to 270 Ω.

LED direction indicators. Any throttle in this chapter, or any other throttle for that matter, can be equipped with LED direction indicators, Fig. 2-9. These are easy to install and add a nice extra touch.

3 Simple projects

IF YOU'VE BECOME a little bored with hard-shell scenery, making trees, and ballasting track, one of the simple projects in this chapter may create a pleasant diversion. None requires a printed circuit and all use a minimum of components. Each adds a nice touch of realism to your layout.

Constant brightness headlights with a bridge rectifier

A model locomotive headlight is usually a 12-V to 16-V bulb wired across the motor. The lamp's brightness varies with the motor speed — most unprototypically, unless the prototype has a weak generator and flat batteries!

One way to achieve constant brightness is to exploit the voltage-dropping characteristic of semiconductor diodes. Replace the bulb with a 1.5-V to 2-V grain-of-wheat bulb or a Pacific Fast Mail "micro-miniature" light, put two diodes in series with one motor lead, and you'll obtain constant brightness whenever the motor draws current. That is, the bulb will receive a steady voltage (usually about 1.4 V) regardless of the voltage to the motor. Add two more diodes connected in reverse to the first pair, and the motor can turn in either direction and still supply a fixed 1.4 V to the lamp.

But why use four separate diodes? Just take a bridge rectifier, jumper its DC leads, cut one motor lead, connect the ends of the motor lead to the bridge rectifier's AC leads, and you've got compact, easy-to-install constant lighting, Fig. 3-1.

Constant brightness lighting for locomotives with can motors

A check of the simple constant brightness circuit, Fig. 3-1, shows that motor current, flowing through the series-connected bridge rectifier diodes, produces the power to light the lamp. A motor drawing 0.1 A through two silicon diodes, (voltage drop 1.4 V) can dump 0.14 W to light the lamp. Super-efficient can motors, now becoming more and more popular in all scales, often draw as little as 0.025 A when running slowly with no load. That isn't enough power to light the lamp properly (it produces only 0.035 W), so we need a different system.

A voltage regulator solves the problem. These ICs give a constant output voltage over a wide range of input voltages. In Fig. 3-2 a bridge rectifier supplies the voltage regulator input with positive DC regardless of the track polarity (this system can be used on both AC and DC track power). The regulator gives a constant 1.5-V output, just what we need. The LM317T is adjustable, and the 220-Ω and 39-Ω resistors in this circuit set the output at 1.5 V for any input from 4 V to 25 V. The capacitor ensures that the input to the regulator is high even for low track voltages. Be aware that because the capacitor charges to the peak value of the track voltage pulse, this system will work at lower track voltages with pulse throttles than with filtered DC throttles.

A constant 5-V power supply

The 5-V output version, Fig. 3-3, can light three PFM or No. 49 lamps in series, and is ideal for passenger trains. Mount the regulator on a heat sink or cooling plate and you can supply nine or twelve lamps in three or four parallel groups of three lamps in series. The voltage regulator runs hot, so should not contact plastic.

Track pickup can be from the coach axles. Figure 3-3 shows the 5-V version fitted to an AHM/Rivarossi ready-to-run coach that came with metal wheels and axle pickups. Wires with miniature plugs and sockets between cars can be used to transfer the output voltage down the train. Keep in mind that because power for the lights comes from the throttle, a train with three or four lighted cars will draw an extra 0.2 A to 0.25 A from that throttle.

An LED headlight

If you prefer LED headlights, you can modify the constant brightness circuit in Fig. 3-2 to provide the 2.5-V output required to turn on an LED. Change the 39-Ω resistor to 220 Ω. Add a 33-Ω resistor in series with either LED lead, and be certain to

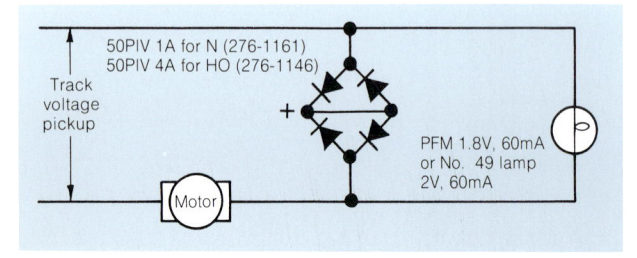

(Left above) In this Atlas HO FP7, I've installed (using silicone sealant as the adhesive) a piece of printed circuit board material copper side up to serve as a heat sink for the bridge rectifier. (Above) Here the bridge rectifier has been installed. It is wired in series with one of the motor leads and powers a small PFM bulb. For clarity I've removed the bulb from its housing in the headlamp and placed it above a small piece of white cardboard. All lighting wiring is insulated from the metal frame.

Fig. 3-1 CONSTANT BRIGHTNESS LIGHTING WITH A BRIDGE RECTIFIER

50PIV 1A for N (276-1161)
50PIV 4A for HO (276-1146)

Track voltage pickup

PFM 1.8V, 60mA
or No. 49 lamp 2V, 60mA

connect the LED in the correct polarity. I use this circuit to operate a high-light-output yellow LED as an HO headlight. The color matches tarnished reflectors, which were common before sealed-beam headlights became the norm.

Locomotive roof flashers

Many railroads now use hazard flashers mounted on the roofs of diesel cabs. You can simulate such a flasher with a red flashing LED containing its own integrated circuit, which is available from Radio Shack (276-036) and Litronix (FRL4403). It can operate from 2 V (1 flash per second) to 10 V (9 flashes per second). If you use the 5-V voltage regulator circuit I've just described, the LED will flash about 3 times per second. Be certain the longer LED lead goes to positive. The only disadvantage with this LED is that it's a little big for HO scale.

A flasher IC. The National Semiconductor LM3909 IC (276-1705) is also useful, Fig. 3-4. With it, you can flash any type or color of LED at a selectable rate. The LM3909 can be supplied from the constant 5-V power supply. Vary the flashing rate by changing the value of the capacitor: 2200 µF at 6 VDC gives about 80 flashes per minute, 100 µF gives about 160 flashes per minute, about the same as the Litronix FRL4403 flashing LED.

The advantage of using the LM3909 is that you can select a miniature LED, more appropriate for HO or N, and also use a red LED for a warning signal, yellow for caution, or green for all clear. By the way, Litronix, Inc. (address on page 4) is an excellent source of miniature LEDs. For example, the Litronix high-light-output yellow LED is cylindrical (CQV58-3) or dome-shaped (CQX33-2) and only 0.228" in diameter; the firm even sells a tiny LED that's only 0.1" in diameter (LD481).

A gyrating headlight

To round out these simple and realistic lighting effects, we can call once more on the 555 IC to make a gyrating headlight, Fig. 3-5. In this device the 555 switches two PFM micro-miniature lamps on and off alternately. Power to the IC comes from the track by way of the 5-V voltage regulator circuit. The lamps are rated at 1.8 V, 60 mA and each requires a 68-Ω limiting resistor, which can be increased to 82 Ω if the lamps flash too brightly. The key to representing the gyrating headlight is to carefully drill the plastic lens already on your loco so that it will accept the pair of PFM lamps. Use a No. 55 or No. 56 drill. The on-off rate is set by the capacitor at pins 2 and 6 of the 555; a lower capacitance gives a faster flash rate. If you choose too low a value, both lamps will flash so fast as to appear to be on continuously. Each lamp should turn on and off about every half second.

Don't use a lamp with a higher current rating than the nominal 60 mA of the PFM bulbs. The cold resistance of an incandescent lamp filament is much lower than its lighted resistance, and a surge of 200 mA through a cold filament could destroy the

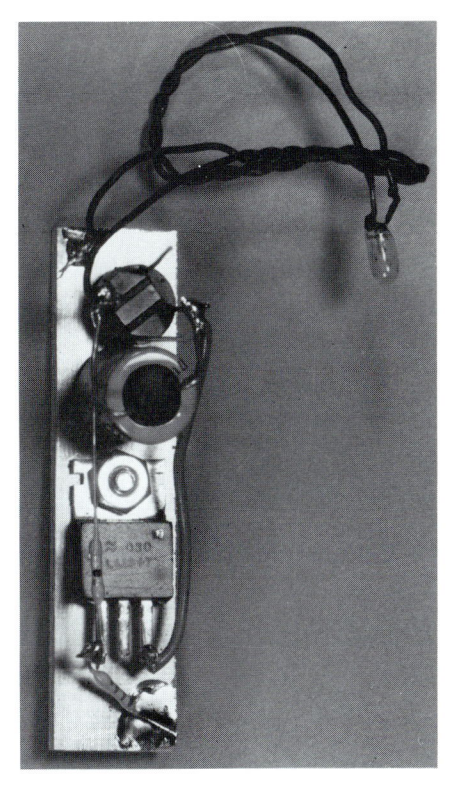

A small printed circuit board serves as a heat sink for the voltage regulator and as a mount for all components.

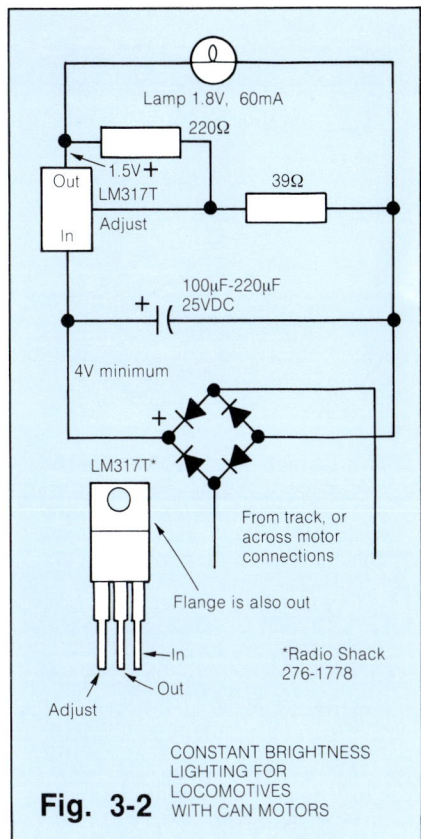

Fig. 3-2 CONSTANT BRIGHTNESS LIGHTING FOR LOCOMOTIVES WITH CAN MOTORS

This constant 5-V power supply is also mounted on a small heat-sinking piece of printed circuit board in an AHM/Rivarossi ready-to-run post office car. It powers three 6-V low-current lamps; Radio Shack bulbs 272-1140 can be used. Always allow for the current draw of such lights when computing power requirements.

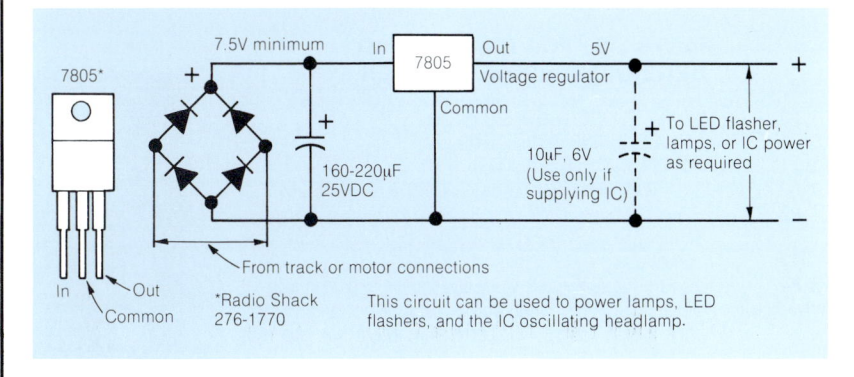

Fig. 3-3 A CONSTANT 5-V POWER SUPPLY

To assemble the LM3909 flasher, solder the leads of the capacitors and LED to the long leads of a wire-wrap DIP socket such as Radio Shack 276-1988, then insert the IC.

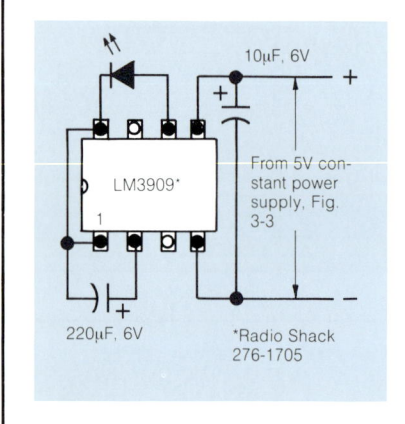

Fig. 3-4 LM3909 LED FLASHER

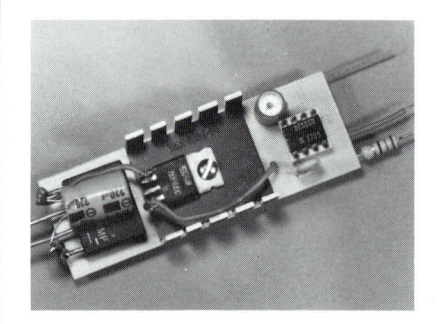

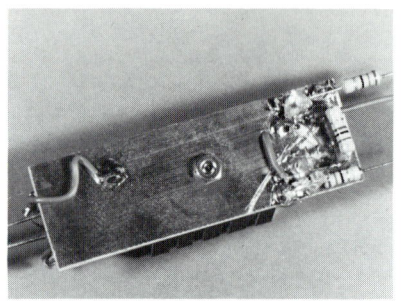

(Left above) The constant 5-V power supply (Fig. 3-3) and the components for the gyrating headlight are mounted on a 1" × 3" piece of printed circuit board. (Right above) The four resistors for the gyrating headlight circuit are on the copper side of the board; all connections are insulated with silicone sealant.

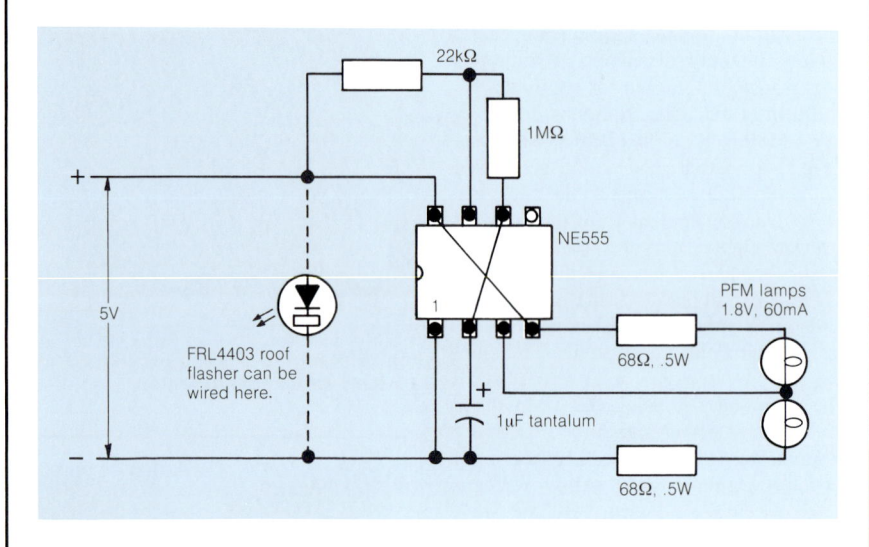

Fig. 3-5 A GYRATING HEADLIGHT

Fig. 3-7 A DUAL-OUTPUT GENERAL-PURPOSE FLASHER

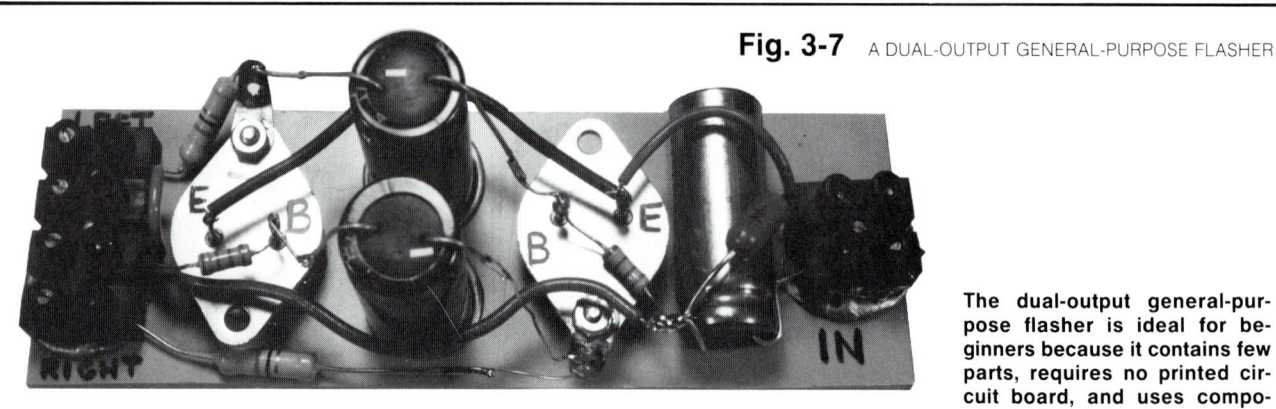

The dual-output general-purpose flasher is ideal for beginners because it contains few parts, requires no printed circuit board, and uses components with wide tolerances.

PARTS LIST FOR DUAL-OUTPUT GENERAL-PURPOSE FLASHER

C1, C2	470-µF, 25-VDC electrolytic capacitors
C3	1000-µF, 25-VDC electrolytic capacitor
D1	200-PIV, 2-A diode (276-1143)
Q1, Q2	10-A, 30-V NPN power transistors in TO-3 case (276-2041)
R1, R2	3.9-kΩ resistors (increasing the value of R1 and R2 gives a slower flash rate, but may result in dimming lamps with a heavy current draw)
R3, R4	22-Ω resistors (these limit the peak current in Q1 and Q2)
Miscellaneous	piece of plastic or printed circuit board, barrier terminals, silicone sealant, SPST NO pushbutton switch (or use relay contacts)
	Note: Test voltages are 25 V at B and E of Q1 and Q2 on the non-flashing side, 1 V on the flashing side.

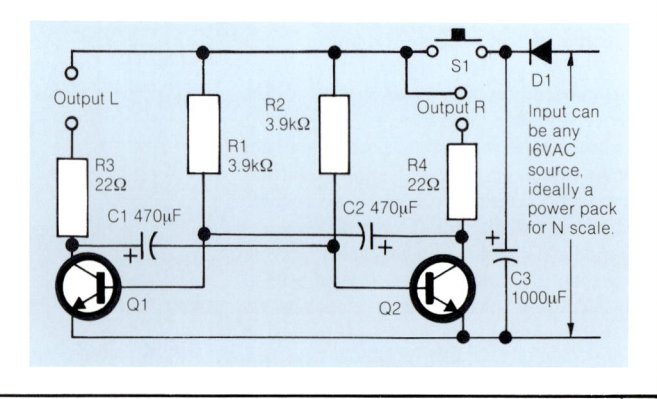

30

chip. You may use No. 49 lamps (these are 2 V, 60 mA) if there's enough space available. Radio Shack 272-1139 (1.5 V, 25 mA) is also suitable; if you choose it, substitute 150-Ω resistors for the 68-Ω resistors shown in Fig. 3-5.

Assembling the gyrating headlight. There's nothing critical about the layout, so you can assemble the device however it's convenient for your locomotive. I mounted the components on a small piece of printed circuit board, Fig. 3-5. Because the circuit is simple, I simply scratched off the copper where I wanted an insulated area. The IC socket rests in oversized holes, and jumper wires between IC socket pins are soldered directly to the pins. To maintain insulation I filled the area around the IC socket pins with silicone sealant to prevent movement of wires and components.

Shortcomings of solid-state lighting circuits

Although they are fun to build, inexpensive, and work well, the lighting circuits I've described aren't the best circuits to use if you only operate locomotives with high-quality motors that run at low voltages. This is because few solid-state devices, especially ICs, work below 4 V. The lowest input voltage for a voltage regulator (the LM317T, for example) is 3.7 V. The exceptional LM3909 will operate at 1.5 V, but a 555 requires at least 5 V.

I describe a sophisticated lighting system in Chapter 7; this system includes a high-frequency constant lighting generator and is suitable for all kinds of locos.

All of the above circuits will work with command control systems that deliver constant voltage to the tracks, though except for the flashers and the gyrating headlamp, it's simpler to use conventional 12-V to 16-V lamps (with resistors to extend bulb life) across the track voltage pickup.

Remote turnout operation

A solenoid-operated switch machine draws a large current, so large that thousands have overheated and have been ruined when inadvertently energized for too long. The switch machine draws up to 12 A at 12 V, 144 W — a lot of power. Fortunately, the switch machine need be powered only for a fraction of a second to operate properly.

Many model railroaders now use capacitor-discharge power supplies to operate switch machines. These charge a capacitor (2200 µF at 25 VDC is typical) with rectified voltage from a 16-VAC input and this energy is snappily discharged into one of the solenoid coils on much the same principle as battery-operated flashguns. The capacitor supplies sufficient power to operate the switch machine, and there's no danger of overheating because the solenoid is energized for a very short time. You'll find a complete description of capacitor-discharge units in my book PRACTICAL ELECTRONIC PROJECTS FOR MODEL RAILROADERS.

Now let's say you want to operate the switch machine from far away. If the leads from the switch to the switch machine have to carry the full 12 A at 12 V, you'll have problems with voltage drop in the long leads and may lose up to 6 V in 50 or 60 feet of wire. Heavy-gauge wire provides a partial solution, but the best answer is to devise a way to trigger the capacitor with leads that need carry only a small current.

Here's my solution, Fig. 3-6. I provide an SCR for each switch machine solenoid and use the SCR to switch the capacitor. A small current at the gate of the SCR turns it on, dumping the energy stored in the capacitor into the solenoid coil. The SCR turns off when the capacitor is empty, and the capacitor recharges in 5 to 10 seconds when you return three-position switch S1A/S1B to its center position. An LED lights to show that the capacitor is charged. The leads from S1A/S1B carry less than 100 mA, so they can be as long as needed.

The two SCRs, R1, C, and the terminal strip are mounted on the copper side of a

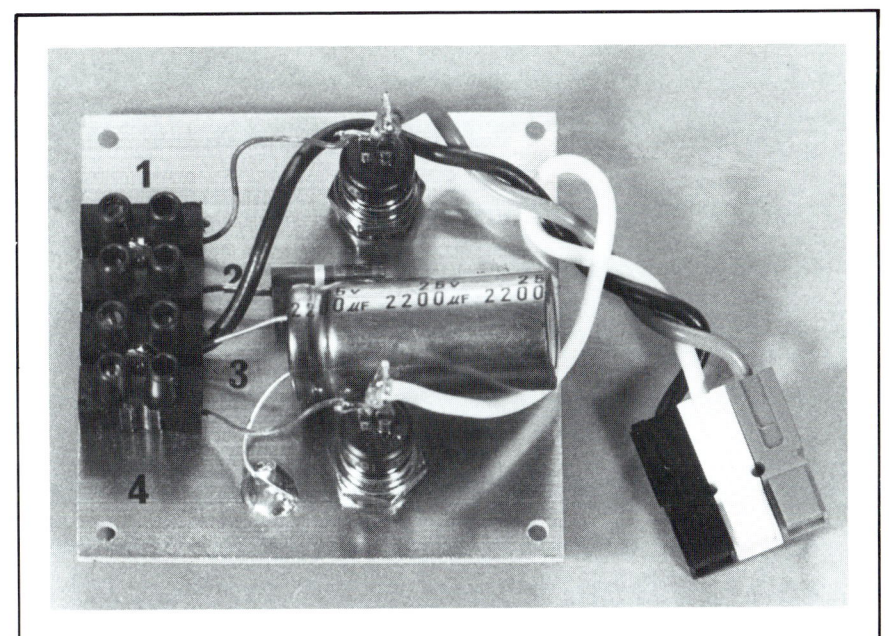

One lead of R1 and C, and the anode of each SCR are soldered directly to the copper side of a 3" × 3" printed circuit board. This board is mounted next to the turnout. The switch and LED charge indicator can be mounted many feet away.

PARTS LIST FOR REMOTE TURNOUT OPERATION

C	25-VDC or 35-VDC, 3000-µF electrolytic capacitor
D	1-A, 400-PIV rectifier diode (276-1103)
R1	2-W to 5-W, 150-Ω to 220-Ω resistor
R2	0.5-W, 1-kΩ resistor
S1A, S1B	2-pole, 3-position switches. These must have non-shorting contacts. If you can't find a 3-position switch and use Radio Shack 275-1836 or Centralab PA1003 or PA2003, note that only 3 positions are used on these 6-position switches.
SCR1, SCR2	25-A (250-A surge), 100-PIV silicon controlled rectifiers such as Motorola C230A or C231A
Miscellaneous	3" × 3" printed circuit board, barrier terminal, connectors to switch machine (optional)

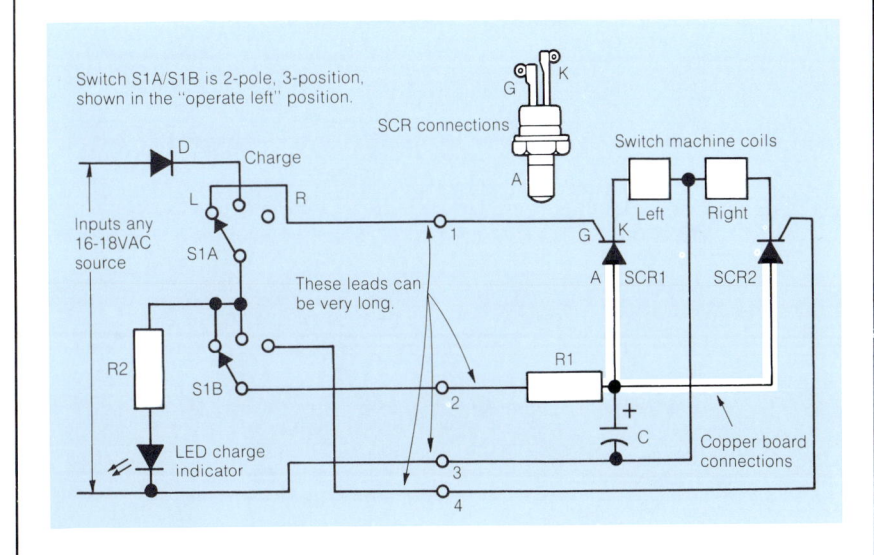

Fig. 3-6 REMOTE TURNOUT OPERATION

Fig. 3-8 LIGHT-SENSITIVE TRAIN DETECTOR

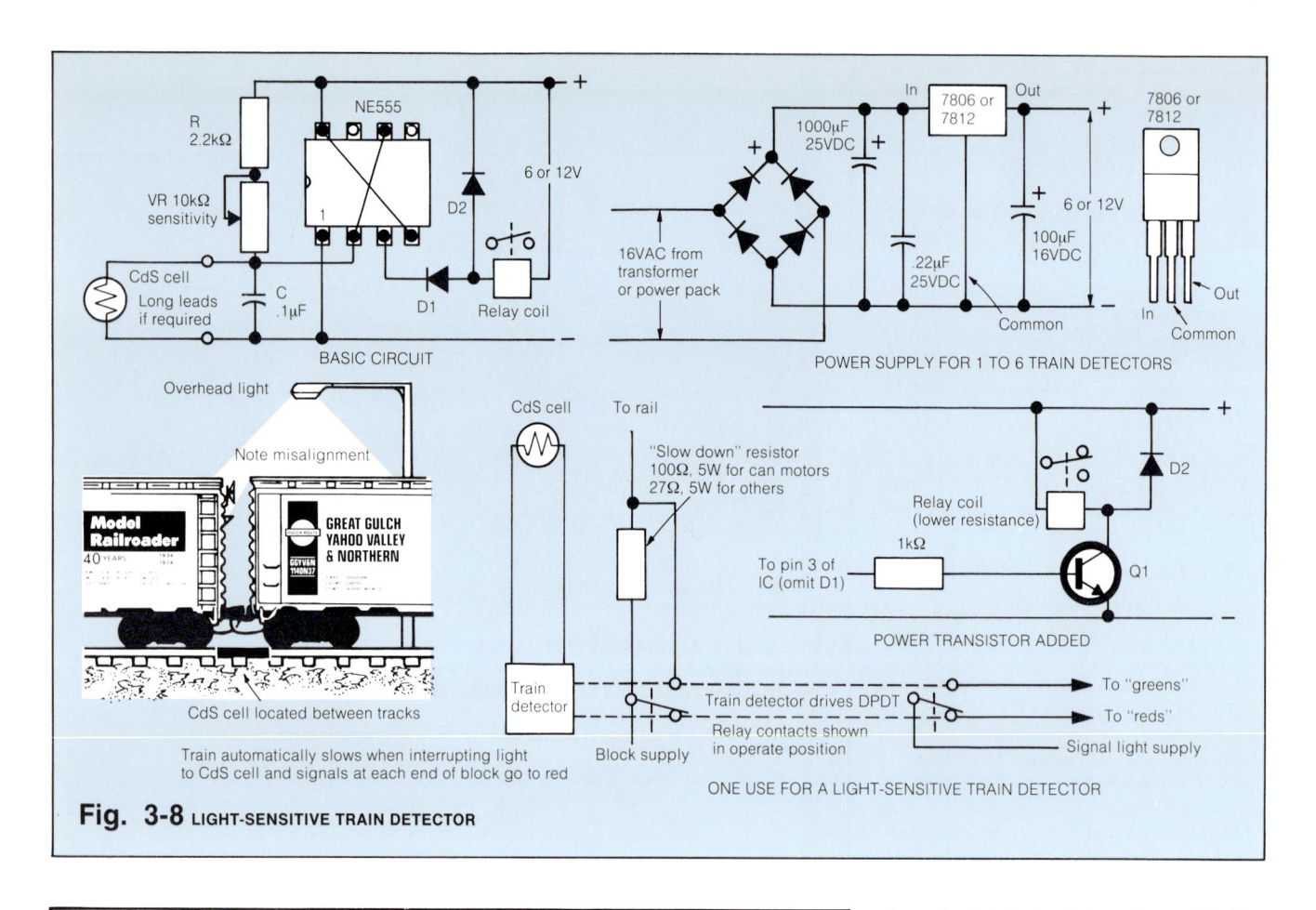

PARTS LIST FOR LIGHT-SENSITIVE TRAIN DETECTOR

C	0.1-µF, 100-VDC film capacitor (for electrical noise suppression)
D1, D2	1-A, 200-PIV rectifier diodes, 1N4002 (276-1102)
IC	NE555 (8 pin) (276-1723)
CdS	cadmium sulfide photoconductive cell (276-116)
R	2.2-kΩ resistor
Relay	6 V or 12 V, coil resistance not less than 160 Ω, contacts as required (12 V, DPDT is 275-206; 6 V, SPDT is 275-004)
VR	10-kΩ potentiometer (for sensitivity adjustment) (271-218 or 271-335)
Miscellaneous	IC socket adapter board (276-024) or perf board, IC socket (276-1995)
Notes:	If the CdS cell measures more than 3 kΩ in ambient light, use 4.7 kΩ for R and 47kΩ for VR. Q1 is a a 40-V, 5-A NPN transistor (276-2041); the voltage regulator is a 6-V or 12-V regulator, 7806 or 7812 in a TO-220 case (12 V is 276-1771); and the bridge rectifier is 4 A, 100 PIV (276-1171).

piece of printed circuit board material. The heavy line in Fig. 3-6 shows connections that go straight to the copper. Note that the anode of each SCR bolts directly to the copper. The switch, R2, D, and the LED are mounted on the layout control panel. Any source of 16 VAC to 18 VAC, even the smallest transformer, can supply the unit.

A dual-output general-purpose flasher

This little gadget, Fig. 3-7, can be used to operate grade-crossing flashers, to ring bells, or to operate relays. It can be hand-wired on a piece of plastic or printed circuit board and you can assemble the unit in an hour.

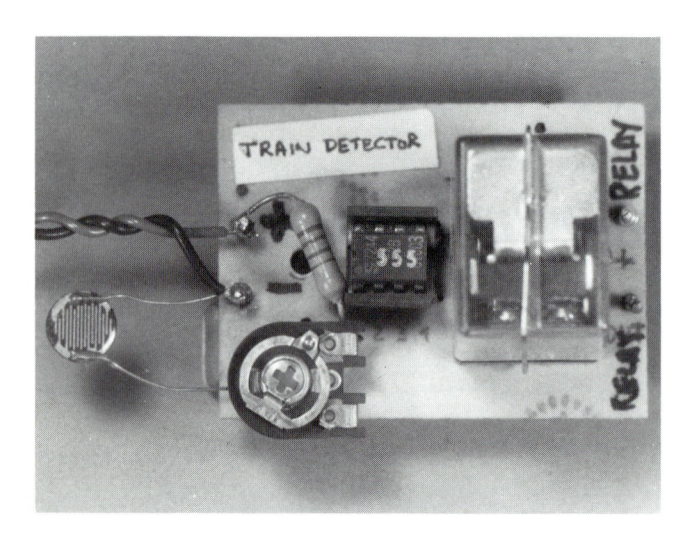

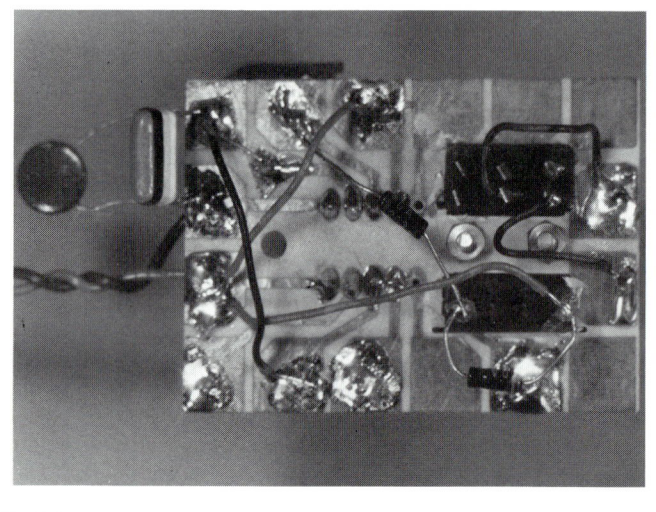

I've mounted all of the train detector components and a 12-VDC, DPDT miniature relay (275-206) on a 1½" × 2⅛" printed circuit IC socket adapter board.

The flash rate using the components specified is about 80 flashes per minute, with the two outputs alternating. You can vary the rate from about 20 to 200 flashes per minute by changing the values of C1 and C2.

The circuit can handle loads up to about 0.5 A. For grade-crossing flashers, wire two grain-of-wheat bulbs in series at each output and add more pairs of bulbs for additional crossings.

For heavier loads, install a relay at one output and replace the load on the other output with a 200-Ω to 220-Ω, 5-W resistor. If you use a 12-V relay, add a resistor equal in value to the resistance of the relay coil. For example, a Radio Shack 275-206 relay with a coil resistance of 160 Ω needs a 180-Ω resistance in series. The relay coil also needs a 200-PIV, 1-A diode (1N4002) across the coil, cathode to positive.

You can ring a small electric bell with this device. Short together any switch contacts on the bell, wire it to one output, and install a 200-Ω to 220-Ω, 5-W resistor at the other output. Load the bell with epoxy, pennies, or modeling clay until it sounds like a loco or crossing bell.

A light-sensitive train detector

This detector, Fig. 3-8, uses a CdS cell to turn on a 555 IC whenever layout light is shadowed by a train. For example, if you mount the CdS cell between the track, its resistance increases whenever a train passes over it and the increased resistance triggers the 555, energizing the load.

The load can be almost anything you desire. It can be simply a 12-V to 16-V grain-of-wheat signal lamp (in which case D1 and D2 are not needed), or it can be a relay that switches on crossing lights and bells, aligns turnouts, disconnects a block behind the train to prevent rear-end collisions, or automatically brakes the train.

The relay coil should be a 12-V type with a resistance of not less than 150 Ω, but you can add a power transistor to operate lower-resistance relays. Diodes D1 and D2 prevent voltage spikes from damaging the 555 and must be installed in the polarity shown.

Because the light or relay is on only when the CdS cell is in shadow, the relay may

A headlight and a roof flasher greatly enhance the realism of any diesel locomotive.

hiccup with a slow train as light filters through between the cars. Avoid this problem by installing an off-center yard light to illuminate the CdS cell.

Potentiometer VR adjusts the sensitivity of the circuit. Moving the wiper toward plus increases the amount of light required to turn off the 555 and decreases the amount of shadow required to turn it on. The potentiometer allows for the wide variations of ambient light levels on layouts and compensates for different CdS cells. I've specified values for R and VR that match the Radio Shack CdS cell called for in the parts list, but if you use a photoconductive cell with a higher resistance, you may have to increase the value of R to 4.7 kΩ and change VR to 47 kΩ.

Figure 3-8 also shows the circuit for a power supply suitable for one to six train detectors, more if all of the detectors aren't operated at the same time. Use a 12-V voltage regulator with 12-V relays, a 6-V regulator with 6-V relays.

I built my detectors on a Radio Shack IC socket adapter board. The IC socket adapter board is a pre-drilled printed circuit board that accepts one 6-pin to 16-pin IC or IC socket, and that has extended copper leads for easy soldering. I removed some of the copper to insulate the socket of the 12-V, 160-Ω DPDT relay shown.

33

④ Intermediate and advanced projects

THIS CHAPTER contains five projects that range from intermediate to advanced. They are an improved current-sensitive train detection system, a current-sensitive detection system that can also sense direction, an animated grade crossing system complete with light and sound effects, a circuit for programmed turnout control, and an automatic reversing loop. If you're ready to build any of them, you're well beyond the elementary level, so I've kept the explanations of theory of operation and construction techniques brief.

Current-sensitive train detector

Linn Westcott's Twin-T is undoubtedly the most widely used current-sensitive train detector; it's described in full in PRACTICAL ELECTRONIC PROJECTS FOR MODEL RAILROADERS. There is also an update on the Twin-T in the August 1980 issue of MODEL RAILROADER. With the Twin-T a minute current — about 0.01 mA — across the track switches off a package consisting of three transistors and two diodes. One of the transistors powers a light, LED, relay, or some other device.

Good as it is, the Twin-T has two drawbacks. First, the leakage across the track is often made to pass through conductive paint on the axles of unpowered or unlighted cars, and conductive paint can be hard to find. Second, the Twin-T is so sensitive that it can be tricked into false detection by tiny currents leaking across turnout frogs in humid weather.

My design is similar to the Twin-T but overcomes these drawbacks. Instead of conductive paint, I simply solder a 680-Ω resistor across the axle, Fig. 4-1. And, my design requires at least 2 mA leakage to operate, so it's not subject to false detection. As shown in Fig. 4-1, a small amount of throttle voltage causes a current

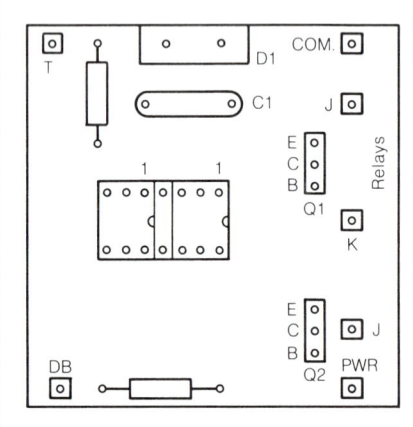

CURRENT-SENSITIVE DETECTOR CIRCUIT BOARD (component side). Shown full size 2″ × 2″.

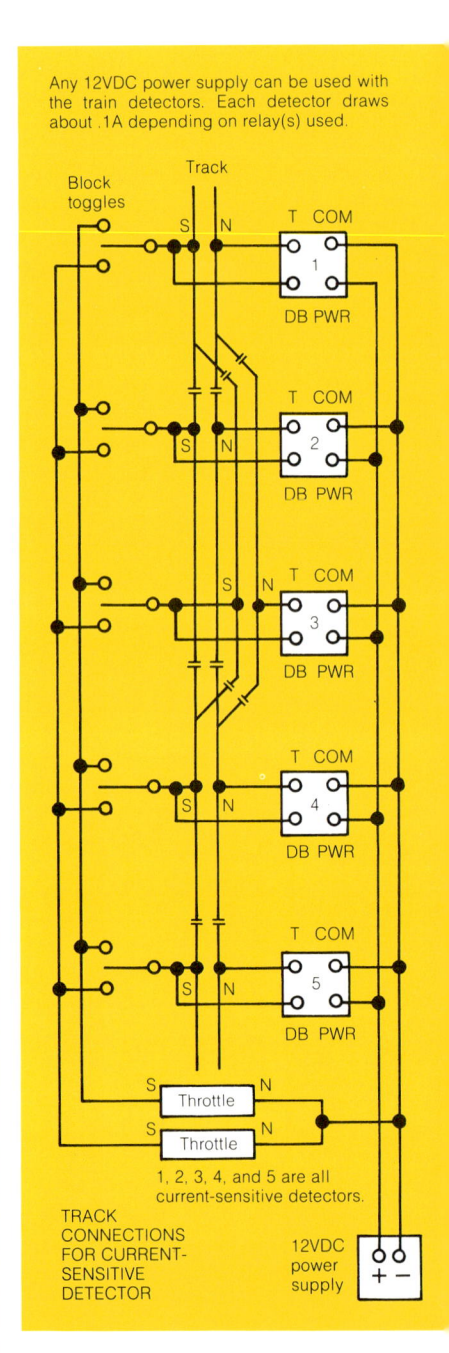

Fig. 4-1 CURRENT-SENSITIVE TRAIN DETECTORS

1, 2, 3, 4, and 5 are all current-sensitive detectors.

Any 12VDC power supply can be used with the train detectors. Each detector draws about .1A depending on relay(s) used.

TRAIN DETECTION SYSTEMS CHECKLIST

	Magnetic (Reed or Hall-Effect)	Optical (CdS)	Current-Sensitive (e.g. Twin-T)
Records block in use*	No	No	Yes
Senses track power	No	No	Yes
Modifications to rolling stock	Yes	No	Yes
Can use with command control systems	Yes	Yes	Yes
Can use with sound-on-rail systems	Yes	Yes	No
Can use with hf lighting	Yes	Yes	No
Layout location	Trackside	Trackside	Below layout
Affected by ambient light (need sensitivity adjust)	No	Yes	No
Can sense both directions of travel	Yes	No	Some types, yes

This chart will simplify selection of a track detection system. Some generalizations have been made; for example, the Twin-T can be used with some sound-on-rail systems, but the wiring-up becomes more complicated than the answer deserves.

*Block in use indicates capacity to detect a single stationary item of rolling stock over any specified length of track.

PARTS LIST FOR CURRENT-SENSITIVE DETECTORS

C1	0.1-µF, 100-VDC film capacitor
C2, C3	47-µF or 100-µF, 25-VDC electrolytic capacitors
D1	100-PIV, 2.5-A bridge rectifier (General Instruments KBF-02 or Radio Shack 276-1171. Use 276-1180 for O scale. The bridge rectifier must withstand short-circuits across the track, so do not substitute a lower-rated part.)
D2, D3, D4	200-PIV, 1-A silicon diodes, 1N4148 or 1N4002 (276-1102)
O1, O2	DC-input optoisolators, 4N35, 4N36, or 4N37 (For the basic detector, use an AC-input optoisolator such as General Electric H11AA1 [best], or H11AA2, or CNY35.)
Q1, Q2	4-A, 40-V NPN Darlington amplifiers in TO-126 or TO-220 case, Texas Instruments TIP120, TIP121, or TIP122; Motorola MJE2090, MJE2091, 2N6037, 2N6038, 2N6039, 2N6043, 2N6044, or 2N6045 (276-2058)
Miscellaneous	2" × 2" printed circuit board, approximately 2" × 5" sheet plastic, soldering pins, 14-pin DIP IC socket (276-1999) (Use an 8-pin socket [276-1995] for the basic detector.), silicone sealant, appropriate relay(s)

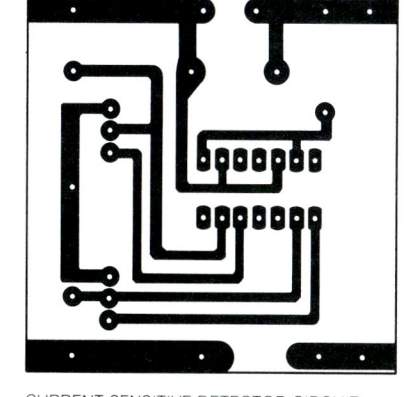

CURRENT-SENSITIVE DETECTOR CIRCUIT BOARD (foil side). Shown full size 2" × 2".

In order to detect unpowered or unlighted rolling stock, solder a 680-Ω resistor across the axle.

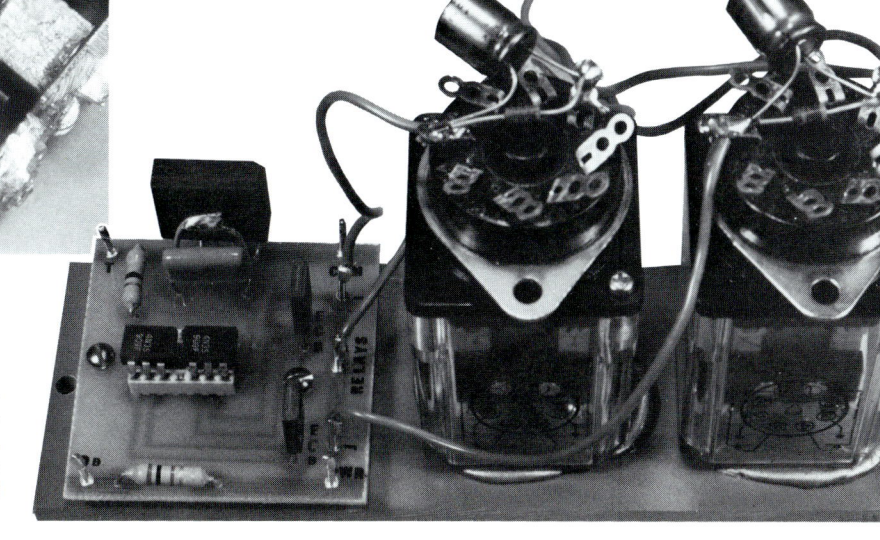

The bidirectional current-sensitive train detector uses two DC input optoisolators and two relays. The printed circuit board and the relays mount on a single piece of plastic.

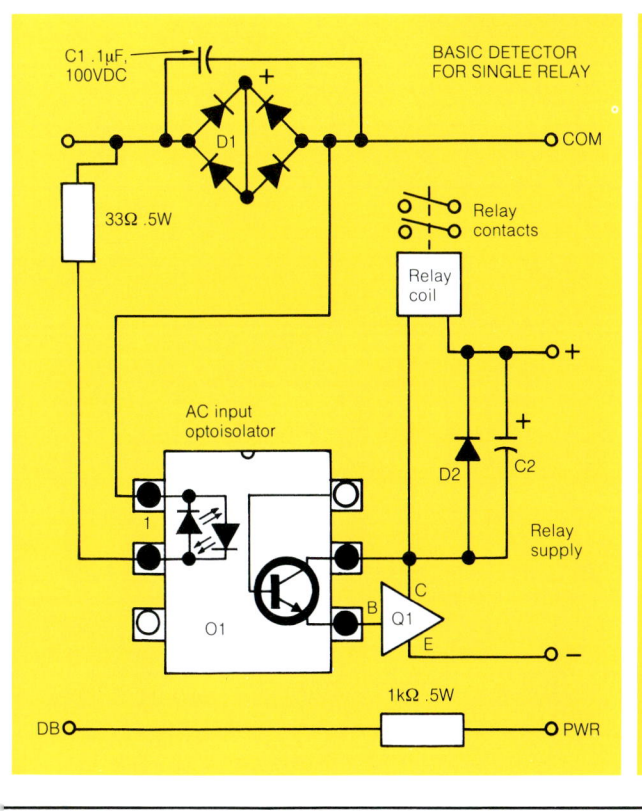

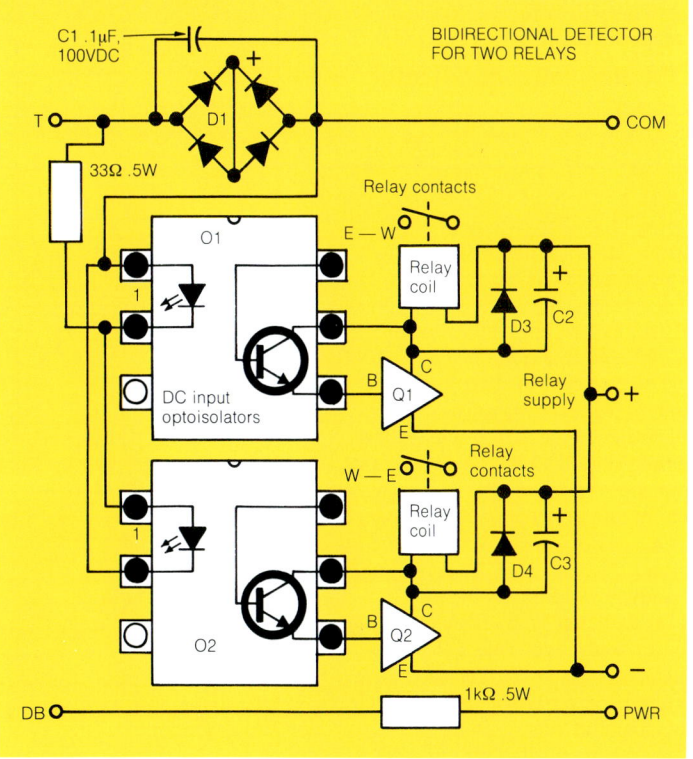

BASIC DETECTOR FOR SINGLE RELAY

BIDIRECTIONAL DETECTOR FOR TWO RELAYS

35

of at least 2 mA to pass through any locomotive or lighted car or caboose (or any car equipped with a "680-Ω axle") in the block being detected.

This develops either a positive or a negative voltage across the "DC shorted" bridge rectifier in series with the track power. The voltage across the bridge is supplied to an AC-input optoisolator, which contains LEDs that work from either input polarity and that turn on an electrically isolated internal transistor switch. Most optoisolators have a "current transfer ratio" of 20 percent to 100 percent, which means that the 2 mA of current operating the internal LED is transferred as between 0.4 mA and 2 mA of transistor switch current. This current is amplified by a Darlington amplifier, Q1, to a level that can operate any lamp or relay.

When a train is running in the block at any speed, the voltage applied to the optoisolator's input is limited to a safe maximum of 1.4 V by the bridge rectifier in series with the track. If track voltage is applied without a train in the block, the optoisolator receives no signal and does not operate. On the other hand, when a train is in the block, sufficient current passes through the locomotive, lighted car, or the car equipped with the "680-Ω axle" to operate the optoisolator from the auxiliary 12-VDC power supply. This is true whether or not track power is present.

Note that if a transistor throttle set at low output voltage is switched to the block, the circuit can produce an error because the very low internal resistance of the throttle will bypass the axle resistor, light, or motor resistance and indicate an empty block. If you have this problem, induce the 2-mA leakage by connecting a 5.6-kΩ, 0.5-W resistor across the C and E connections of the throttle power transistor or Darlington amplifier. This will have no effect upon the operation of the throttle.

A bidirectional detector

To build a direction-sensing train detector, substitute two DC-input optoisolators for the AC-input component used in the basic version. The LEDs in the optoisolators are wired together externally, in opposite polarity. One optoisolator switches with one track polarity and the other switches with reversed track polarity. This feature is convenient for bidirectional signaling on single track, because the relevant relay contacts can be used to control signals only in the direction of travel. Approach-lit signals for the opposing direction will remain dark.

Rolling stock will be detected by one set of direction relays only. You can select which by reversing the polarity of the auxiliary DC power supply leads to the optoisolators.

Readily available 12-V, 4PDT relays used for E-W and W-E sensing give you the option of four completely independent sets of contacts, on and off, for each direction. The relays may control signals, switches, lights, sound effects, or whatever else you desire. Parenthetically, observe that relays are better than IC logic switches for these

Fig. 4-2 ACTION CROSSING

The action crossing incorporates detector, timers, flashers, sound generators for bell and horn, an audio amplifier with a layout-mounted loudspeaker, and a power supply. Most components mount on a 4″ × 4″ printed circuit board.

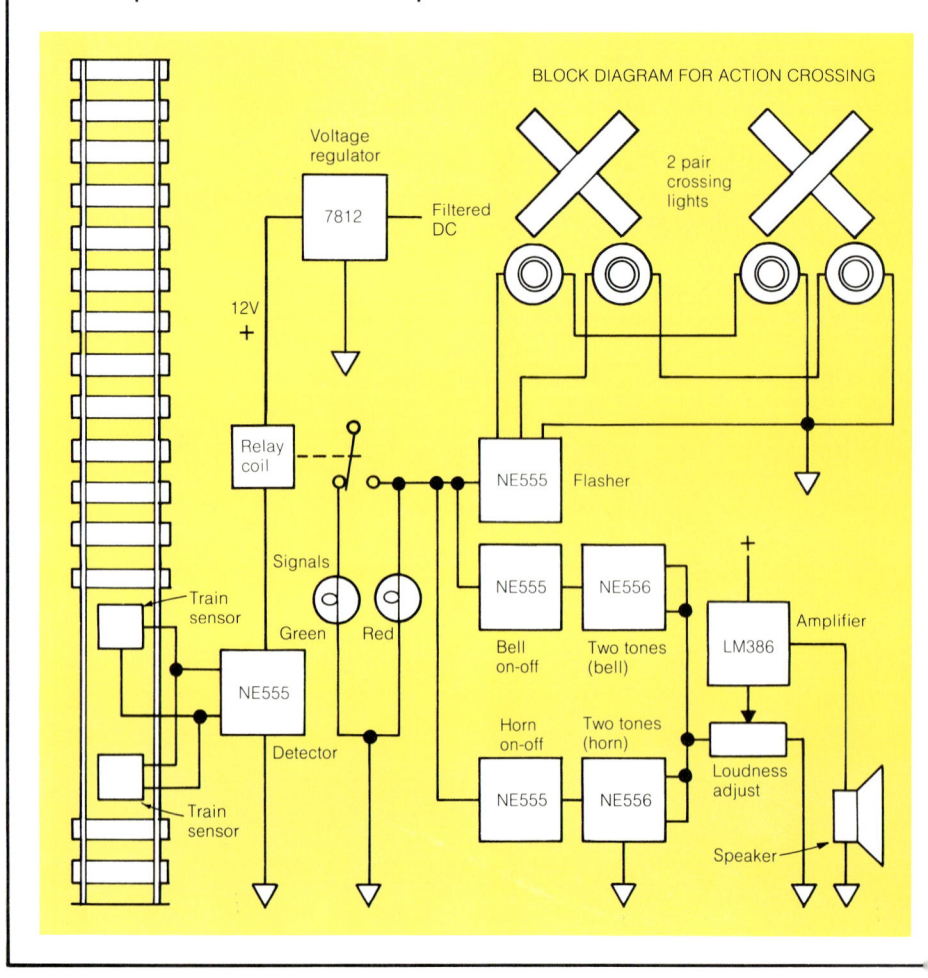

36

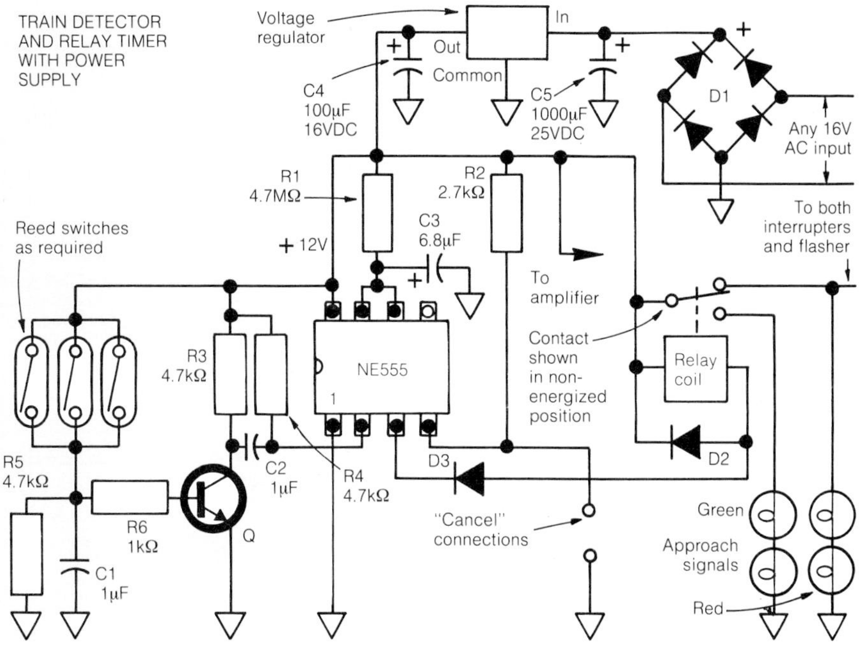

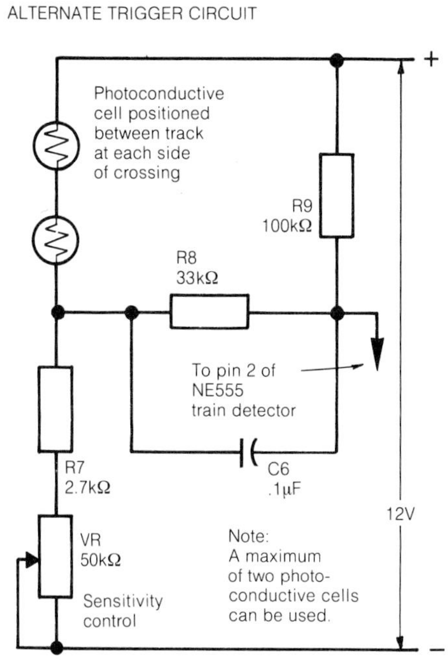

CIRCUIT OF BELL OR HORN SOUND GENERATOR

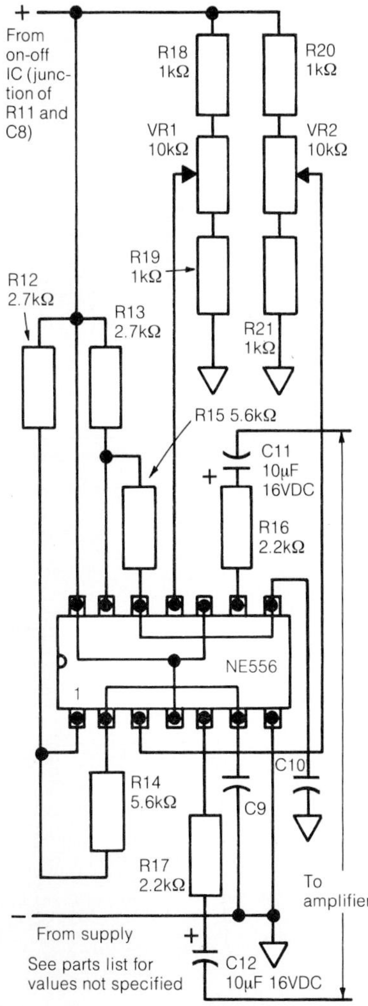

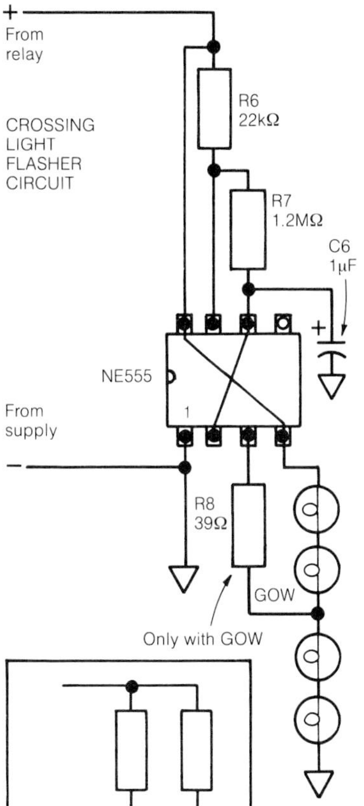

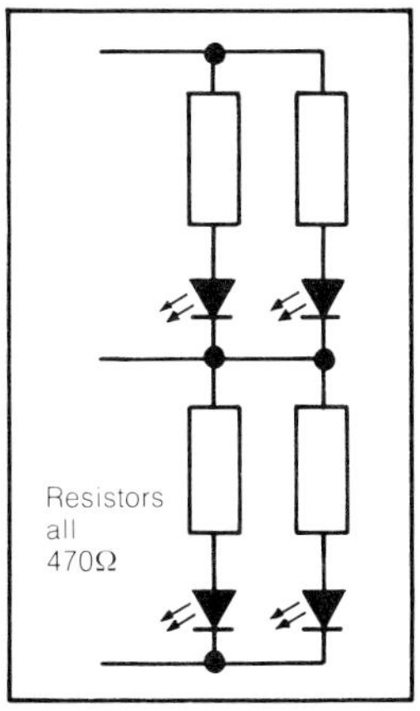

Use this circuit with LEDs.

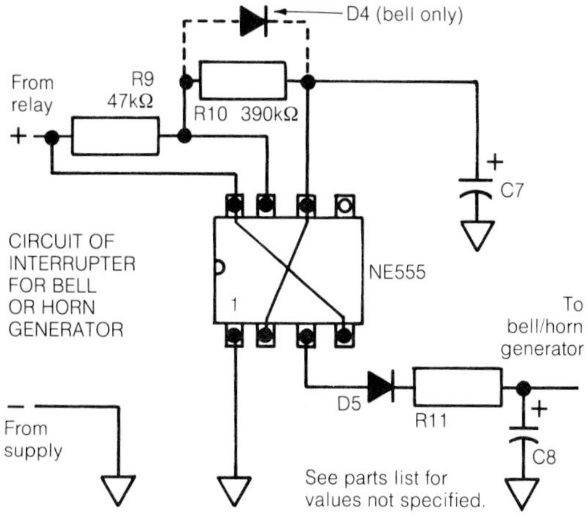

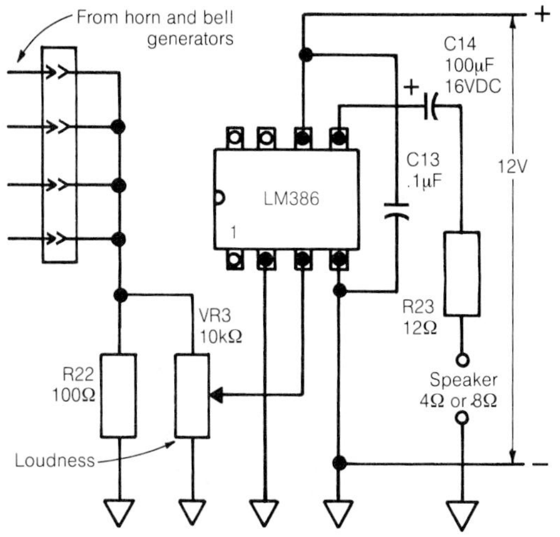

AMPLIFIER CIRCUIT FOR ACTION CROSSING

Hole locations for ACTION CROSSING PRINTED CIRCUIT BOARD. Shown full size 4" × 4".

Colored lines indicate jumpers on this side of board.

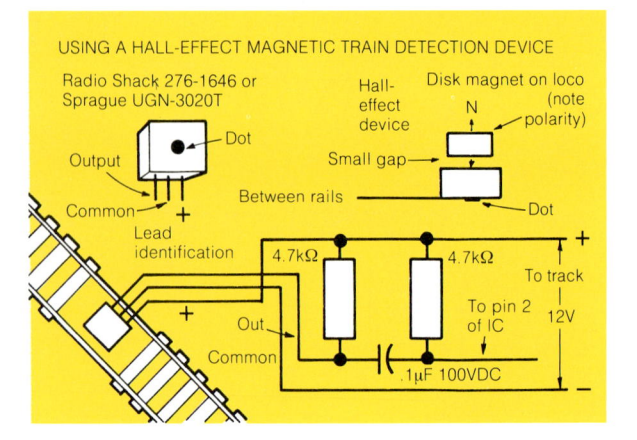

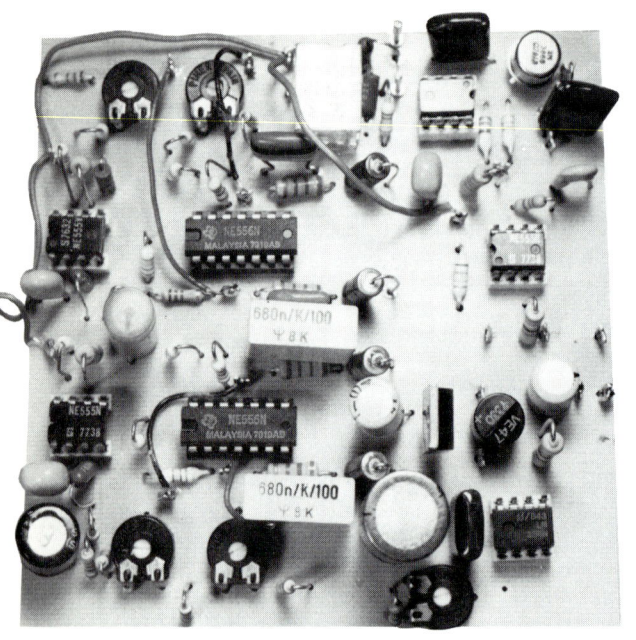

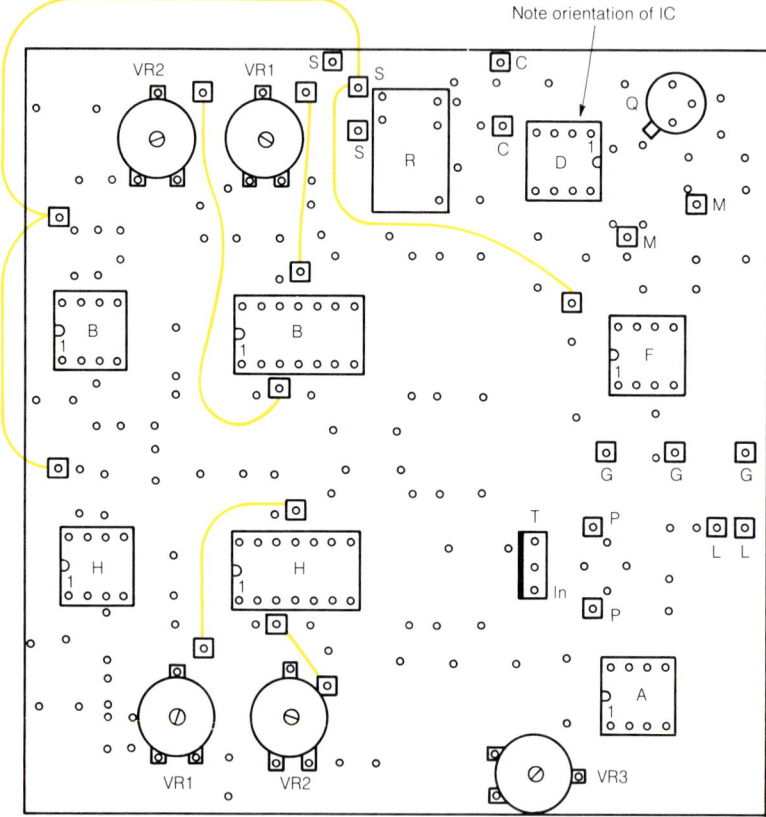

Note orientation of IC

USING A HALL-EFFECT MAGNETIC TRAIN DETECTION DEVICE

Radio Shack 276-1646 or Sprague UGN-3020T

- Dot
- Output
- Common
- Lead identification

Hall-effect device

Disk magnet on loco (note polarity)
- N
- Small gap
- Between rails
- Dot

4.7 kΩ   4.7 kΩ
To track
To pin 2 of IC
12V
.1 µF 100VDC
Out
Common

Prepare the printed circuit board, then mount the components and make connections as shown here.

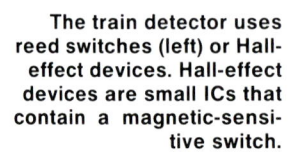

The train detector uses reed switches (left) or Hall-effect devices. Hall-effect devices are small ICs that contain a magnetic-sensitive switch.

PARTS LIST FOR ACTION CROSSING

TRAIN DETECTOR AND RELAY TIMER WITH POWER SUPPLY

C1, C2	0.1-µF, 50-VDC disk or film capacitors
C3	6.8-µF, 16-VDC tantalum or solid aluminum capacitor
C4	100-µF, 16-VDC electrolytic capacitor
C5	1000-µF, 25-VDC electrolytic capacitor
D1	100-PIV, 1-A bridge rectifier (Must be at least 1 A.) (276-1152)
D2, D3	100-PIV, 0.2-A silicon diodes, 1N914, 1N4148 (Must be at least 0.2 A.) (276-1152)
IC	NE555 (8-pin) (276-1723)
Q	0.3-A, 30-V NPN general purpose silicon transistor, 2N2222A (276-2030)
R1	4.7-MΩ resistor (Note high value.)
R2	2.7-kΩ resistor
R3, R4, R5	4.7-kΩ resistors
R6	1-kΩ resistor
relay	12-V, 200-Ω SPDT relay (275-003) (276-216 will do, but add a 68-Ω, 1-W resistor in series with the relay coil, as this is a 5-V relay.)
voltage regulator	12-V, 1-A voltage regulator, µA7812 (276-1771)
Miscellaneous	8-pin IC socket (276-1995), magnets for rolling stock (64-1880), miniature reed switches between track (275-1610) Note: If the crossing is triggered frequently, the voltage regulator may overheat. Should this happen, add a 30-Ω (approximate), 5-W resistor in series with either AC input lead.

CROSSING LIGHT FLASHER

C6	1-µF, 16-VDC tantalum or solid aluminum capacitor (272-1419)
IC	NE555 (8-pin) (276-1723)
R6	22-kΩ resistor
R7	1.2-MΩ resistor (Note high value. Higher resistance increases on time.)
R8	39-Ω resistor (R8 is for grain-of-wheat lamps; if using LEDs, obtain 4 470-Ω resistors.)
Miscellaneous	8-pin IC socket (276-1995)

INTERRUPTER FOR THE BELL AND HORN GENERATORS (ONE EACH REQUIRED)

C7	1-µF, 16-VDC tantalum or solid aluminum capacitor for bell, 6.8-µF, 16-VDC tantalum or solid aluminum capacitor for horn
C8	100-µF, 16-VDC electrolytic capacitor for bell, 22-µF, 16-VDC electrolytic capacitor for horn
D4, D5	100-PIV, 0.2-A silicon diodes, 1N914, 1N4148 (276-1122) (D4 used with bell only.)
IC	NE555 (8-pin case) (276-1723)
R9	47-kΩ resistor
R10	390-kΩ resistor (Higher value slows rate of interruption, lower value increases rate of interruption.)
R11	100-Ω resistor for bell, 270-Ω resistor for horn
Miscellaneous	8-pin IC socket (276-1995)

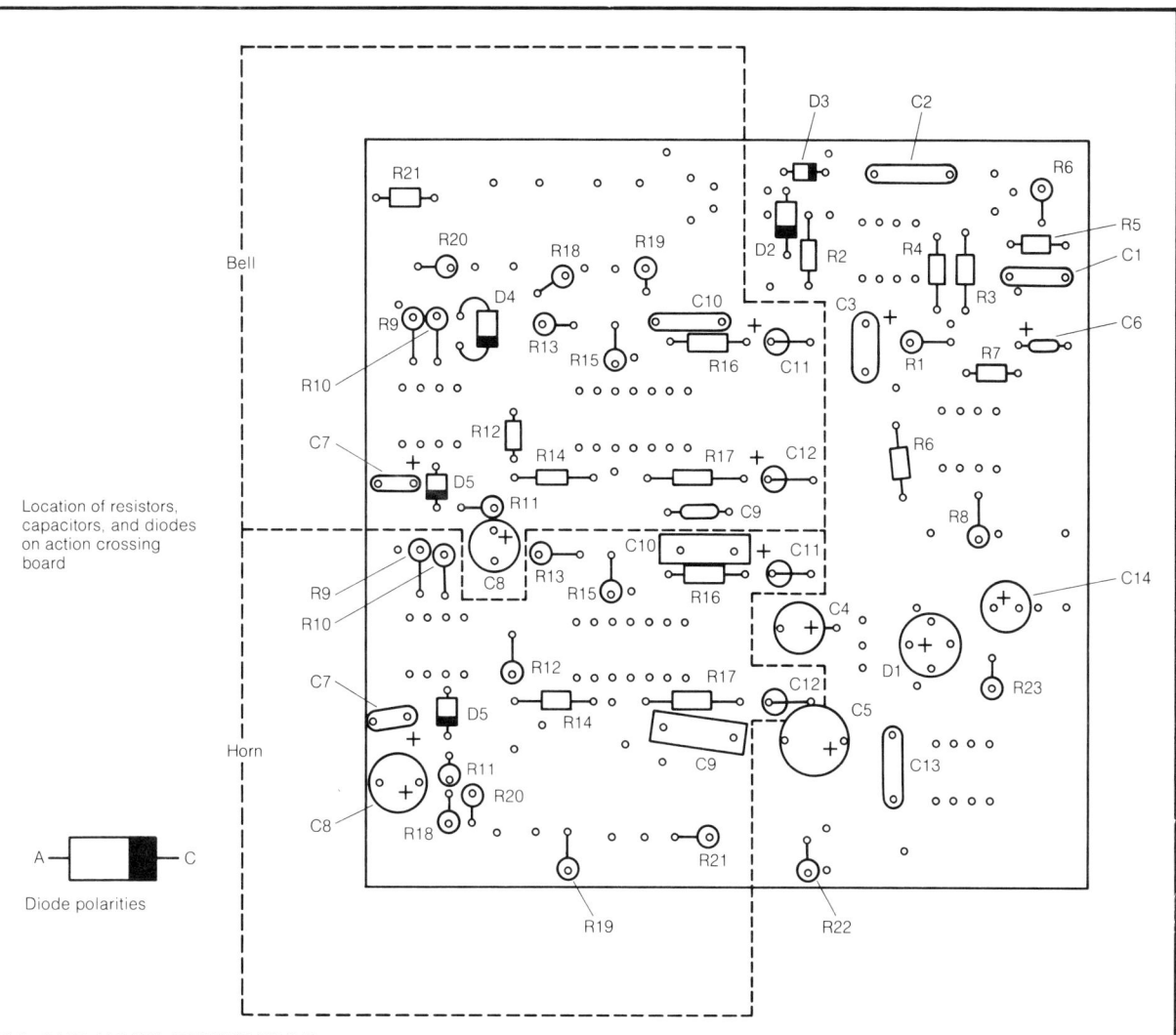

Location of resistors, capacitors, and diodes on action crossing board

Bell

Horn

A ▭ C
Diode polarities

BELL AND HORN GENERATOR
(ONE EACH REQUIRED)

C9, C10	0.01-μF, 100-VDC film capacitors for bell, 0.68-μF, 100-VDC film capacitors for horn
C11, C12	10-μF, 16-VDC electrolytic capacitors
IC	NE556 (276-1728)
R12, R13	2.7-kΩ resistors
R14, R15	5.6-kΩ resistors
R16, R17	2.2-kΩ resistors (Increase to 4.7-kΩ if horn is too loud relative to the bell.)
R18, R19	1-kΩ resistors
R20, R21	
VR1, VR2	10-kΩ potentiometers for tone adjustment (271-335)
Miscellaneous	14-pin IC socket (276-1999)

AUDIO AMPLIFIER

C13	0.1-μF, 100-VDC disk or foil capacitor
C14	100-μF, 16-VDC electrolytic capacitor
IC	LM386 (276-1731)
R22	100-Ω resistor
R23	12-Ω resistor
VR3	10-kΩ potentiometer for volume adjustment (271-335)
Miscellaneous	8-pin IC socket (276-1995), 4" × 4" printed circuit board, soldering pins Note: The Vector R407DP dry-transfer photoresist materials described on page 10 are a big help in preparing the printed circuit board.

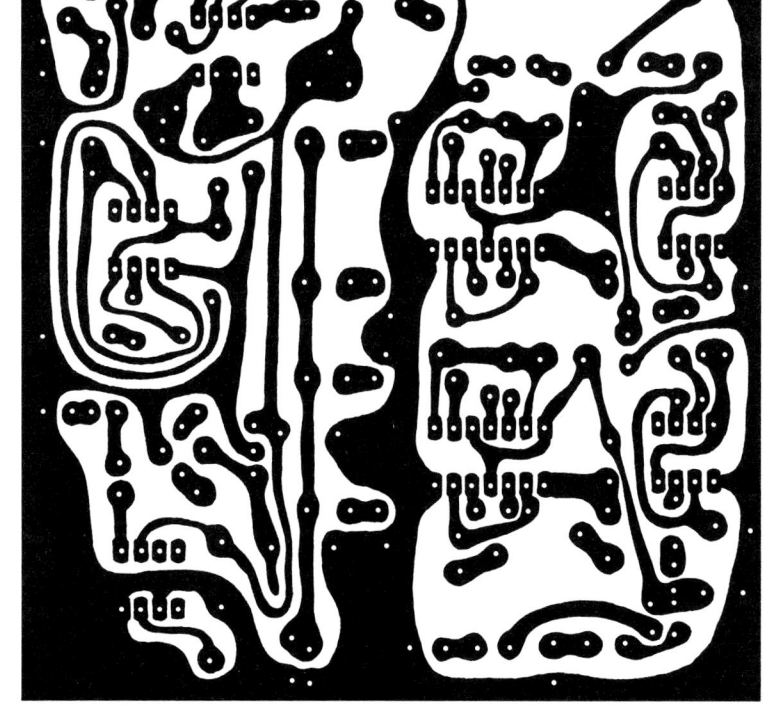

ACTION CROSSING BOARD (foil side). Shown full size 4" × 4".

39

applications. This is because the relays are completely electrically isolated, so that you can easily integrate these train detection systems with your existing layout wiring.

The table on page 34 presents a checklist describing the characteristics of several types of train detectors.

Building the detectors. Printed circuit board patterns are in Fig. 4-1. Prepare the board, then mount the components to the board. Note that the patterns shown are for the bidirectional detector; ignore the inappropriate connections if you're building the basic version. (In case you're wondering, "DB" stands for "detection bias," and this terminal connects to the track just as with a Twin-T.) The optoisolators are in DIPs, so mount them on IC sockets. Be certain the transistor pins are oriented correctly. After the board has been completed, attach it and the relays to a large piece of sheet plastic with silicone sealant.

The action grade crossing

The animated grade crossing, Fig. 4-2, features flashing lights and bells, diesel horn blasts, and automatic red signal aspects at each end of the crossing. The circuit uses several timer ICs and the entire sequence of events lasts 50 seconds; if the train is still in the crossing area, the system recycles and operates for another 50 seconds. Sounds come from a small speaker located under the layout.

Three methods of train detection can be used, two magnetic and one optical. None of these connects to the track, so all are compatible with any type of train control. (Current-sensitive train detectors shouldn't be used with command control systems.) The reed-switch and Hall-effect device versions can control all tracks passing through a multi-track crossing; the photoconductive cell version can control only one track in both directions, but requires no modifications to rolling stock.

How it works. A block diagram of the entire project is in Fig. 4-2. The ubiquitous NE555 IC is the timer. The screening of light from a photoconductive cell, the brief contacting of a magnetic reed switch, or the triggering of a Hall-effect device by the presence of a train starts the NE555 timing and the relay at its output is de-energized.

After the programmed period of time, the NE555 switches itself off and the relay becomes energized. The time is set at 50 seconds by the values of R1 and C3.

The relay contacts (simple SPDT relays are used) change signal approach lights from green to red and supply 12 V to the bell and horn interrupter on-off chips. These are also NE555s, each set to switch on and off at different rates, one corresponding to a bell rate and the other for from 2 seconds to 4 seconds on and off, corresponding to diesel horn blasts. In turn, these interrupters supply power, in their "on" mode only, to the horn generator and the bell generator.

Each generator produces two adjustable tones, which can be blended to make a more realistic sound. The bell sound frequencies are, of course, higher than the diesel horn frequencies. The frequencies are determined by C11 and C12. A lower capacitance value gives a higher pitch.

The four sounds are mixed and passed through a volume control to an LM386 audio amplifier. This puts about 0.25 W of sound power into a 4-Ω, 8-Ω, or 16-Ω speaker; not much power, but enough to make scale people jump at least a millimeter!

So now the bell is ringing, the diesel horn is blowing, the approach signals are red, and the crossing lights are flashing, courtesy of another NE555. With the values shown, in a 50-second operating cycle, the bell rings 100 times, the flasher cycles on-off 25 times, and the diesel horn sounds one long and six short (2-second) blasts.

Train detectors for the action crossing. As I mentioned, you may choose one of three methods of train detection. The first uses reed switches buried between the rails. These switch when a loco equipped with a small ceramic disk magnet passes over them. If all approach tracks are wired with reed switches (connected in parallel) in both directions, the system will always respond correctly.

The second detection method uses Hall-effect devices. These are small ICs that turn on or off in the presence of a correctly polarized magnetic field. They have about the same sensitivity as a reed switch. As with the first method, mount a small magnet on the bottom of the locomotive. The south pole of the magnet must face downward. Note also that Q1 and the components in its base circuit are not used with the Hall-effect switch detector. Each Hall-effect switch draws about 12 mA; if you use several, heed the note on voltage regulator overheating in the parts list.

The third method uses photoconductive cells whose resistance increases when they are shadowed by the train. If a train is stopped in the crossing area, the system will recycle as long as the cell is obscured. If the action stops before the rear of the train has cleared the crossing, the system is turned on again when the locomotive passes the detector on the other side. Thus, the timer and detection circuits are completely effective and prototypical.

An optional cancel circuit. The two "C" contacts on the action crossing printed circuit board can be connected to another track-located reed switch. If this reed switch is activated, the action crossing timer cancels itself immediately. This feature can be used to cut short the 50-second operating period if a fast freight speeds through.

The action crossing circuit board has three jumper wires which connect the bell, the horn, and the flasher sections separately to the positive supply relay contact. Any of the leads can be interrupted by a switch, so you can switch off one or more pieces of the action, if desired. The scale inhabitants may complain at seven diesel blasts every time the twelve-volt express zooms through the crossing, especially if the express is powered by a steam loco!

Building the action crossing. Prepare the printed circuit board, drill holes, and mount components. Be certain the diodes, electrolytic capacitors, and ICs are correctly oriented.

Circuits for the crossing light flasher, bell or horn sound generator, interrupters for the bell or horn generator, and the audio amplifier are shown individually, but all components shown mount on the large printed circuit board. However, each can be used separately if desired, with a pushbutton for manual operation. A printed circuit board is not necessary for these simpler circuits. One quick solution is to hand-wire the components using wire-wrap IC sockets. These sockets have leads almost 1" long to which the few resistors or capacitors required can easily be soldered. Figure 3-4 on page 30 of the LM3909 LED flasher circuit shows the technique.

Choosing a loudspeaker. The speaker has an enormous effect on sound quality. Use the largest diameter possible. The bell sound tends to "breathe" and it's a good idea to weight the speaker cone with an ounce or two of metal to help reduce this effect. If you weight the cone, mount the speaker with the cone facing up or down. Don't use a non-enclosed speaker; at the very least, mount it on a square piece of plywood whose sides are twice as long as the speaker's diameter. Bell sounds are difficult to generate electronically and this one sounds a little cracked. But then, not all prototype bells are perfect!

Action crossing variations. As I mentioned, portions of the system can be operated individually. For example, if you need a crossing flasher, build the circuit of Fig. 4-2 and connect it to 12-V filtered DC through an on-off switch in the plus or minus lead. Use a 12-V voltage regulator in the supply because most ICs of this kind are damaged at 16 V.

Similar comments apply if you need a diesel horn generator: Construct the horn generator and audio amplifier circuits of Fig. 4-2, and connect to 12 V via a normally open pushbutton switch.

Programmed turnout control

Even a relatively small model railroad usually has a yard with perhaps nine to a dozen turnouts. There are three more or less standard ways of threading a freight train through such a yard:

● Throw the turnouts one at a time, manually or with electric switch machines to establish the route before picking up the throttle to move out the train. This is either fiddly or both fiddly and noisy: The clump of some switch machine solenoids is enough to shake out the track nails.

● Establish a route program and allow switch contacts on the solenoid switch machine to supply power to the next turnout down the line. This is still noisy and still shakes track nails loose.

● Use diode-matrix route control — see Chapter 5 of PRACTICAL ELECTRONIC PROJECTS FOR MODEL RAILROADERS. This bypasses the need for switch machine contacts, but fires all five to ten switch ma-

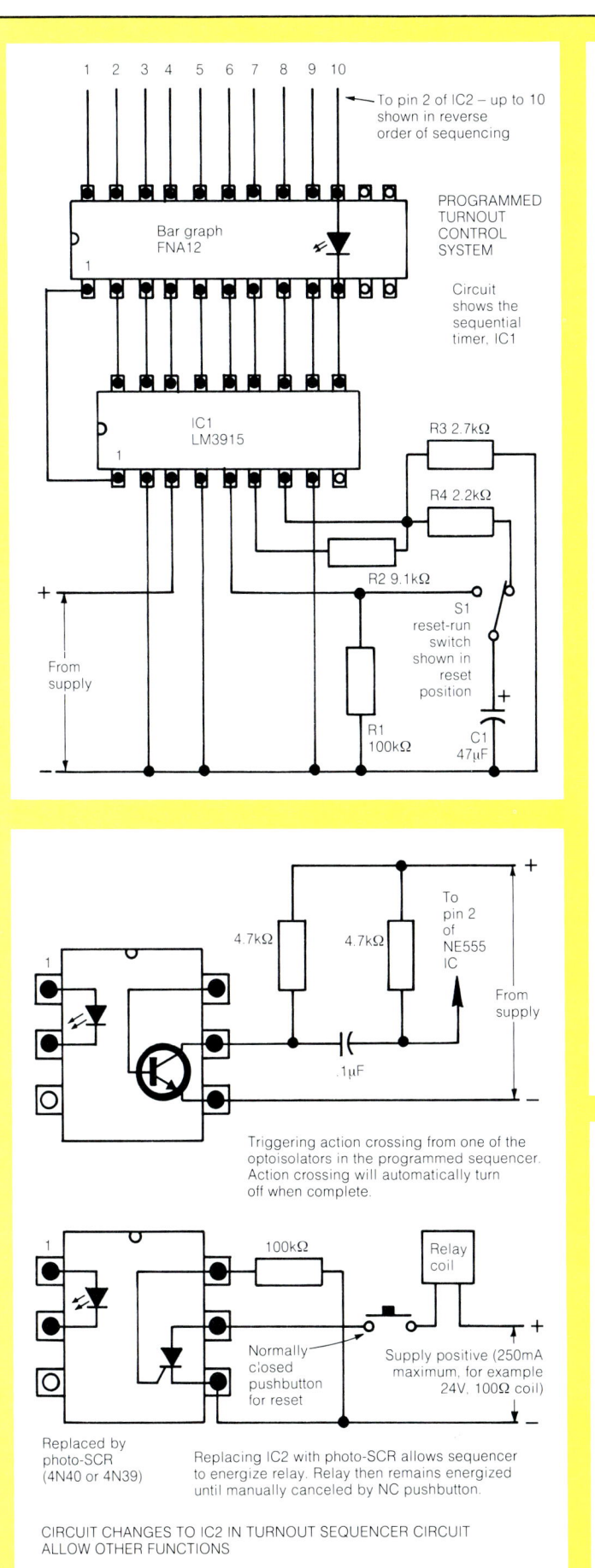

FIG. 4-3 PROGRAMMED TURNOUT CONTROL

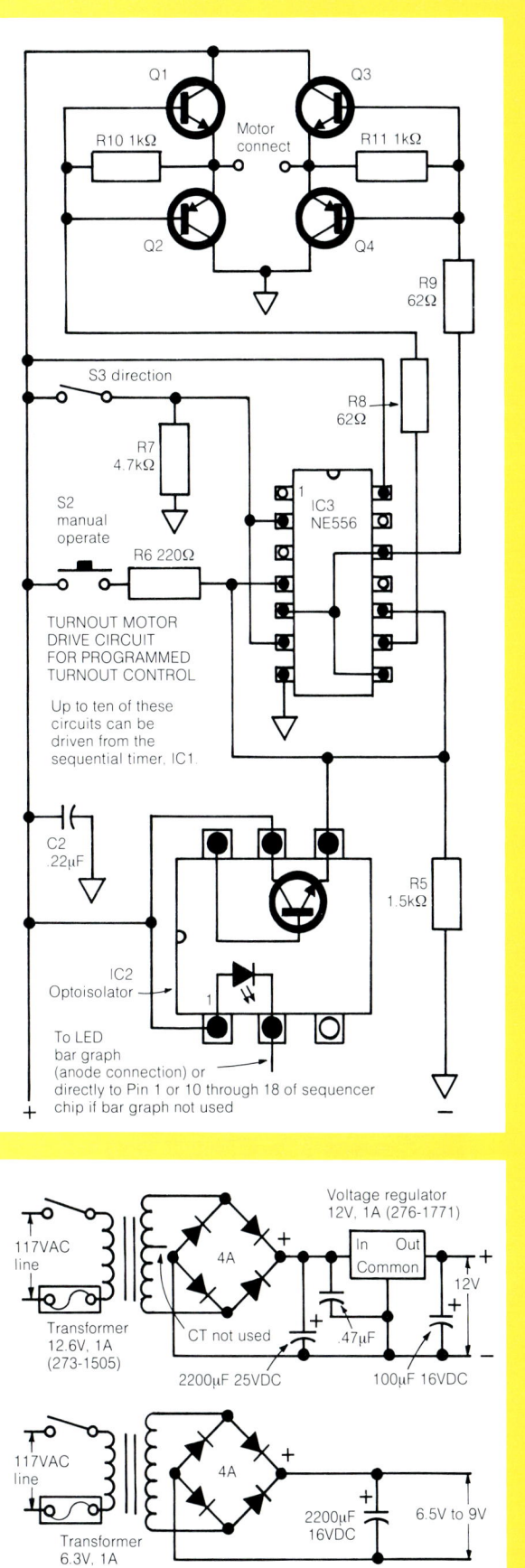

chines at once, possibly with enough vibration to shake a narrow gauge steamer off the track!

If you're opposed to the non-prototypical thunder, there is the option of motor-driven (as opposed to solenoid-driven) switch machines. In recent years a couple of manufacturers have produced motor-driven switch machines that include both printed circuit limit switches and auxiliary switch contacts built into the mechanism. Also, in the January 1977 MODEL RAILROADER, Gordon Odegard told how to make slow-motion switch machines from low-rpm motors, cams, gears, and limit switches. Both commercial and homemade motor-driven switch machines lend themselves to programmed turnout control.

The circuits of Fig. 4-3 can control up to ten motor-driven switch machines using a single small DC power supply for both the circuit and the motors. No wire carries more than 1 A, so heavy wire is not needed. The method of operation is simply to set the direction of each turnout with an SPST slide switch (one per turnout), and then turn on the "program run" switch. Each motor in sequence receives a 3-second power application. Thus, over a 30-second period, up to ten turnouts are thrown smoothly and prototypically.

The "program set" and "program run" switches can be located on a control panel remote from the yard, or along the edge of the yard close to each turnout. Each turnout can be operated independently at any time by positioning its program set switch and operating its own independent run push-button.

How it works. An LM3915 IC is used as a sequencer, measuring the rate of discharge of capacitor C1. As the capacitor charge falls, switches turn on and off in the chip, one by one. The switches operate the LED in an optoisolator, which in turn applies a pulse to an NE556 IC. This chip is connected to give two outputs when enabled by the optoisolator signal. The outputs change polarity when a 0 or a 1 voltage is applied by external switch S2. At this point, a low-current motor could be driven directly from these two polarity-reversible outputs. However, the motors in the Mann-Made switch machines I used need a 1-A starting current and a 0.3-A to 0.4-A running current. Therefore, the NE556 outputs drive a bridge-connected current amplifier consisting of two PNP and two NPN power transistors.

The sequence time can be easily adjusted by changing the value of R1. Use a lower value to shorten the time. For very long times, requiring a high value of R1, use a tantalum or low-leakage electrolytic capacitor for C1.

An optional bar graph LED display is interposed between the LM3915 sequencer and the optoisolators. This visually indicates which turnout motor or circuit is operating at any given time. It can be omitted by applying shorting jumpers across its opposite terminals on the circuit board.

Note that the printed circuit board con-

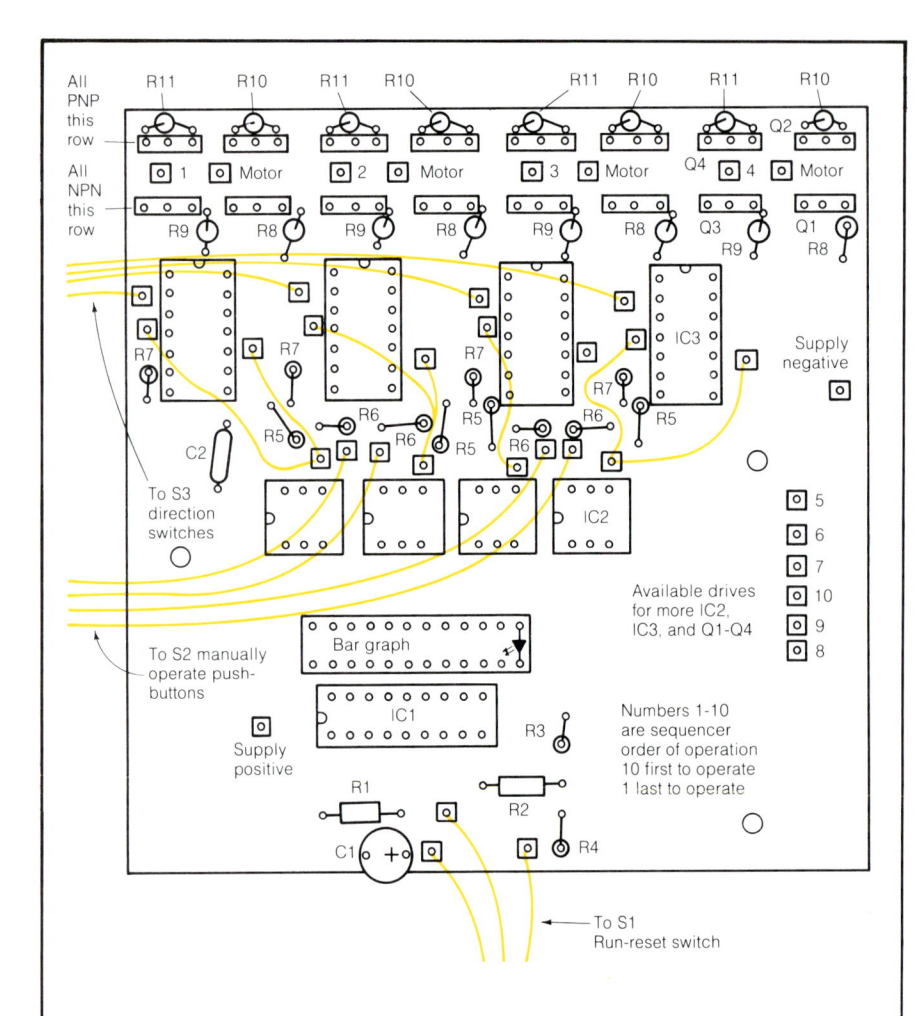

Fig. 4-3A PROGRAMMED TURNOUT CONTROL

tains the sequencer and bar graph display for up to ten switch machines but has space for only four sets of optoisolators and current amplifiers. If you want to control more than four switch machines, simply make additional circuit boards and mount the optoisolators, ICs, and transistors. Then connect these to the sequencer and bar graph board with jumpers to terminals 5 through 10.

If these terminals are not used, they should be joined together and connected to the supply positive. To save construction time, two or three printed circuit boards can be clamped together and drilled simultaneously; they can also be etched at the same time.

Variations. As I mentioned, the electric motors I used drew 0.3 A to 0.4 A with 9-V input to the switch machine (some voltage is lost through the drive transistors). The NE556 can supply 0.1 A to 0.2 A, so if you plan to use motors that draw very little current, Q1 through Q4 can be omitted. In that case, connect the motor directly to R8 and R9, and reduce R8 and R9 to 12 Ω.

If the sequencer power supply is reduced from 12 V to 5 V, the optoisolators will still operate (no circuit changes are required), and you can replace any or all of them with logic-interface circuitry. In this way the sequencer can control any number of railroad functions. You can even trigger a timer circuit from the sequencer, so random control function intervals can result. For example, an NE555 timer can be triggered by arranging for a negative-going pulse at one of the sequencer outputs. Depending on the component values, the timer could supply or cut off power to a block for a time ranging from 30 seconds to 5 minutes. Or, you could run the entire action crossing sequence described earlier in this chapter.

Also, you can replace one or more of the optoisolators with a light-activated silicon controlled rectifier (photo-SCR) in the same type of 6-pin package. The photo-SCR can

PARTS LIST FOR PROGRAMMED TURNOUT CONTROL

Bar graph	bar graph (Fairchild FNA12 is shown in photo. This has 12 LEDs; 2 are not used. Bar graphs with 10 LEDs such as Litronix RBG1000 and IEE LR7164R [276-081] are also suitable.)
C1	47-µF, 10-VDC electrolytic capacitor (Use a tantalum or low-leakage electrolytic capacitor if R1 exceeds 100 kΩ.)
C2	0.22-µF, 100-VDC film capacitor
IC1	LM3915N (276-1708)
IC2	optoisolator (4 per board), 4N29, 4N30, 4N32, 4N33, 4N35, 4N36, 4N37, FCD850 (276-133) (Radio Shack 276-132 is a TIL111 and may not work properly because it does not have a 100-percent current transfer ratio.)
IC3	NE556 (4 per board) (276-1728)
Q1, Q2	3-A, 40-V NPN power transistors in TO-126 or TO-220 case (8 per board), TIP31A (276-2017)
Q3, Q4	3-A, 40-V PNP power transistors in TO-126 or TO-220 case (8 per board), TIP32A (276-2025)
R1	100-kΩ resistor (Higher value gives longer on times.)
R2	9.1-kΩ resistor
R3	2.7-kΩ resistor
R4	2.2-kΩ resistor
R5	1.5-kΩ resistor (4 per board) (Increase to 2.2-kΩ if motors do not start reliably. There should be at least 7 V across each R5 when the sequencer triggers the IC3 to which it is connected.)
R6	220-Ω resistor (4 per board)
R7	4.7-kΩ resistor (4 per board)
R8, R9	62-Ω resistors (8 per board)
R10, R11	1-kΩ resistors (8 per board)
S1	SPDT slide or toggle switch (RUN-RESET) (275-635)
S2	NO pushbutton switch (4 per board) (275-1547 contains 5 of these switches.)
S3	SPST slide or toggle switch (DIRECTION) (4 per board) (275-401)
Miscellaneous	4" × 4" printed circuit board, soldering pins, ribbon cable to connect switches. Some turnout motors may operate too fast or cause the turnout to jam when operated on 12 V. If you have this problem, wire a 2-Ω to 5-Ω, 1-W resistor in series with either motor lead, or power the complete system with a 7808 8-V voltage regulator. No other component changes are required.

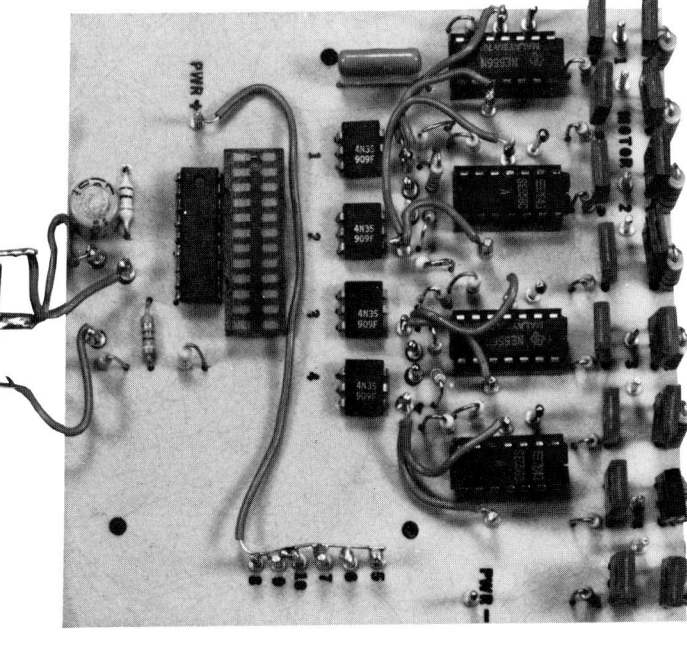

The circuit shown here and in the patterns is for four turnouts; terminals 5 through 10 allow as many as ten turnouts to be controlled sequentially by the LM3915.

The programmed turnout control is for use with motor-driven turnouts such as this Mann-Made switch machine. Lubricate the slide and worm with a plastic-compatible grease before installation and apply a dab of silicone sealant to further secure the drive nut to the slide.

turn on a relay to control any layout effect. The relay remains energized until canceled by a normally closed pushbutton switch.

Voltage checks on the sequencer. Pins 1 and 2 of IC2 should read 1.5 V (pin 1 positive) only when that specific sequence is operating.

Pin 6 of IC2 should read less than 0.5 V when not operating and at least 8 V when operating or when S2 is pushed.

There should be 8 V across pins 9 and 12 of IC3 when operating or when S2 is pushed. Polarity should reverse when S3 is thrown.

Motor polarity should be positive at the left terminal on the printed circuit board, when S3 is open. When not operating, voltage across the motor connections should be less than 0.25 V. When operating, the motor voltage should be the supply voltage less 1.5 V.

The most likely causes of problems are poor solder connections. If you've checked for these, and one motor out of four still doesn't work, try substituting IC2s and/or IC3s.

Operation of IC1 is verified by the bar graph indicator. If one LED does not light, it's probably because of a poor solder connection. If they all light, check C1 and R1; the sequencer is probably running so fast that the LED indicators appear to be on constantly.

Automatic reversing loop control

Nobody likes reversing loops. Even John Armstrong, author of TRACK PLANNING FOR REALISTIC OPERATION, shows weak imitations he calls "reverted loops." Unfortunately, many layouts need reversing loops to accommodate continuous runs: Each end of a "hambone" layout is probably a reversing loop. And, special wiring is necessary even with command control; in fact, self-powered on-board radio-controlled trains are the only kinds that don't need special electrical wiring, gaps, or switches for reversing loops.

What happens, of course, is that a train changes direction between the time it enters the loop and when it exits. Therefore, the polarity of the lead-in/lead-out track must be reversed before the train exits, and the track must be isolated with gaps in all rails leading into and out of the loop in order to avoid a short-circuit, Fig. 4-4.

Electromechanical automatic reversing loop control. Figure 4-4 shows the circuit for an electromechanical reversing loop control. A DPDT relay, operated by the turnout motor, sets the polarity of the reversing loop to correspond with whichever way the turnout is thrown. The contacts are shown connecting loop RS to lead-in track N. Thus, the train enters the loop on the right, and before it exits to the left, the turnout is aligned left. Loop RS now connects to lead-in track S. Exit train, reversed and running.

Many solenoid-operated HO switch machines incorporate enough auxiliary switch contacts to accomplish this switching, but such contacts are neither long-lived nor reliable. That's why I prefer to use a motorized switch machine and a DPDT relay. Note that in this case, the motor is powered by AC (using internal diodes to rectify the voltage). Some manufacturers may specify external diodes.

If you don't obtain correct reversing loop polarity after the turnout motor is installed, reverse the N and S track connections.

Electronic automatic reversing loop control. So far, so good. Now you can install a pair of train detectors in the loop for automatic turnout operation. The right location for these detectors is a train length into the loop, on each side of the loop. As the loco passes either sensor, the turnout position should change automatically to correspond with exit in that continuing direction. This in turn guarantees, via the turnout-switch relay, that exit polarity is also correct. The circuit in Fig. 4-4 uses two light-sensitive train detectors (page 33). Each detector switches a DPDT relay. The relays' contacts are interlocked so that they can't operate simultaneously, and so that nothing happens if the turnout is already correctly set for the approaching locomotive. The relay contacts replace the turnout direction switch of the electromechanical automatic reversing loop control.

If the turnout control direction is opposite to that needed, interchange the extend and retract leads. If you use 12-V relays — and all three can be the same type — you can use a 12-VDC voltage regulator power supply like the one described on page 33. Suitable relays include Radio Shack 275-206. The 6.3 VAC required for the turnout motor can be supplied by Radio Shack transformer 273-1384 or 275-050. Observe all the precautions in Chapter 1 about working with 117 VAC when wiring the transformers.

The train detector photoconductive cells must be a train length into the loop to avoid the possibility of the turnout operating with the caboose still on it. The cells should also be separated from each other by a train length because once both have been tripped by the train, re-tripping the first detector would change the turnout direction. Each cell must be obscured for at least 3 seconds for the turnout motor to operate properly.

The return loop control automatically alternates in direction. In other words, trains alternately run in opposite directions around the loop.

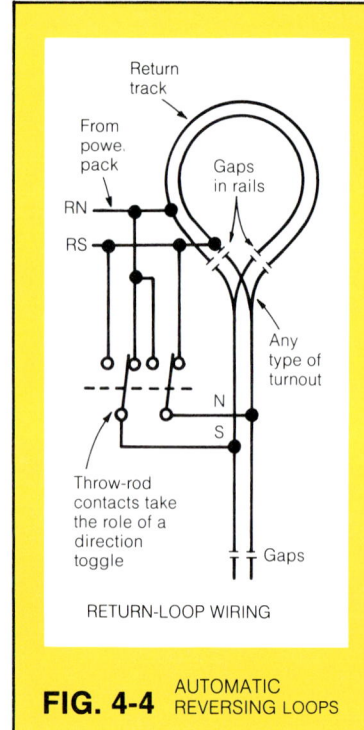

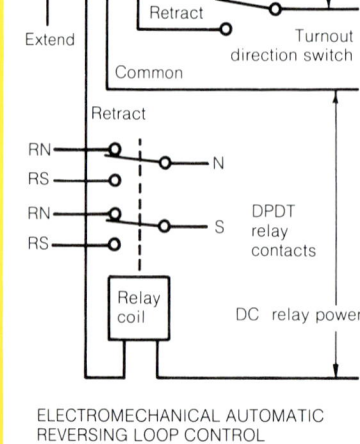

FIG. 4-4 AUTOMATIC REVERSING LOOPS

RETURN-LOOP WIRING

ELECTROMECHANICAL AUTOMATIC REVERSING LOOP CONTROL

ELECTRONIC AUTOMATIC REVERSING LOOP CONTROL

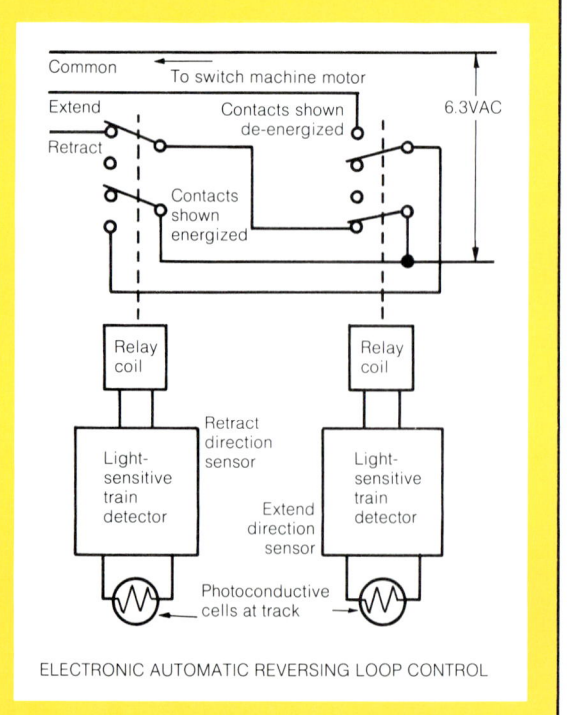

5) Sound circuits

IN THE PAST, most on-board or trackside sound systems for steam, diesel bell or horn used discrete components. Now custom integrated circuits are used in many electronic toys and games. These integrated circuits can't be purchased individually, and they're packaged for automatic assembly, not hand assembly. Nevertheless, many of these budget-priced toys can be easily adapted for use as steam chuff or bell sounds. Three such toys are shown here, purchased from Sears, Woolco, and Radio Shack. This chapter will offer hints on adapting these toys for use as sound devices. These modification tips should apply to similar devices you may buy from the toy store.

Also included in this chapter are projects for diesel horn, steam chime, bell (if you don't go the toy route), and a ringer circuit to pulse a bell or diesel horn on and off automatically.

The ringer circuit can be used to synchronize steam chuff with track voltage and, hence, locomotive speed.

The sound circuits can be packaged and used as a deluxe system that sends sounds through the track to the locomotive. This package will not work with command control, so a filtered DC throttle circuit operable with this system is shown.

On-board or trackside?

Stand-alone sound systems have the advantage of simplicity. A locomotive bell would normally only be used in stations or yards. Thus, you can put small speakers or piezoelectric sound devices in trackside buildings — and switch sound to them as appropriate via a selector switch in the control panel. The same applies to steam chimes or diesel horns. Steam chuff is a different matter; it belongs on-board. Incorporating sounds to send through the track is more complex, but the choice is yours.

The near future?

Texas Instruments sandwiched what was termed the "first talking ad" between a couple of *Business Week* pages late in 1989. The chip can be programmed for 45 seconds of any sound for two dollars each (in million lots!). Also, several telephone answering machines have ICs that will record and play back sounds in the voice frequency spectrum. When available to the hobbyist, these devices will provide one more option for realistic sound. The principles illustrated in this chapter help to show how they could be used for model railroading.

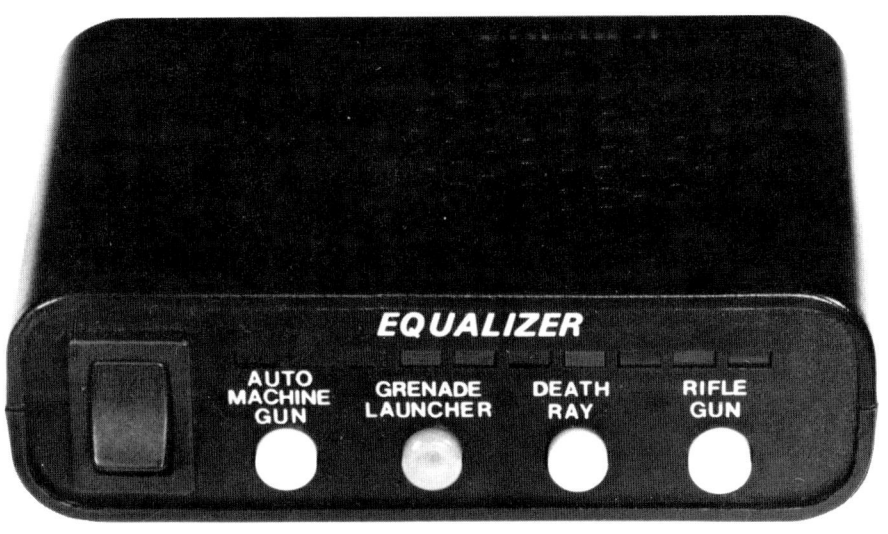

The Equalizer is another sound generating toy. The "auto machine guns" can be used as a steam chuff source.

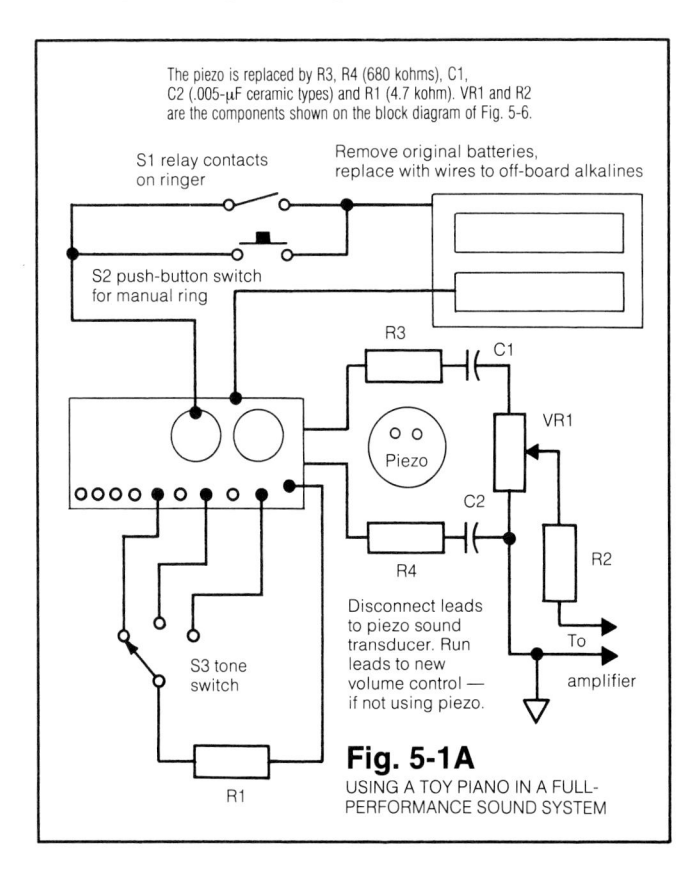

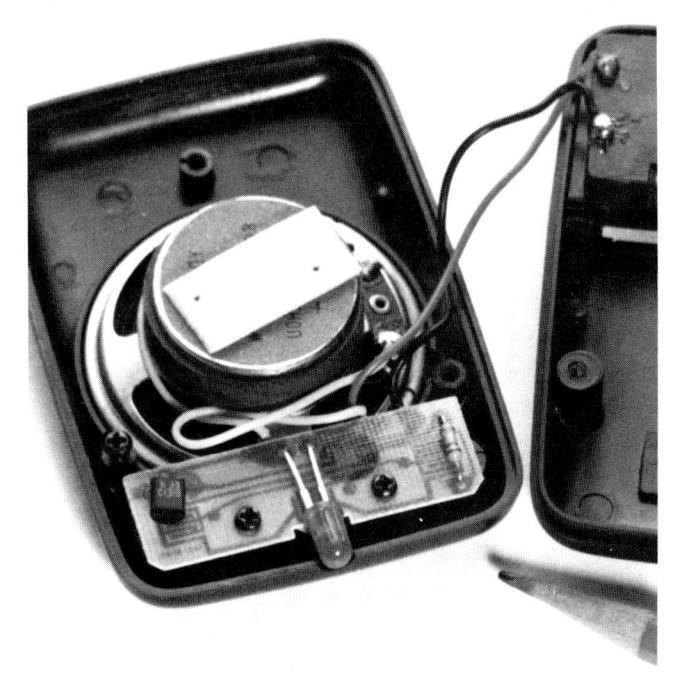

Fig. 5-1A
USING A TOY PIANO IN A FULL-PERFORMANCE SOUND SYSTEM

The piezo is replaced by R3, R4 (680 kohms), C1, C2 (.005-μF ceramic types) and R1 (4.7 kohm). VR1 and R2 are the components shown on the block diagram of Fig. 5-6.

The Avenger is a gun/bomb/phaser noise machine from the Canadian 1990 Radio Shack catalog. The simple electronics may be easily modified for steam sound in most scales. The 8-ohm speaker fitted is a 2"-diameter unit that can be used as is in O or G scales.

Toy drum synthesizer with cover removed. This type of toy can be easily modified for use as a steam chuff generator. The size restricts it to O or larger scales.

Fig. 5-1B SCHEMATIC FOR BELL GENERATOR USING AN IC

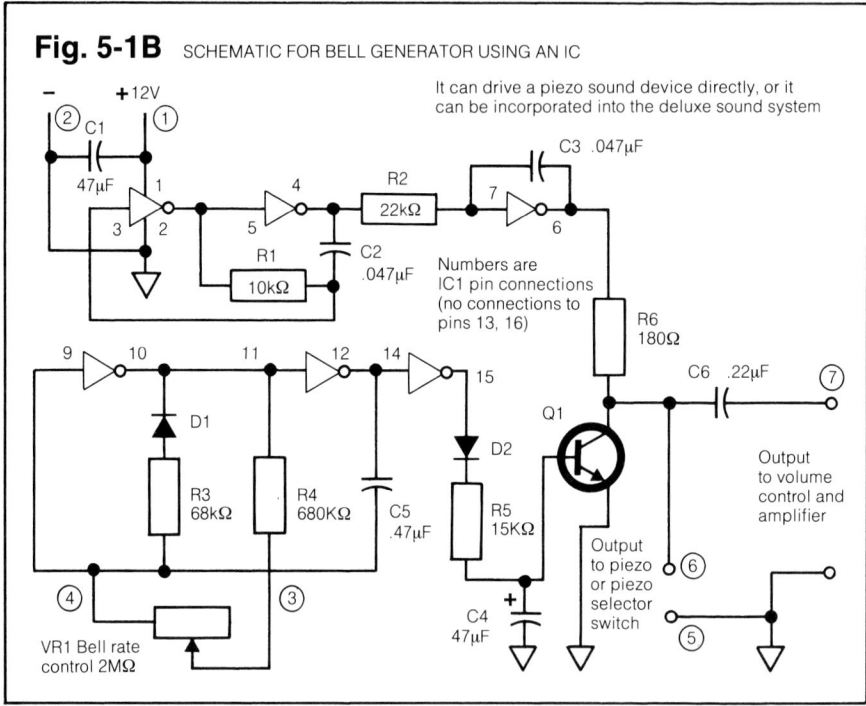

It can drive a piezo sound device directly, or it can be incorporated into the deluxe sound system

Steam chuff

Frustration-relief "adult" toys such as The Avenger and Terminator have machine-gun-like sounds along with bomb and phaser sounds. Usually just one resistor is inside that varies the rate of sound. Increasing its value to around 1 megohm slows the rate until it's virtually continuous. Using a cam or a wheel-driven magnet/reed switch combination to turn the 3-volt battery power on and off gives a good steam chuff representation. A better sound, with an adjustment, is available from an electronic toy drum synthesizer. In this case there's usually a volume control, a larger battery, and a physically larger circuit board. Use is restricted to O and large scales. The on-off switch for the chuff is not the battery power, but in the input circuit from the "drumstick." One of the trembler switches in the stick is replaced by the magnet/reed switch combination.

If you build one of these chuff circuits into the deluxe sound system the magnet/reed switch is replaceable by the output relay contacts in the ringer circuit. The notes at the end of the parts list indicate which components to change to synchronize the chuff rate with the locomotive speed.

These chuff toys seem to use speakers as the sound source. The smallest is 2" diameter, which precludes on-board use for HO or N scale. A smaller speaker can be used. The one shown in the N scale package photo is from Mouser Electronics and is 1" diameter. Even this is too large for N, unless you carefully trim the edges. A dynamic type of earphone replacement can be used, but it won't be as loud.

The Avenger circuit board will certainly fit in N, using the earphone and watch-type batteries. The current draw is about 50 milliamps from 3-volt batteries using the 2" speaker supplied with the unit. With an 8-ohm earphone, it's only 20 milliamps. Avenger circuits do not include loudness controls, but you can add a fixed resistor of 4.7 to 15 ohms (½ watt) in series with either speaker lead to cut things down. Scale sound requires less volume than you might anticipate.

Some brass locomotives have a metal cam that can be used as the chuff switch. Since the on-board chuff is insulated from the track supply because of the battery power source, this cam can be used even though one side of the battery is connected to the locomotive frame.

You might feel an N gauge magnet and reed switch is impractical, but Hamlin (distributed by Newark Electronics with locations in many states) produces an Alnico bar magnet that's .06" x .06" on end and 0.5" long. The Hamlin part is H31, the Newark part 33F1090. A miniature matching reed switch is Hamlin MINI-2S-115, Newark 33F1067. The magnet can be cemented along an axle, with the reed on the tender bottom. I'd hate to estimate, however, how long the rotating axle could stand the unbalance of the magnet mass.

Ding dong

In the photo, a simple musical piano with

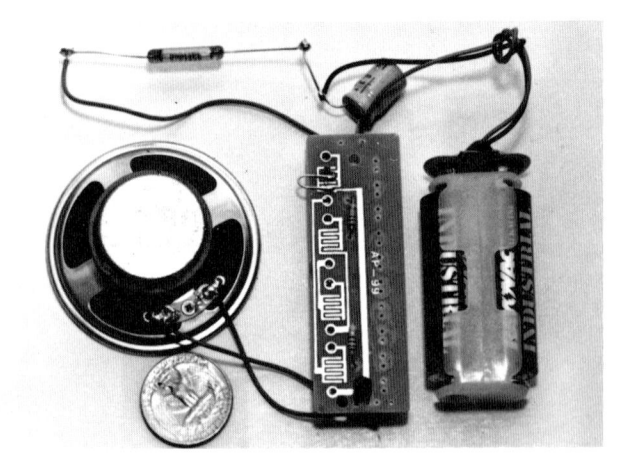

The Equalizer showing the components for steam sound in the larger scales. The LEDs are removed, and the push-button contacts for the "gun" are shorted. The chuff switch is a reed switch in series with one of the battery leads. A 330-μF 4-VDC capacitor is added across the battery to aid in longer battery life.

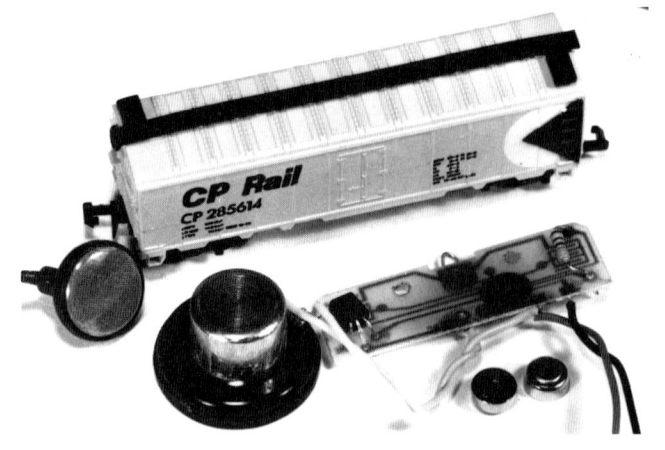

The Avenger board will fit in an N gauge box car. The 3-volt power must come from a pair of watch batteries. The speaker shown is a 1"-diameter unit, part number 25RF006 from Mouser Electronics. You'll need to cut it down slightly or use a dynamic earphone.

46

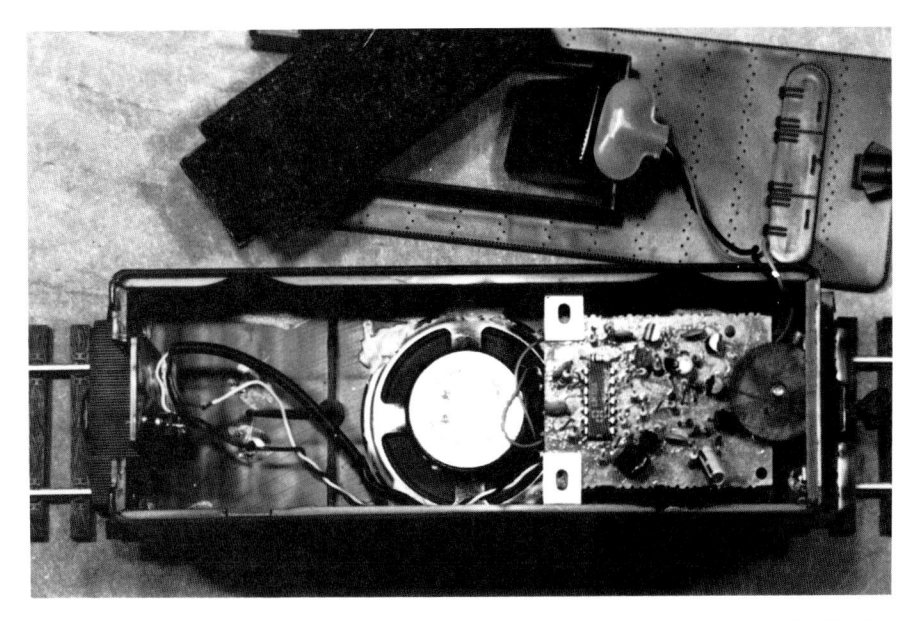

Here's the drum synthesizer installed in an O scale tender. A few holes are drilled in the tender base for sound transmission. The on-off and volume control project slightly from a slot in the tender rear, and the length-of-chuff switch is just at the fireman's ear! The 9-volt battery is located under the coal load.

The chuff switch is a reed switch fixed to the tender truck and switched on by a magnet cemented to the inside of a tender wheel. A G scale model is shown, but the principle is applicable to all scales. There are many locomotive models that include a built-in cam switch that can be used.

built-in reverberation is the basis for one bell. A straightforward single integrated circuit plus a transistor is the other. Either can drive a piezo directly, so if you need bell sound in yards or stations a strategically located piezo wired through a selector switch will do a good job. In most instances a piezo makes better bell sound than a speaker, largely because its frequency response peaks in the bell band.

A three-position, one-pole switch will select three locations. A Radio Shack 275-1385 will do. For piezos, 273-073 or 273-074 is suitable. All parts numbers are from the 1990 Radio Shack catalog.

The toy piano is modified simply by removing the keyboard and selecting the three or four most appropriate notes for a bell. Another three- or four-position switch then replaces the keyboard contacts. Usually the positive battery supply is the common connection, and IC pins are the other connections. Figure 5-1A illustrates typical wiring. The watch-type batteries are replaced by heavy-duty cells; the unit shown operates on 3 volts. A simple NO (normally open) push-button switch is added to give manual control — one push, one ring. But as shown in the photo of the finished assembly, a ringer circuit has been added to provide the option of an automatic ring. The toy used was less than three dollars, and it supplies an excellent bell tone — it's far better as a bell than as a piano!

This circuit can be integrated into a deluxe sound system; Fig. 5-1A shows how the piezo is discarded — or left in position, it doesn't matter — and what components are added to integrate it into the power amplifier. There's no point in replacing the battery with power from the amplifier main board because the batteries are good for a year or more. The other bell circuit is built from scratch using a CD4049 integrated circuit. The lower three sections of the chip (Fig. 5-1B) operate as the "clapper," and the upper three gates are the tone oscillator. The clapper or ringer frequency is variable with VR1, which is a panel control and not part of the printed circuit board. Transistor Q1 turns the bell tone on sharply and off slowly, aided by D2, C4, and R5. Increasing or decreasing the value of C4 will alter the decay time of the sound. A smaller value gives a shorter decay.

The clapper rate is determined largely by the value of C5. A larger value here slows the ringing rate, should this be outside the range of VR1. Capacitor C2 determines the tone of the bell: A larger value gives a lower pitch. Note that this circuit can also be used as a stand-alone bell driving a piezo — or several piezos switch-selected. For this, C3 is not used and R2 is shorted or simply replaced with a jumper wire. Without these changes, the output is low enough that the piezo can scarcely be heard. With R2 and C3 included the output can still drive the power amplifier of the deluxe system, and it also has a more triangular and more bell-like tone.

Take care handling the CD4049, because as a CMOS-type IC it's susceptible to damage from static electricity. Read the handling

(Above) Here are the toy piano internal components. The wax blob contains the single IC used. (Right) In this photo the toy piano components have been converted to a bell with three switch-selected tones. A ringer circuit is included with adjustable ring timing. Two supplies are used, one for the ringer and one for the bell. The unit may be built into a through-the-rails sound system, when the ringer would be powered by the main unit.

47

Fig. 5-2 DELUXE SOUND SYSTEM

AMPLIFIER AND POWER SUPPLY. Shown full size 3" × 2".

AMPLIFIER AND POWER SUPPLY

STEAM WHISTLE/DIESEL HORN. Shown full size 3" × 2"

STEAM WHISTLE/DIESEL HORN

BELL SOUND GENERATOR. Shown full size 3" × 2"

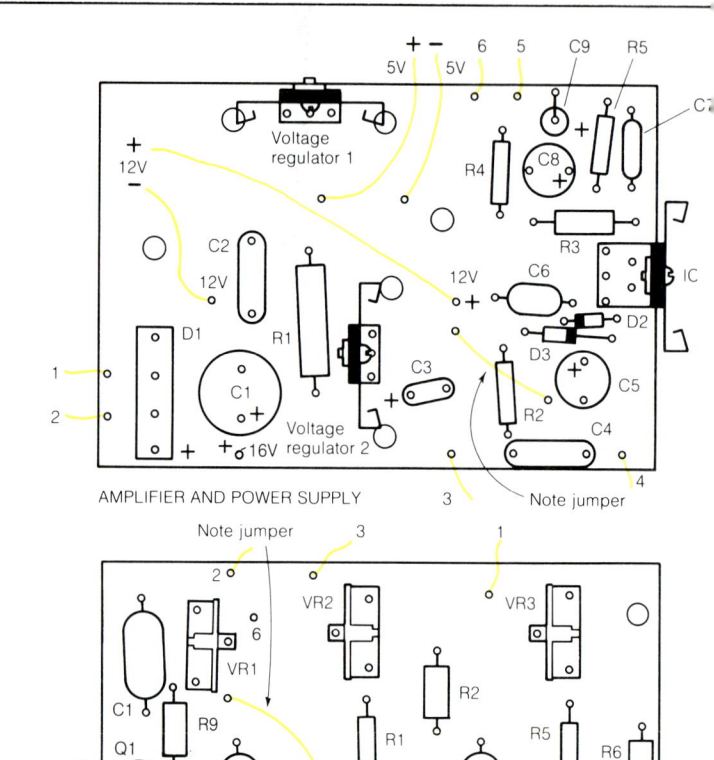

BELL SOUND GENERATOR

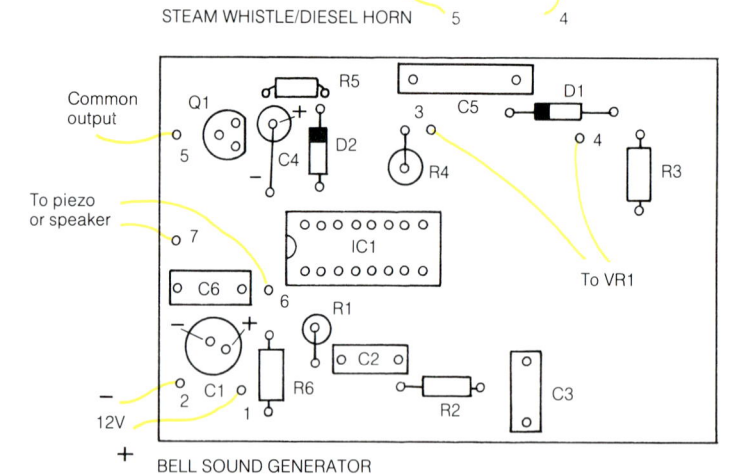

PARTS LIST FOR DELUXE SOUND SYSTEM STEAM WHISTLE/DIESEL HORN

C1, C2, C3, C4	0.22-µF, 50-VDC to 200-VDC film capacitors
C5, C6	10-µF, 16-VDC electrolytic capacitors
D1, D2	100-PIV, 0.5-A to 1-A silicon diodes, 1N914, 1N4148 or similar
D3	10-V zener diode, 1N758(A), 1N5240(A or B), BZY88/C10
Q1	Small signal NPN transistor, 2N2222A, ECG123A or similar
IC1, IC2	NE566, LM566 (Signetics or National Semi), Philips/ECG ECG994M, NTE NTE994M
R1, R5	3.9-kohm resistors
R2, R6	390-kohm resistors
R3, R7	1-Mohm resistors
R4, R8	4.7-kohm resistors
R9	470-ohm resistor
R10	8.2-kohm resistor
S1	1-pole, 3-position switch (or use a multi-position switch with a mechanical stop added)
VR1	2-kohm potentiometer (adjust steam hiss)
VR2, VR3	5-kohm potentiometers (adjust tones)
VR4A, VR4B	two 1-kohm linear taper potentiometers on single shaft Mouser Electronics 31VW301. May also be assembled from Centralab NP-1000-S, NR-1000-S, shaft coupler DC-2 and shaft UP-A-300. Or use two slide potentiometers side by side. Mouser Electronics ME-321-9200-1K or Stackpole Slide-Trol 30V6942
Miscellaneous	2" × 3" printed circuit board, 8-pin IC sockets, soldering pins, knobs

Note: For diesel horn version, C3, C4 are 0.47-µF, and R9, R10, Q1, D3, C1, and C6 can be omitted unless air hiss accompaniment is wanted.

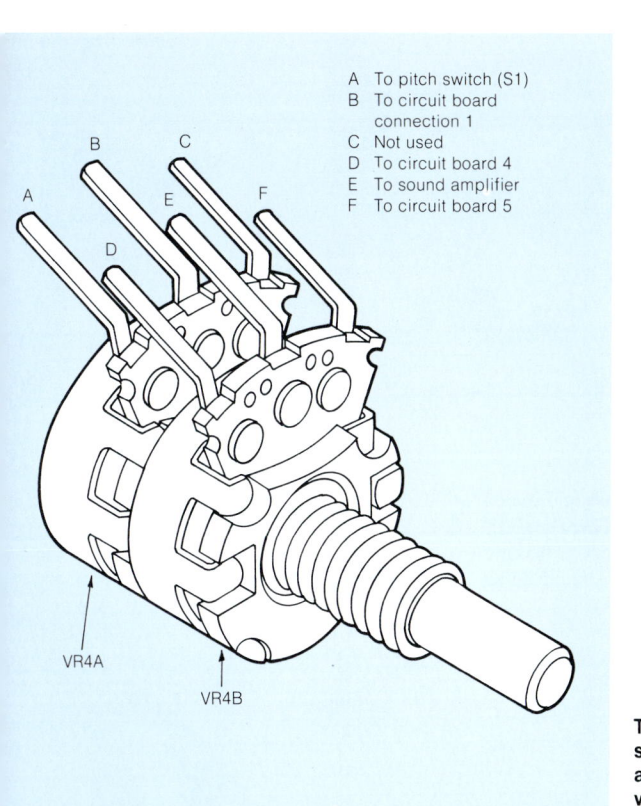

A To pitch switch (S1)
B To circuit board connection 1
C Not used
D To circuit board 4
E To sound amplifier
F To circuit board 5

HOW TO WIRE THE DUAL PITCH-LOUDNESS POTENTIOMETERS VR4A AND VR4B FOR STEAM WHISTLE SOUND

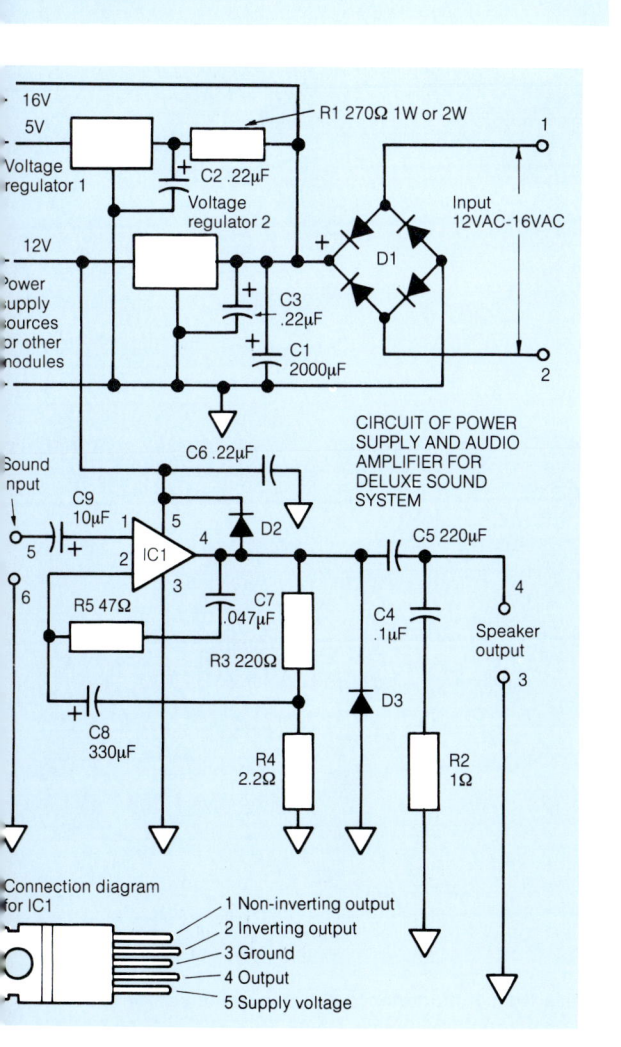

POWER SUPPLY AND AUDIO AMPLIFIER MODULE

C1	2000-µF or 2200-µF, 25-VDC electrolytic capacitor
C2	0.22-µF, 50-VDC to 200-VDC film or tantalum capacitor
C3	0.22-µF, 25-VDC tantalum capacitor
C4	0.1-µF, 50-VDC to 200-VDC film capacitor
C5	220-µF or 330-µF, 16-VDC electrolytic capacitor
C6	0.22-µF, 50-VDC to 200-VDC film or tantalum capacitor
C7	0.047-µF, 50-VDC to 200-VDC film capacitor
C8	330-µF or 470-µF, 16-VDC electrolytic capacitor
C9	10-µF, 16-VDC electrolytic capacitor
D1	100-PIV, 2-A to 4-A bridge rectifier (276-1171)
D2, D3	100-PIV, 1-A silicon diodes, 1N4001 through 1N4005 (276-1102)
IC1	TDA2002, TDA2002A (SGS), or LM383 (276-703)
R1	270-Ω, 1-W or 2-W resistor
R2	1-Ω resistor
R3	220-Ω resistor
R4	2.2-Ω resistor
R5	47-Ω resistor
voltage regulator 1	5-V, 1-A voltage regulator in TO-220 case, 7805 (276-1770)
voltage regulator 2	12-V, 1-A voltage regulator in TO-220 case, 7812 (276-1771)
Miscellaneous	2″ × 3″ printed circuit board, heat sinks for IC1 and both voltage regulators (276-1363), soldering pins

Note: All electrolytic capacitors are printed circuit mount types.

The module that contains the DC power supply and audio amplifier supplies 5 V and 12 V to the other modules and provides 1.5 W of speaker power.

CIRCUIT OF POWER SUPPLY AND AUDIO AMPLIFIER FOR DELUXE SOUND SYSTEM

Connection diagram for IC1
1 Non-inverting output
2 Inverting output
3 Ground
4 Output
5 Supply voltage

CIRCUIT FOR STEAM WHISTLE GENERATOR

Note: items inside color line are mounted on printed circuit board

49

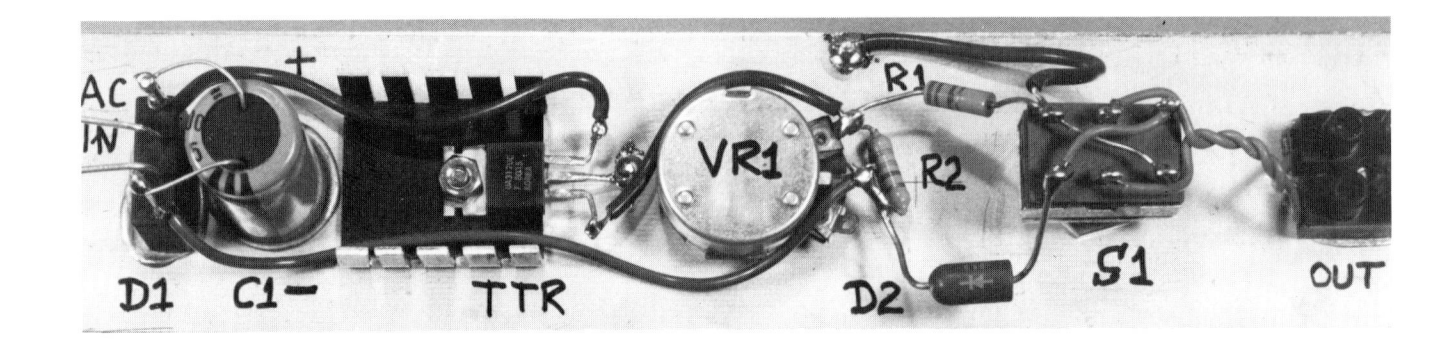

notes on page 7. Never touch the pins on a cold, dry day. Once the IC is plugged in, the danger is minimal.

Bell clapper or ringer

The CD 4049 bell has its ringer built in, but the modified toy piano needs a clapper. The bell ringer circuit is shown in the diagram. A 555 timer integrated circuit is wired as an oscillator, slowly opening and closing the relay at the output. The relay contacts are used to switch the bell power supply on and off at a rate determined by control VR1. In the low resistance position, the rate is fast. The other component that determines the clapper rate is C2. A higher value slows things down. Thus this circuit can also be used as a steam chuff switch, replacing the reed switch and magnet of the on-board chuff generators, if VR1 is replaced by a cadmium sulfide photocell. The cell is to be illuminated by a 12- to 16-volt grain-of-wheat lamp that is connected to the track voltage of the sound-equipped locomotive. Thus the value of VR1 now varies according to the lamp brightness, and it's now related to locomotive speed.

The lamp and CdS cell must be enclosed in a small lightproof box. The rate of chuff will be proportional to the separation of lamp and cell, so this will need some setup. The value of C3 may need to be reduced to about 2.2µF. The book EASY TO BUILD ELECTRONIC PROJECTS FOR MODEL RAILROADERS (Kalmbach) illustrates this in detail; page 57 shows the simple wiring needed. This book, incidentally, also includes a diesel sound generator circuit.

Again, the clapper, slowed by increasing C2 to 6.8µF or 10µF, can be used to turn on and off the diesel horn sound generator described next, to replace manual control, or perhaps as an occasional option to manual control.

Note that C2 must always be a film or a tantalum capacitor. An ordinary electrolytic type is too leaky to provide consistent ring rates.

The clapper will operate from 5, 9, or 12 volts, but in each case the relay coil must be the same rating as the supply voltage, and the relay coil resistance must not be less than 100 ohms or the IC could be damaged.

The relay shown in the photographs is actually a reed relay, consisting of a reed switch in a magnetic coil. It's RS No. 275-233 in the 1990 catalog. Reed relays are fast and reliable because the contacts are low mass and sealed in a vacuum or an inert gas. There's absolutely no worry about layout vapors making the contacts dirty. Track itself should be so lucky!

Steam chime

The steam chime board also serves as the basic design for the diesel horn. The necessary changes are shown on the parts list. Two 566

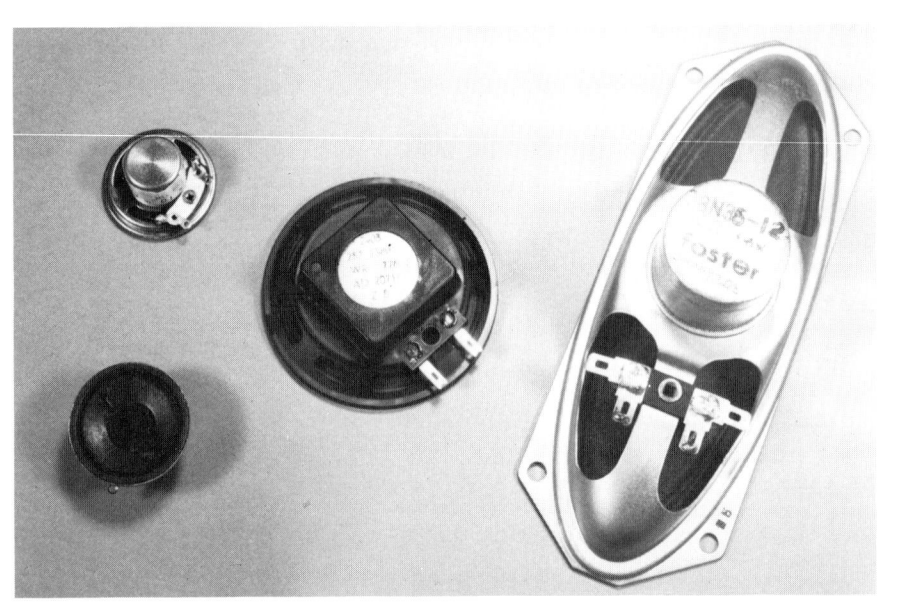

(Top) These speakers range in size from 1" diameter to 2" x 6", and the center speaker, manufactured by Philips, has an easily trimmed plastic frame. (Above) Silicone sealant is perfect for mounting speakers because there's no danger of warping the frame. Note also the 220-µF, 25-VDC coupling capacitors that protect the speaker from damage by track voltages.

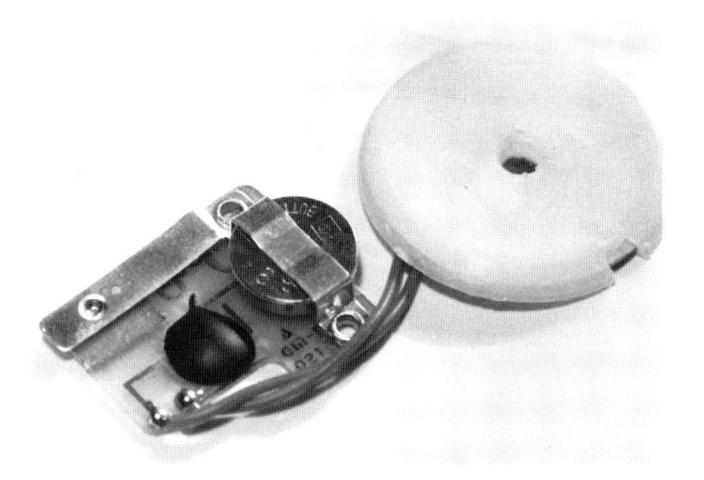

This shows the electronics in a musical Christmas card. With an on-off switch added, the piezo sound unit will replay the first "ring" over and over. In effect, it makes a low-budget bell.

function generator clips, IC1 and IC2, are connected to produce triangle wave forms of two different frequencies mixed in equal proportions. The frequency is varied by the amount of DC current flowing into each pin 6. This enables a pitch control to be used, so that the chime or horn can be varied smoothly in pitch or frequency. The same circuit is used for each frequency. In this way, front panel switch S1 (plus D1, D2, and D3) lets you choose from three discrete kinds of whistle or horn characters.

VR4A/VR4B, also a front panel control, varies the pitch and volume of the combined sounds. Turning VR4A counterclockwise lowers the pitch; clockwise raises the pitch. VR4B is mounted on the same shaft as VR4A and is a volume control, tracking the pitch. This twin device controls pitch and loudness simultaneously.

The common knob provides no sound at fully counterclockwise. Clockwise yields increasing whistle volume and pitch, accompanied by increased steam background hiss. By rotating the common control back and forward, you can obtain a good simulation of an

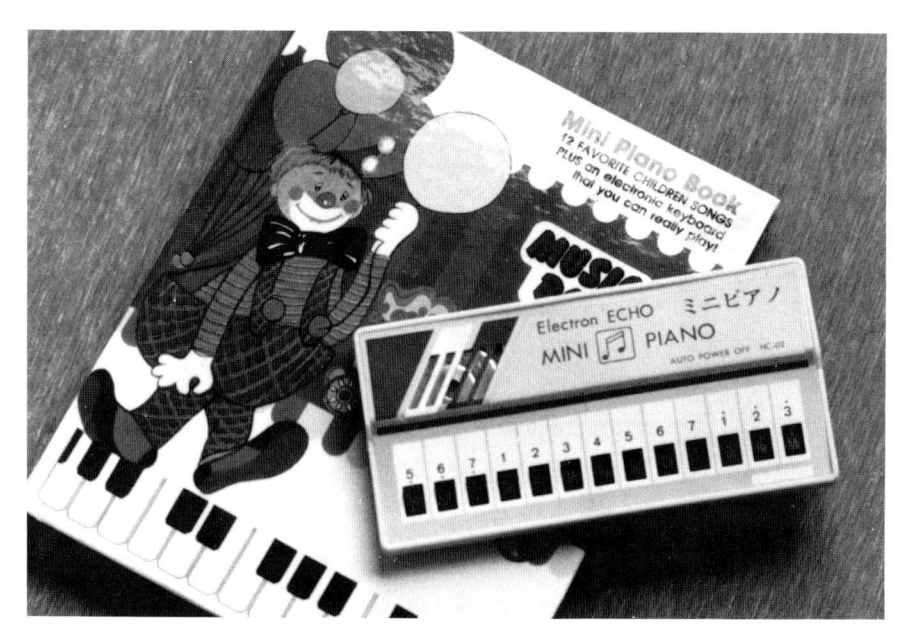

(Above) Front panel layout for the modified toy bell and ringer modules. (Below) This toy piano can be made to produce a range of bell tones for model railroads.

The bell ringer can also be used as a steam chuff switch or to turn horn sound on and off.

The bell ringer from below. The circuit is assembled on a Radio Shack pre-drilled board

51

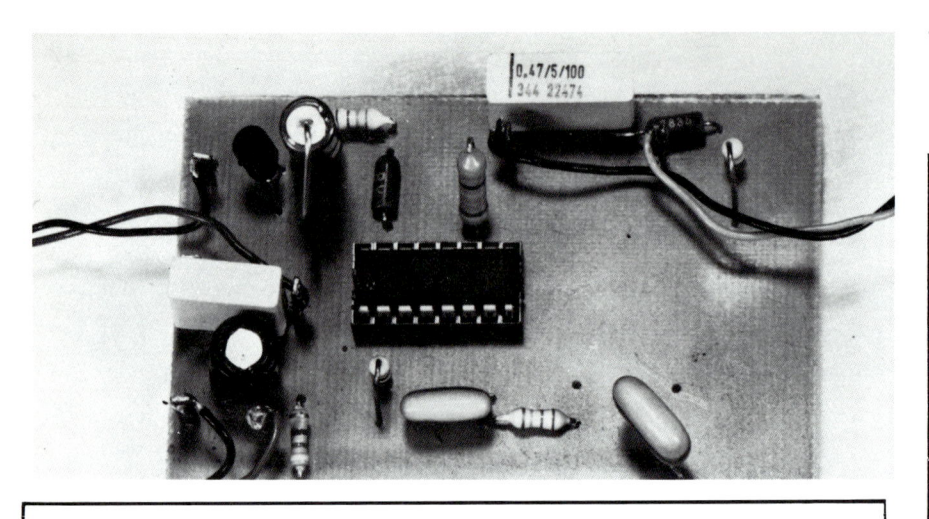

The bell generator module

PARTS LIST FOR BELL RINGER MODULE

R1, R2	10-kohm resistors
VR1	500-kohm potentiometer
C1	10-µF 25-VDC electrolytic capacitor
C2	4.7-µF 25-VDC tantalum capacitor or film type: Do not use an ordinary electrolytic type
C3	0.01-µF 50-VDC ceramic or film capacitor
IC1	555 timer integrated circuit
D1, D2	general purpose diodes, e. g., 1N4002
RL1	relay with single-pole switch contacts (S1): Can be a 5, 9, or 12V type, depending on supply voltage used for the module

Miscellaneous: printed circuit board (RS 276-159), 8-pin IC socket, on-off switch

Note: This module can be used as a horn switch, when C2 should be increased to 10µF, or as a steam chuff switch, when VR1 must be replaced with a cadmium sulfide photocell lit by a lamp wired to loco supply voltage. Both to be in a lightproof housing. Start rate of chuff depends on separation of lamp and CdS cell.

PARTS LIST FOR PURE DC THROTTLE

C1	1000-µF, 25-VDC electrolytic capacitor (276-1032)
D1	100-PIV, 2.5-A bridge rectifier (276-1171)
D2	100-PIV, 2.5-A diode (276-1143)
R1	270-Ω resistor
R2	3.3-kΩ resistor
S1	DPDT switch, center off (275-1533 or 275-620)
voltage regulator	1-A voltage regulator in TO-220 case, National Semiconductor LM317T or Fairchild UA317UC (276-1778)
VR1	10-kΩ audio (best) or linear taper potentiometer (271-1721)
Miscellaneous	2" × 8" printed circuit board (to assist in cooling the voltage regulator), heat sink (276-1365), barrier terminals, knob, silicone sealant

Note: An additional 470-µF, 25-VDC capacitor; a 1-Ω, 1-W to 5-W resistor; and two 2-millihenry to 3-millihenry, 2-Ω to 3-Ω chokes are required for sending sound through the rails. You may use the choke from Radio Shack crossover coil 40-1296.

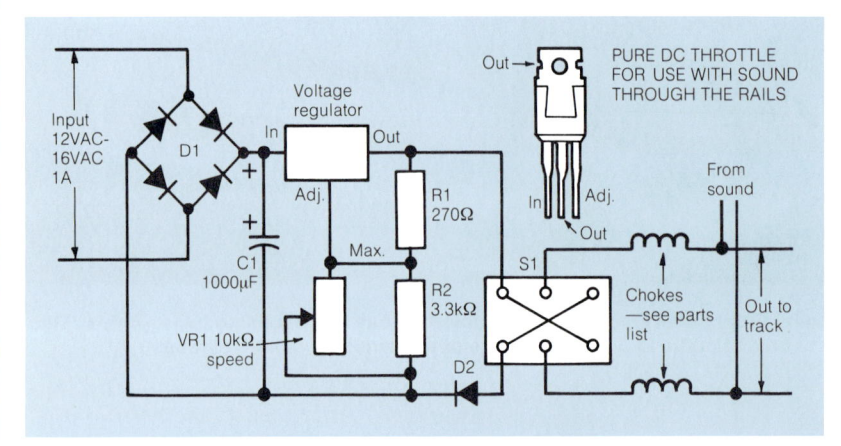

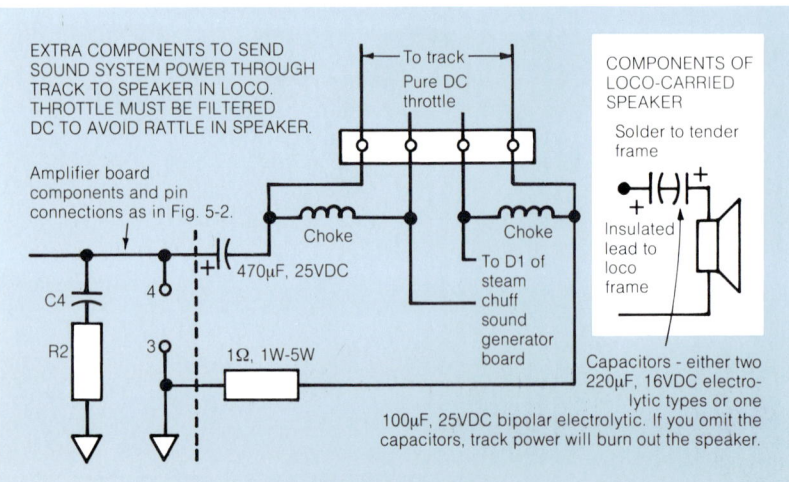

Fig. 5-3 PURE DC THROTTLE FOR SOUND THROUGH THE RAILS

---

old-time engineer "playing the chimes." The hiss of the accompanying steam is generated by zener diode D3, amplified by Q1, and adjusted to the right "mix" by VR1. The noise output from a zener is not a design specification, so you may have to select the device from four or five for most noise. A package of five usually costs less than $1.50.

If the pitch range of the control is excessive to your taste, connect a fixed resistor of 1 kohm across VR4A. Two separate side-by-side slide potentiometers could replace VR4A/VR4B. With two fingers the loudness and pitch controls could be adjusted independently or moved in opposite directions. The parts list furnishes a source for these. The slide potentiometer is recommended for the diesel horn version, and practice can yield a model Doppler effect. You may choose to omit the steam hiss components for the diesel horn. The parts list shows which ones to omit, but it's a matter of personal choice. Some real-life diesels fit hardly more than a glorified car horn, and you never hear steam from that! Truckers' air horns are different, as jaywalkers can testify.

Packaging modules

Both the bell sound possibilities will drive a sound unit — a piezo or speaker — directly. The steam chime and diesel horn modules need an amplifier to operate on their own. The amplifier and power supply module that allow them to be used as stand-alone sound on the layout are shown in Fig. 5-2.

You may want to incorporate all sounds in one assembly; the block diagram in Fig. 5-6

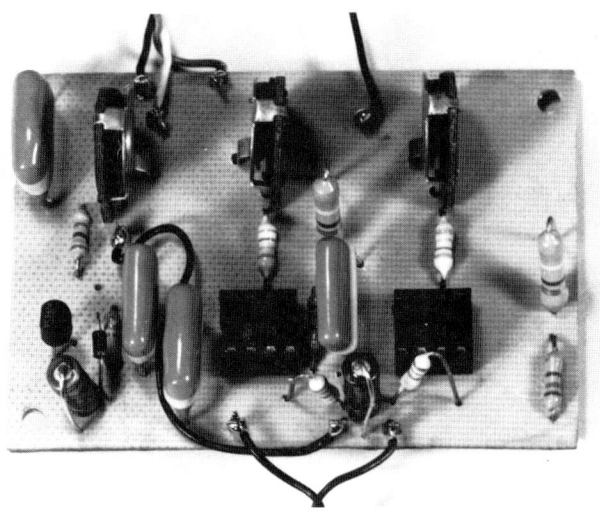

The steam whistle (chime) generator board

The diesel horn board is similar to the steam whistle board with a value change of two capacitors. The steam (air) hiss components may also be omitted. See parts list.

shows how each module can drive one common amplifier and power supply. Each VR2 shown sets the correct sound level for each module at the speaker output. The fixed resistor shown in series with each VR2 slider may need adjustment; reduce the value if the volume is insufficient. For a steam chuff unit that is modified from a toy with a speaker output, replace the supplied speaker with a fixed resistor of 47 ohms, and connect it to the steam chuff VR2 with an added capacitor (C6 in the block diagram) of 10µF 16VDC. Piezos can be replaced with 1 kohm resistors and the output routed to a VR2, as shown.

Figure 5-6 illustrates a completely integrated deluxe sound system using five modules. It could also include both manual and automatic switched operations for horn and bell on the front panel.

The speaker for this deluxe system can be wired as suggested: Use a rotary switch to select speakers, one at a time, located at strategic parts of the layout, so that the sound comes from each appropriate area required.

Sound through the rails

Another feature of the deluxe sound system is the option of sending the sound through the rails to a speaker mounted in the train or locomotive. Sound cannot be sent through the rails when using a pure pulse throttle, such as an SCR type. If the pulse amplitude is substantially cut or eliminated, the other throttle described in Chapter 2 may be used. Pulses make a rattling sound in a speaker, and it's impractical to filter the sound out. A pure DC throttle, however, is a practicality, particularly with the modern multi-pole motors used in most locomotives. A suitable design is shown in Fig. 5-3. This uses an LM317T adjustable voltage regulator, provides pure DC output, and includes automatic short-circuit protection. (This throttle will not provide effective slow running possibilities with cheap motors.)

To send sound through the rails, you'll need a 1-ohm, 1-W to 5-W resistor, a 470-µF 25-VDC capacitor, and two chokes. The chokes, used to block the sound signals from being shorted out through the throttle, should be 2 to 3 millihenrys, 2 to 3 ohms maximum resistance. The woofer coil from Radio Shack crossover networks 40-1296 or 40-1299 can be used.

The train-mounted speaker, Fig. 5-3, is protected from track voltage (which would otherwise burn it out) by two 220-µF 25-VDC electrolytic capacitors wired back to back in series with one speaker lead.

Speakers

One-inch-diameter speakers are easily available. These fit into HO locomotives, tenders, and boxcars, and may squeeze into some N gauge rolling stock. Don't be tempted to slice off edges to make a speaker fit unless it has a plastic, not metal, frame. Metal filings in the voice coil magnetic gap will ruin the sound. For N scale you are probably limited to an 8-ohm dynamic replacement earphone. The sound won't be loud, nor will it be of exciting quality. For O and G scale, at least a 2" speaker can be accommodated with good sound. Some sound

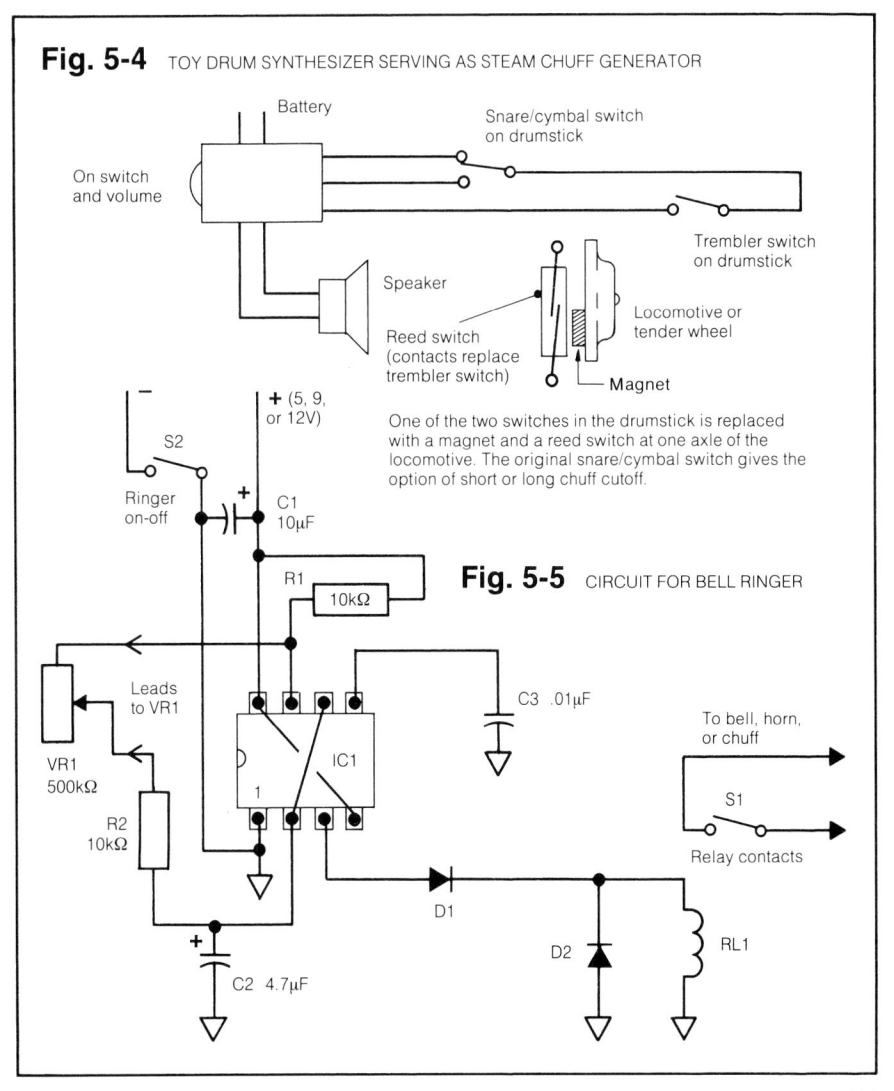

Fig. 5-4 TOY DRUM SYNTHESIZER SERVING AS STEAM CHUFF GENERATOR

One of the two switches in the drumstick is replaced with a magnet and a reed switch at one axle of the locomotive. The original snare/cymbal switch gives the option of short or long chuff cutoff.

Fig. 5-5 CIRCUIT FOR BELL RINGER

Fig. 5-6

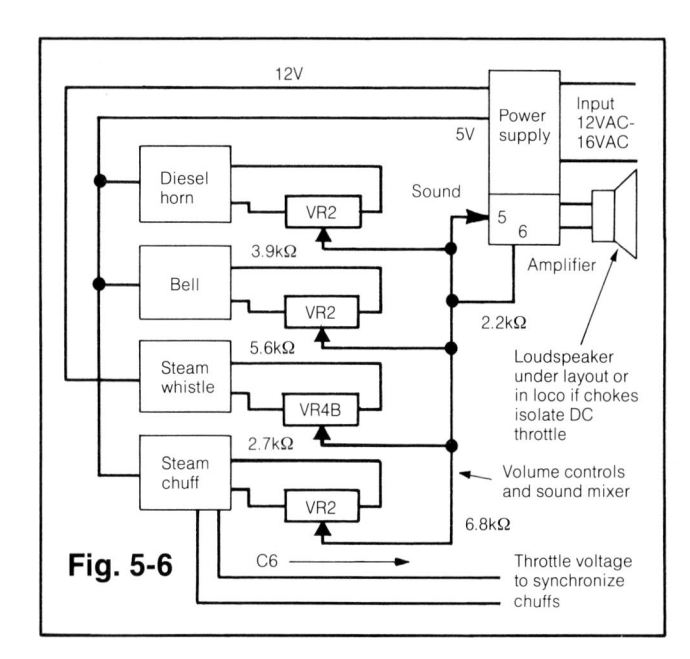

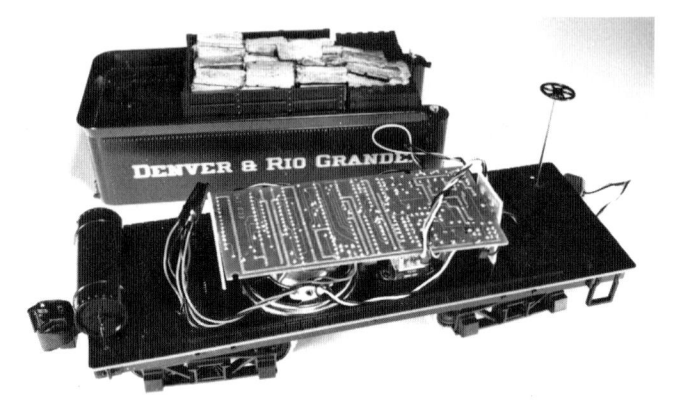

[Diagram showing: 12V, 5V, Power supply, Input 12VAC-16VAC, Diesel horn, Bell, Steam whistle, Steam chuff, with VR2 (3.9kΩ), VR2 (5.6kΩ), VR4B (2.7kΩ), VR2 (6.8kΩ), 2.2kΩ, Sound, pins 5, 6, Amplifier, Loudspeaker under layout or in loco if chokes isolate DC throttle, Volume controls and sound mixer, C6, Throttle voltage to synchronize chuffs]

This digitized sound unit by P.H. Hobbies Inc. has a chuff, bell and whistle. Note the size of this unit. To be fitted in this Delton G scale C-16, a smaller speaker than the one supplied was required. Custom IC designs and new assembly techniques could shrink this design 75 percent or more, but such "talking" ICs are on the threshold of arrival.

kits for G use 3" or larger speakers, but before you buy, be sure the height of the speaker supplied allows room for the electronics and battery.

Speaker enclosures

Mount the speaker so sound radiating from the front can't easily travel to the back of the cone and produce sound cancellation. Perforations are advisable so that sound can get out of the locomotive or car. Silicone sealant is the easiest adhesive to hold speakers, even those mounted under the layout. Clamp or block the speakers in position until the sealant is set. If screws or nuts and bolts are used, speaker frames could rattle.

Piezo sound transducers

These are suitable for bell sounds or similar higher frequency notes, but they have a narrower band of sound frequencies than all but tweeter speakers. In fact piezos are often used in hi-fi systems as tweeters. Even so, if you're really in a corner for space, try one. They're more effective on 9-volt or higher voltages.

Supplier information

Armed with a Mouser Electronics and a Newark Electronics catalog, you should be able to locate most of the components specified in this chapter.

Mouser Electronics can supply twin and slide potentiometers, miniature speakers and earphone replacements, as well as packages of resistor and capacitor assortments.

The phone number in the U. S. A. and Canada is (800) 34-MOUSER. A minimum order applies.

Newark Electronics can supply a full range of Hamlin reed switches and magnets, other switches of all makes and models, and dual potentiometers.

Check your Yellow Pages, because you can find Newark Electronics branches in most states and in Ontario and Quebec provinces in Canada.

Radio Shack stores also carry most, but not all, components, and the list of available components shrinks annually. The 566 IC (this should not be confused with the 556) should be available from Signetics, National Semiconductor distributors, or Philips/ECG or NTE, which are available from dealers everywhere. Or get a hold of an issue of *Radio Electronics* among the component advertisers. At the time of this writing, another good source is American Design components, (800) 776-3700, or in New Jersey, (201) 941-5000.

PARTS LIST FOR BELL SOUND GENERATOR

R1	10 kohm resistor
R2	22 kohm resistor
R3	68 kohm resistor
R4	680 kohm resistor
R5	15 kohm resistor
R6	180-ohm resistor
VR1	2 or 5 megohm potentiometer, Mouser Electronics 31VA602 or 31VA605
C1, C4	47-µF, 25-VDC electrolytic capacitors
C2, C3	0.047-µF 50-VDC film capacitors
C5	0.47-µF 50-VDC capacitor or film type, not electrolytic
C6	0.22-µF 50-VDC film capacitor
IC1	CD4049 hex inverter
Q1	General purpose NPN small signal transistor, e.g., 2N2222A or equivalent

Miscellaneous: 2" x 3" printed circuit board, 16-pin IC socket, solder pins

Note: A small speaker or a piezoelectric transducer can be driven directly. Omit C3 and short R2. A piezo gives a better sound; Radio Shack carries several types.

6 Signaling systems

MODEL RAILROAD equipment manufacturers offer a wide variety of signals and MODEL RAILROADER frequently publishes articles on how to build signaling equipment. This chapter presents designs for connecting signals to circuits that will operate them realistically. (If you're not familiar with the ways full-size railroads design and use signal systems, read John Armstrong's book, ALL ABOUT SIGNALS, and if your library goes back that far, also read Boomer Pete's [Al Kalmbach's] excellent article, "What the Signals Say," in the August 1954 issue of MODEL TRAINS.)

Simple sequential switching

You can use this simple switching circuit, Fig. 6-1, to automatically change a signal from green to red and back to green again. The circuit is built around a 555 timer chip, and the length of the cycle can be adjusted by changing the value of C1 as noted in the parts list. If you prefer manual control of the timing, replace R1 with a 1-MΩ resistor in series with a 4.7-MΩ or 5-MΩ potentiometer. Lead length is not important.

Assembly. I built my switch on a wire-wrap IC socket. I then attached the switch to the base of the signal with silicone sealant, which I also smeared over the exposed leads to insulate them. My signal uses 12-V grain-of-wheat bulbs; if you use LEDs, reduce the power supply to 5 VDC and install 100-Ω resistors in the positive leads of the LEDs.

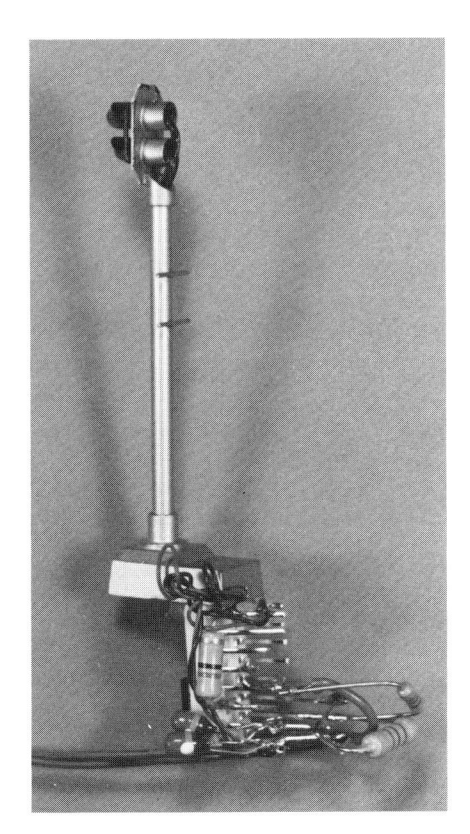

Relay 3-color signal system

You can easily use the simple light-sensitive train detector in Chapter 3 (page 33) or the bidirectional train detector in Chapter 4 (page 36) to drive DPDT relays (such as Radio Shack 275-206 for a 12-V train detector, or 275-215 for a 5-V detector) that control 3-color signals. If you use 4PDT relays (such as Radio Shack 275-214), you can even add automatic train control to the signaling system. Remember that the light-sensitive detector can be operated on any layout, regardless of gauge or control system and that the bidirectional train detector can't be used with command control systems.

Figure 6-2 shows how to wire 3-color signals for five blocks. The train is in block 4, and only the block 4 relay contacts are switched from the static or non-detected position. The upper contact set switches off the green light in block 3 (the block from which the train is exiting), and switches on the red light in block 3 and the yellow in block 2. The lower contact set turns off the green in block 2. Thus, the signal sequence, from block 5 to block 1, is green-green-red-yellow-green, and as the train moves into block 5, the red and yellow aspects move forward a block, leaving all other aspects green. For the opposite direction, on a bidirectional single-track line, the opposite facing signals will all be green, which is hardly prototypical. However, you could solve this problem with a switch that turns off all signals in the direction of travel opposite to that being used.

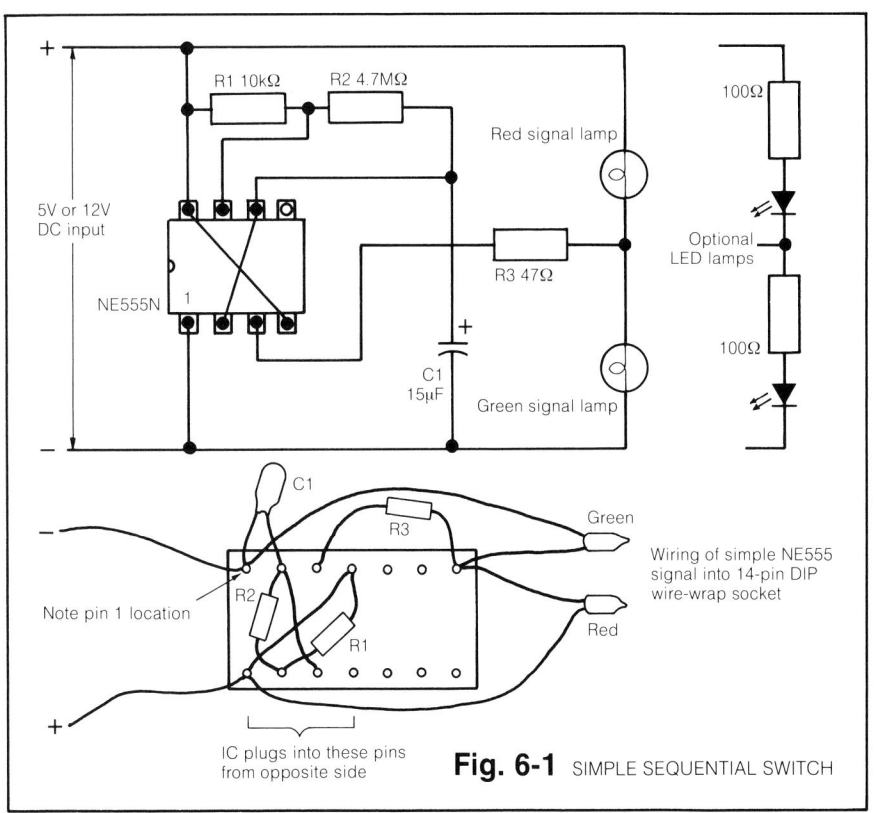

The simple sequential switch automatically changes this signal from red to green to red and so on at a rate set by timing capacitor C1. Use a 12-VDC power supply for grain-of-wheat bulbs or a 5-VDC supply for LEDs.

Fig. 6-1 SIMPLE SEQUENTIAL SWITCH

PARTS LIST FOR SIMPLE SEQUENTIAL SWITCH

C1	15-µF to 22-µF, 10-VDC or 16-VDC tantalum capacitor (This must be a tantalum; a regular electrolytic will not work.) (Increase C1 to 47-µF for a two minute red, two minute green cycle if desired.)
IC	NE555N (8-pin case) (276-1723)
R1	10-kΩ resistor
R2	4.7-MΩ resistor
R3	47-Ω resistor (This limits currrent load of the IC.)
Miscellaneous	14-pin or 16-pin wire-wrap DIP socket (276-1993), silicone sealant

55

Fig. 6-2 RELAY 3-COLOR SIGNAL SYSTEM

Relays operated by train detectors provide 3-aspect progressive signals.

ADDING AUTOMATIC TRAIN CONTROL

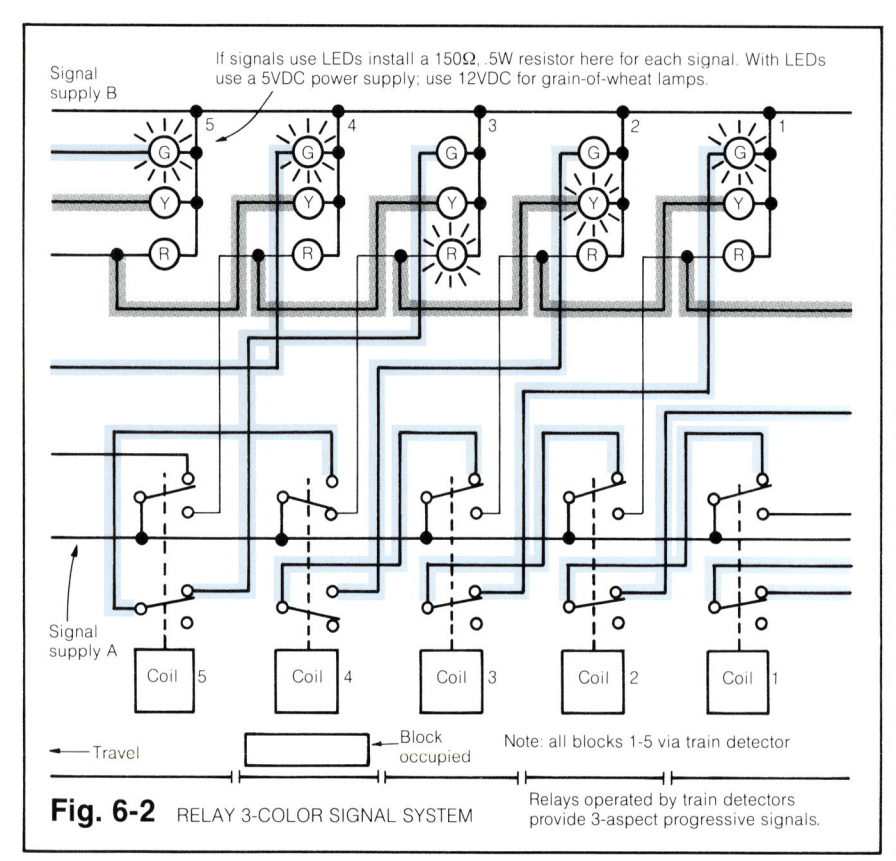

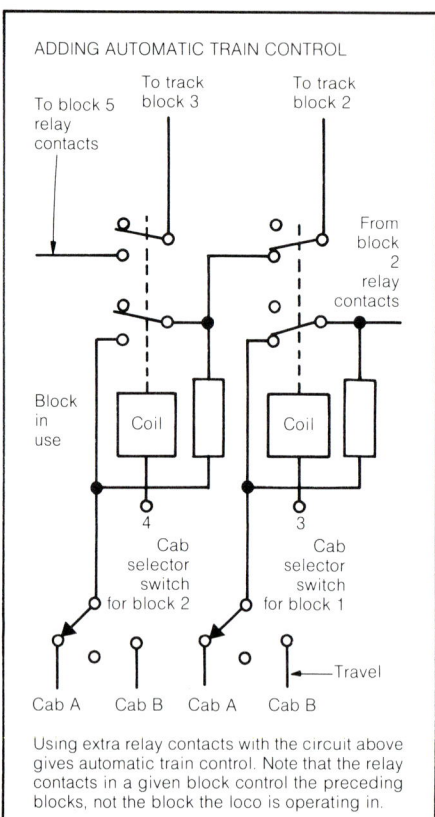

Using extra relay contacts with the circuit above gives automatic train control. Note that the relay contacts in a given block control the preceding blocks, not the block the loco is operating in.

The signal power supply can be 10-V to 12-V AC or DC if the signals have 12-V grain-of-wheat bulbs. (The lower voltage greatly increases bulb life.) If they have LEDs, use 5-V filtered DC in the correct polarity and install a 150-Ω, 0.5-W resistor between the single common lead for each signal and the "B" signal supply.

Adding automatic train control. If you use 4PDT relays with the system I've just described, you can use the other two sets of relay contacts to create a simple form of automatic train control. Again assume that a train is in block 4. The relay contacts are wired to cut off all electricity to block 3 and to halve the voltage in block 2. Thus, any train following closely in block 3 will stop completely, and any distantly following train in block 2 will slow to half speed. When the loco moves into block 5, a train in block 4 stops, a train in block 3 starts at half speed, and block 2 gets full steam ahead.

Logic-output light-sensitive train detector

You can make a light-sensitive train detector, Fig. 6-3, that will provide the 1 and

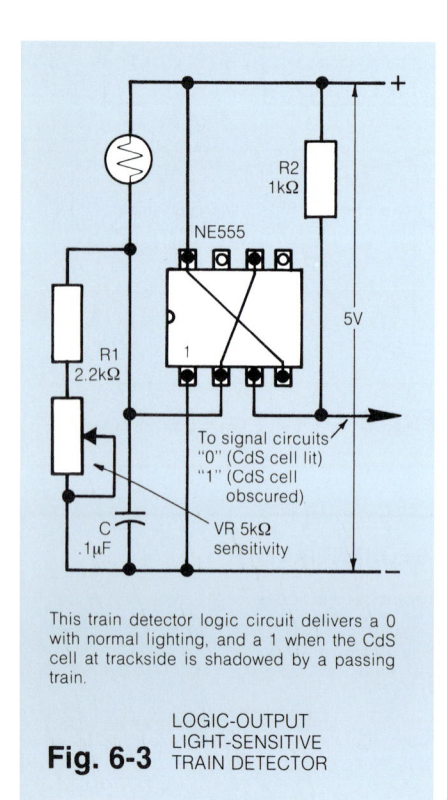

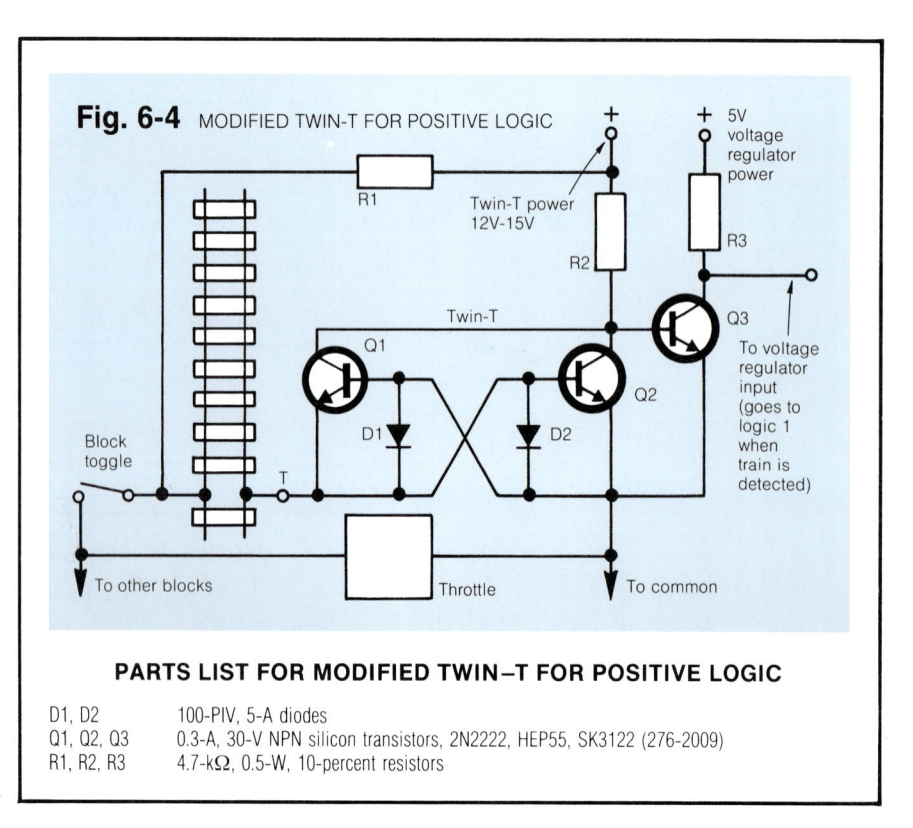

This train detector logic circuit delivers a 0 with normal lighting, and a 1 when the CdS cell at trackside is shadowed by a passing train.

Fig. 6-3 LOGIC-OUTPUT LIGHT-SENSITIVE TRAIN DETECTOR

Fig. 6-4 MODIFIED TWIN-T FOR POSITIVE LOGIC

PARTS LIST FOR MODIFIED TWIN-T FOR POSITIVE LOGIC

D1, D2	100-PIV, 5-A diodes
Q1, Q2, Q3	0.3-A, 30-V NPN silicon transistors, 2N2222, HEP55, SK3122 (276-2009)
R1, R2, R3	4.7-kΩ, 0.5-W, 10-percent resistors

Fig. 6-5 ONE-LED, THREE-COLOR, LOGIC-CONTROLLED SIGNAL

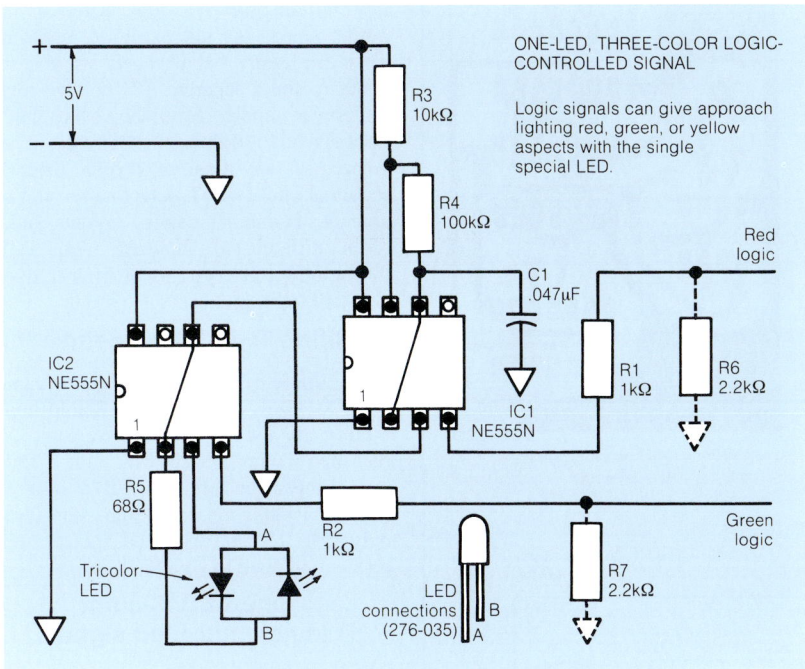

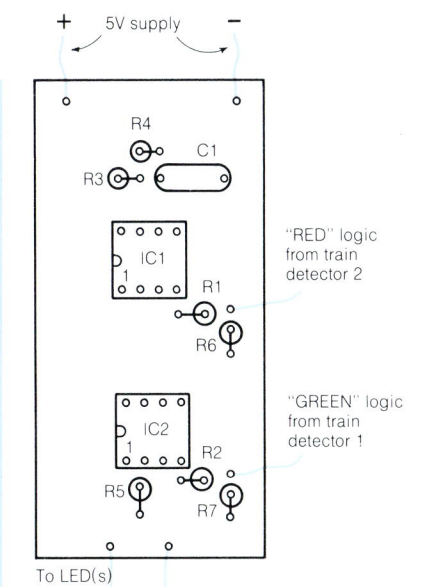

ONE-LED, THREE-COLOR LOGIC-CONTROLLED SIGNAL

Logic signals can give approach lighting red, green, or yellow aspects with the single special LED.

ONE-LED THREE-COLOR SIGNAL BOARD (component side). Shown full size 1¼" × 2½".

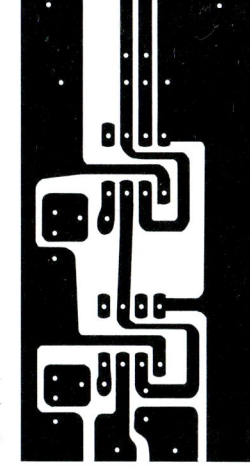

ONE-LED THREE-COLOR SIGNAL BOARD (foil side). Shown full size 1¼" × 2½".

PARTS LIST FOR ONE-LED, THREE-COLOR, LOGIC-CONTROLLED SIGNAL

C1	0.047-µF, 50-VDC to 200-VDC ceramic or film capacitor
IC1, IC2	NE555 (8-pin case) (276-1723)
LED	tricolor LED (276-035) (See text for other suitable LEDs.)
R1, R2	1-kΩ resistors (These are trigger current limiters.)
R3	10-kΩ resistor (This is an oscillator component.)
R4	100-kΩ resistor (This is an oscillator component.)
R5	68-Ω resistor (Use 33 Ω if you use two separate LEDs.)
R6, R7	2.2-kΩ resistors
Miscellaneous	1¼" × 2½" printed circuit board, 8-pin IC sockets (276-1995), soldering pins

(Left) This device is controlled by two light-sensitive logic-output train detectors of Fig. 6-3 and provides red, green, or yellow output from a single tricolor LED. (Right) Here I've mounted the LED in a trackside dwarf signal.

57

SIGNALS FOR ONE BLOCK—ONE-WAY TRAFFIC

Such as on a two-track main line

TRUTH TABLE

INPUTS:		OUTPUTS:		
FN	B	G	Y	R
0	0	1	0	0
1	0	0	1	0
0	1	0	0	1
1	1	0	0	1

ONE-BLOCK, ONE-WAY TRAFFIC SIGNAL BOARD (foil side). Shown full size 1¾" × 2½".

ONE-BLOCK, ONE-WAY TRAFFIC SIGNAL BOARD (component side). Shown full size 1¾" × 2½".

This device, as well as those in Figs. 6-7 and 6-8, contains the circuitry for a logic-output light-sensitive train detector and several of the logic chips listed in Fig. 6-9. The devices are driven by the power supply in Fig. 6-10 and can be interconnected as shown in Fig. 6-12.

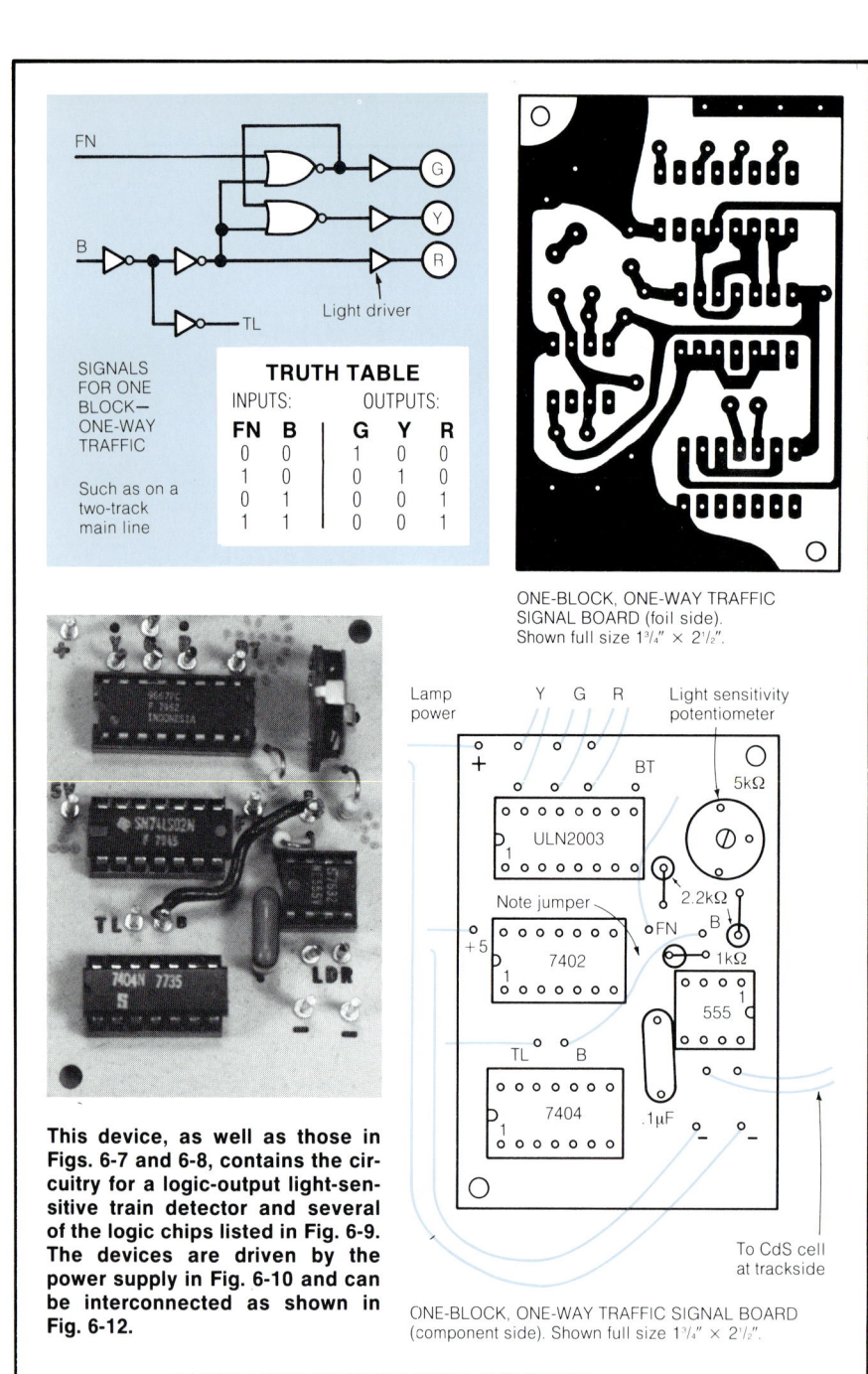

Fig. 6-6 3-LIGHT, LOGIC-OPERATED SIGNAL SYSTEM FOR ONE-BLOCK, ONE-WAY TRAFFIC

The bidirectional train detector of Chapter 4 (page 36) and the widely used Twin-T detector (slightly modified, as described below) will also serve as logic detectors if the output signals do not exceed 5-V positive. This can easily be arranged via the relay contacts and a separate 5-V voltage regulator power supply. Note, however, that the light-sensitive train detector will fit anywhere, on any type of layout. The bidirectional and Twin-T detectors are not suitable for command control layouts and are often difficult to integrate with sound-through-the-rails systems or high-frequency constant lighting.

Modified Twin-T for positive logic

An article by the MR staff in the January 1977 MODEL RAILROADER told how to modify the Twin-T for positive logic. This modified Twin-T is shown, with a few of my changes, in Fig. 6-4. If you already have a Twin-T in NPN transistor format, only Q3, R3, and a 5-VDC power supply connection need to be added.

One-LED, 3-color, logic-controlled signals

An interesting tricolor LED is available from several sources, including Industrial Devices (4301H1/5), Dialight, and Radio Shack (276-035). (Dialight's address is 203 Harrison Place, Brooklyn, NY 11237; telephone [212] 497-7600.) The device is actually one red and one green LED inside a single package. It glows red if a positive voltage is applied, green if a negative voltage is applied, and yellow if the voltage is AC (both LEDs light; yellow is a blend of red and green). Fig. 6-5 shows a control circuit for this LED as well as the printed circuit board layout. I've used it to control a single-LED, tricolor dwarf signal.

The logic signals come from two of the logic-output light-sensitive train detectors I've just described. One detector is located at trackside ahead of the signal with its output connected to the "green logic" input. The signal is not lit until a train shadows the detector, at which time it lights green — provided a train ahead is not shadowing the "red logic" detector. If this happens, the signal shows yellow. However, assuming the track is clear, the signal lights green and the train advances. As it shadows the red logic detector, the signal, now behind, shows red, and goes out as the train clears the second detector. What happens is that the positive logic voltage turns on either IC1 to light the red, or IC2 to light green, with the detector in reversed polarity. Because IC1 is an oscillator, when both logic levels are activated the LED sees both plus and minus signals, so lights yellow.

Resistors R6 and R7 tie the logic signal to 0 when logic detectors are not connected, so you can test the control when it isn't connected to detectors just by touching red logic, green logic, or both, to the 5-V plus terminal.

Adding a second signal. You can connect a second tricolor LED in parallel with the first, but in opposite polarity. The

---

0 outputs necessary to switch logic-controlled signals. It is almost the same as the light-sensitive train detector in Chapter 3 (which is designed to switch relays) except that the positions of the CdS cell and sensitivity control potentiometer VR are reversed and the potentiometer is changed to 5 kΩ for low-resistance CdS cells or 22 kΩ for high-resistance CdS cells. This inverts the action of the detector in that previously the relay at the output was energized only when the CdS cell at trackside was shadowed by a passing train.

Now, if the relay were connected, it would be energized only when a train was not present. If you replace the relay of Fig. 3-8 with resistor R2, Fig. 6-3 (the diodes are no longer required), the detector will signal 0 output if no train is present, and full positive supply voltage output when a train shadows the CdS cell. In conjunction with a 5-VDC power supply, it thus makes available 0 and 1 outputs that can be used as positive logic voltage signals for computer inputs, or for digital ICs of the transistor-transistor logic (TTL) family, including the low-power Schottky group. Many types are available from Radio Shack.

This detector has yet one more advantage: It does not require bounce eliminator circuits, because the detector remains on and supplies a constant voltage regardless of considerable variation in the amount of light striking the CdS cell. (Hall-effect detectors don't bounce either, but for signaling we need a detector sensitive to the presence of a train length, not one that responds only to a train-mounted magnet.)

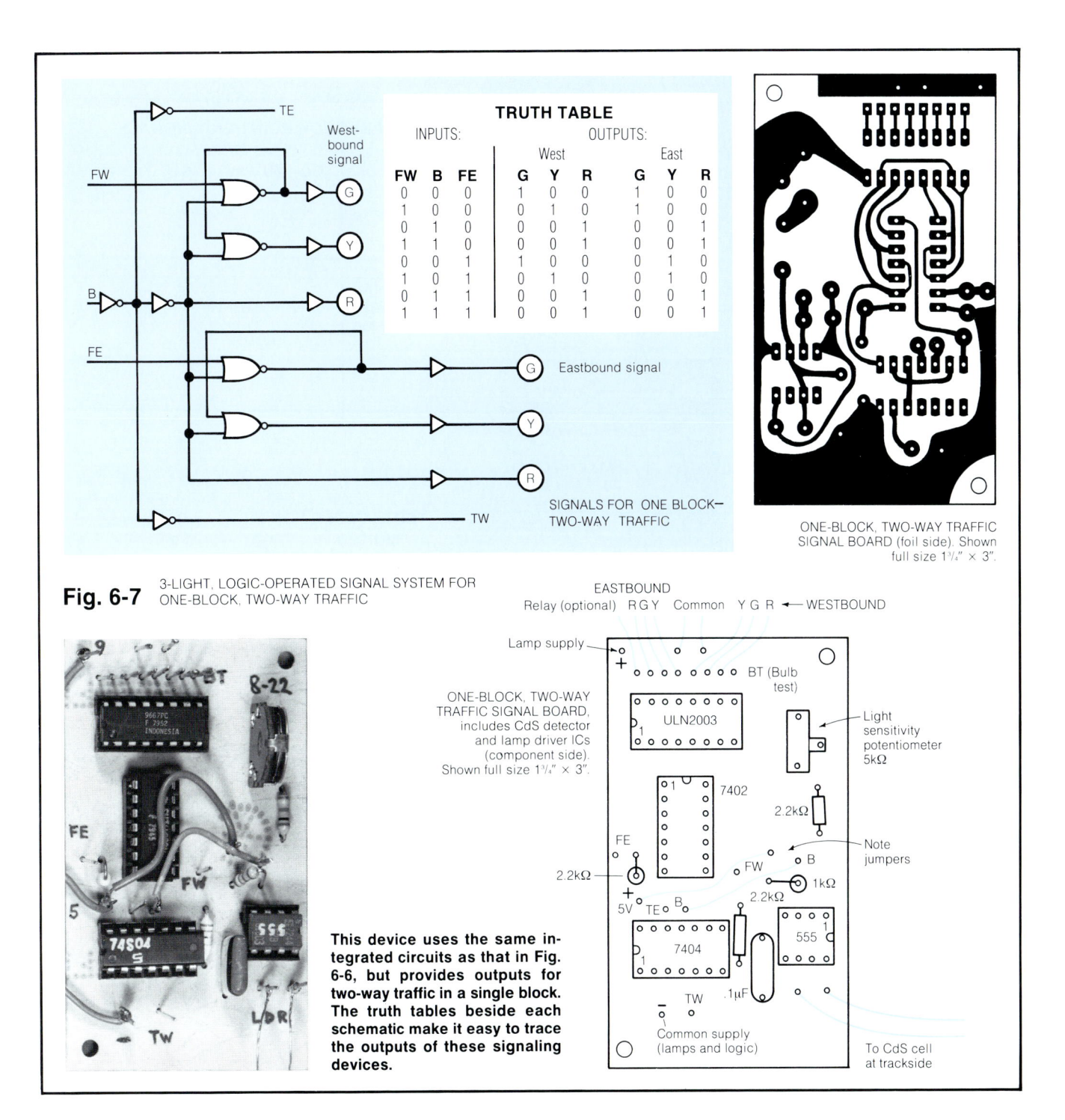

Fig. 6-7 3-LIGHT, LOGIC-OPERATED SIGNAL SYSTEM FOR ONE-BLOCK, TWO-WAY TRAFFIC

TRUTH TABLE

INPUTS:			OUTPUTS:					
			West			East		
FW	B	FE	G	Y	R	G	Y	R
0	0	0	1	0	0	1	0	0
1	0	0	0	1	0	1	0	0
0	1	0	0	0	1	0	0	1
1	1	0	0	0	1	0	0	1
0	0	1	1	0	0	0	1	0
1	0	1	0	1	0	0	1	0
0	1	1	0	0	1	0	0	1
1	1	1	0	0	1	0	0	1

SIGNALS FOR ONE BLOCK— TWO-WAY TRAFFIC

ONE-BLOCK, TWO-WAY TRAFFIC SIGNAL BOARD (foil side). Shown full size 1¾" × 3".

ONE-BLOCK, TWO-WAY TRAFFIC SIGNAL BOARD, includes CdS detector and lamp driver ICs (component side). Shown full size 1¾" × 3".

This device uses the same integrated circuits as that in Fig. 6-6, but provides outputs for two-way traffic in a single block. The truth tables beside each schematic make it easy to trace the outputs of these signaling devices.

second LED will show red when the first is green, so can protect traffic in the opposite direction. Note that R5 should then be reduced to 33 Ω. This simple circuit is useful to protect siding exits in yards. A 5-V voltage regulator power supply can operate several such signals. Each 2-light, 2-detector system draws about 50 mA.

Full-performance 3-light logic-operated signal systems

The following three circuits, shown in Figs. 6-6, 6-7, and 6-8, can be used separately or in combination to produce a complete signaling system for any layout. As in the previous circuit, NE555 light-sensitive logic-output train detectors are used to switch the signals since this detector requires no track voltage connections. Each of the three circuits, for one-way traffic, two-way traffic, or for turnout and block control, uses just three types of TTL ICs to perform the logic switching. These are listed in Fig. 6-9, which also shows their logic functions. (Use Fig. 6-9 and the component location drawings as your parts lists.) This part of each circuit is based on Don W. Hansen's "Using IC's for Signaling," in MODEL RAILROADER, April 1978.

In addition to the logic switching ICs, each board contains the NE555 train detector so that each board can be easily tested on the workbench. Only the CdS cell is at trackside. Also included on each board is a Darlington amplifier chip with seven internal drivers which can be used with grain-of-wheat lamps or LEDs, Fig. 6-10. The ULN2003A Darlington amplifier chip used is specially designed to withstand the cold surge currents of incandescent lamps.

Each ULN2003A also has at least one spare driver which is not used for signal lamp switching and which can be used to drive a 9-V relay simultaneously with any one signal lighting. This relay can be used for automatic block disconnection even with command control systems. The chip also contains the diode reverse-voltage protection needed with relays.

Figure 6-11 shows yet another use for the ULN2003A. The Pennsylvania-type signal normally requires 3 or 4 aspects lit at the same time; using two chips permits each of the 10 lamps on the N. J. International model signal to have separate drive circuits and equal brightness.

Added to each board, and shown in the

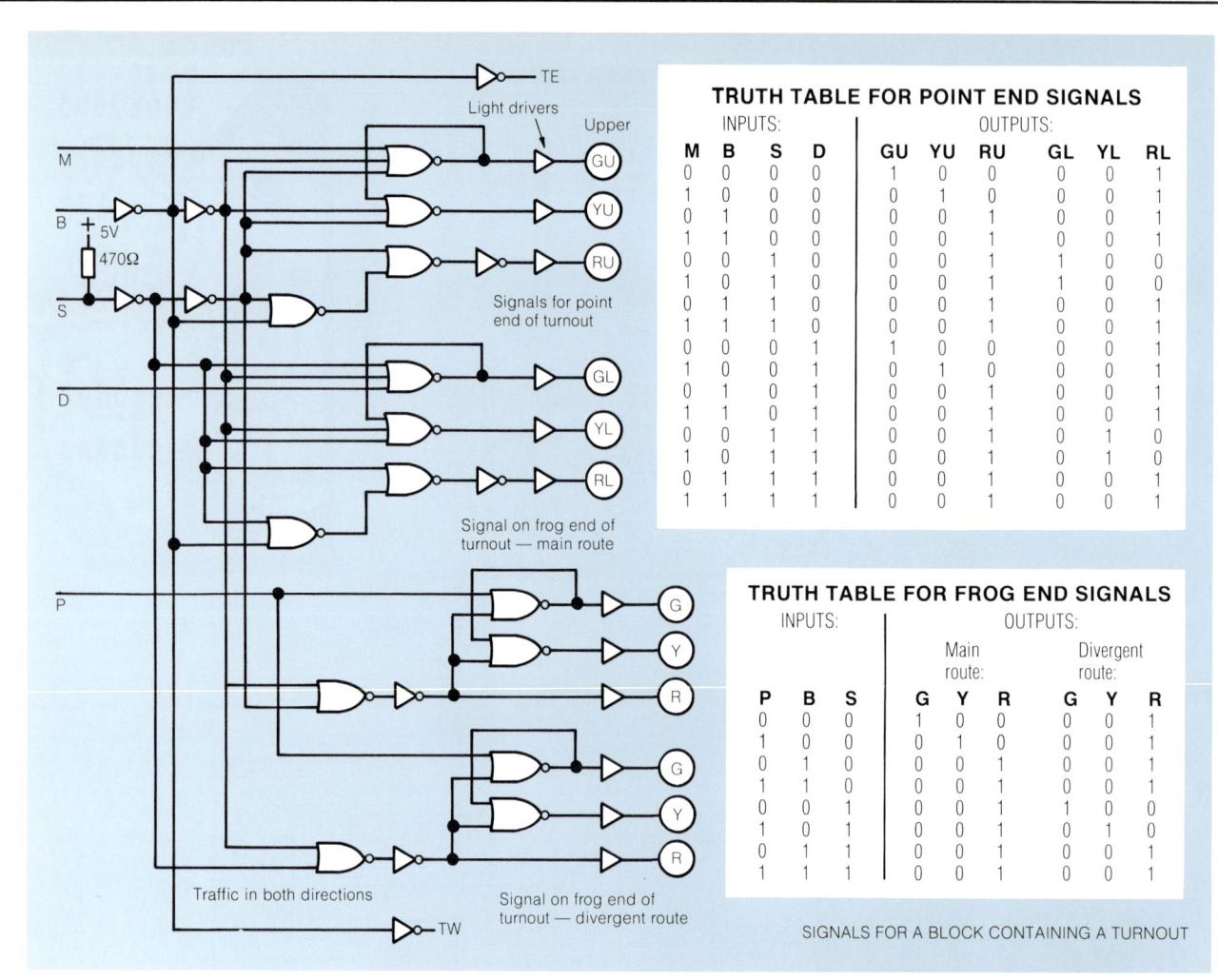

TRUTH TABLE FOR POINT END SIGNALS

INPUTS:				OUTPUTS:					
M	B	S	D	GU	YU	RU	GL	YL	RL
0	0	0	0	1	0	0	0	0	1
1	0	0	0	0	1	0	0	0	1
0	1	0	0	0	0	1	0	0	1
1	1	0	0	0	0	1	0	0	1
0	0	1	0	0	0	1	1	0	0
1	0	1	0	0	0	1	1	0	0
0	1	1	0	0	0	1	0	0	1
1	1	1	0	0	0	1	0	0	1
0	0	0	1	1	0	0	0	0	1
1	0	0	1	0	1	0	0	0	1
0	1	0	1	0	0	1	0	0	1
1	1	0	1	0	0	1	0	0	1
0	0	1	1	0	0	1	0	1	0
1	0	1	1	0	0	1	0	1	0
0	1	1	1	0	0	1	0	0	1
1	1	1	1	0	0	1	0	0	1

TRUTH TABLE FOR FROG END SIGNALS

INPUTS:			Main route: OUTPUTS			Divergent route:		
P	B	S	G	Y	R	G	Y	R
0	0	0	1	0	0	0	0	1
1	0	0	0	1	0	0	0	1
0	1	0	0	0	1	0	0	1
1	1	0	0	0	1	0	0	1
0	0	1	0	0	1	1	0	0
1	0	1	0	0	1	0	1	0
0	1	1	0	0	1	0	0	1
1	1	1	0	0	1	0	0	1

SIGNALS FOR A BLOCK CONTAINING A TURNOUT

Use Vector dry-transfer photoresist patterns and soldering pins when building any of the logic-operated signal systems.

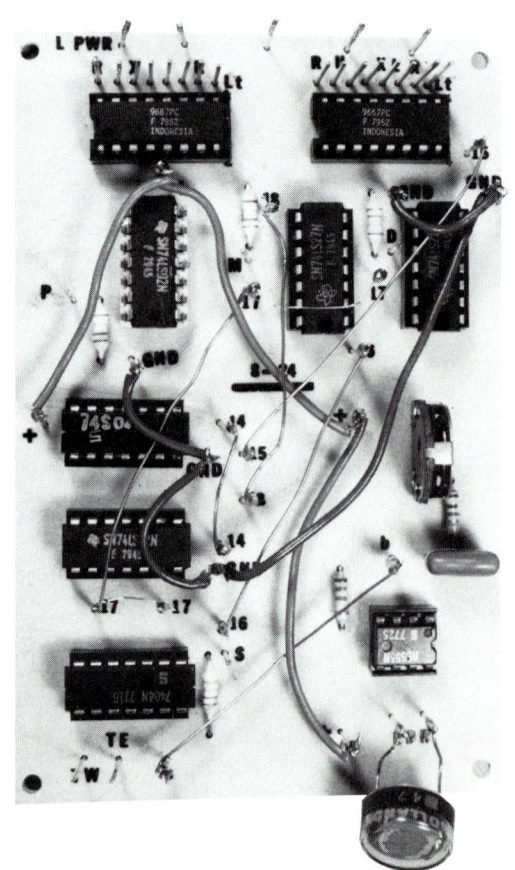

Turnout set to	Next block (contains turnout)	Following block	Aspect
Signals at point end:			
Main route	Clear	Clear	Green over red
	Clear	Occupied	Yellow over red
	Occupied	—	Red over red
Divergent route	Clear	Clear	Red over green
	Clear	Occupied	Red over yellow
	Occupied	—	Red over red
Signals at main route end:			
Main route	Clear	Clear	Green
	Clear	Occupied	Yellow
	Occupied	—	Red
Divergent route	Clear	Clear	Red
	Clear	Occupied	Red
	Occupied	—	Red
Signals at divergent route end:			
Main route	Clear	Clear	Red
	Clear	Occupied	Red
	Occupied	—	Red
Divergent route	Clear	Clear	Green
	Clear	Occupied	Yellow
	Occupied	—	Red

Fig. 6-8 3-LIGHT, LOGIC-OPERATED SIGNAL SYSTEM FOR ONE-BLOCK, TWO-WAY TRAFFIC AND A TURNOUT

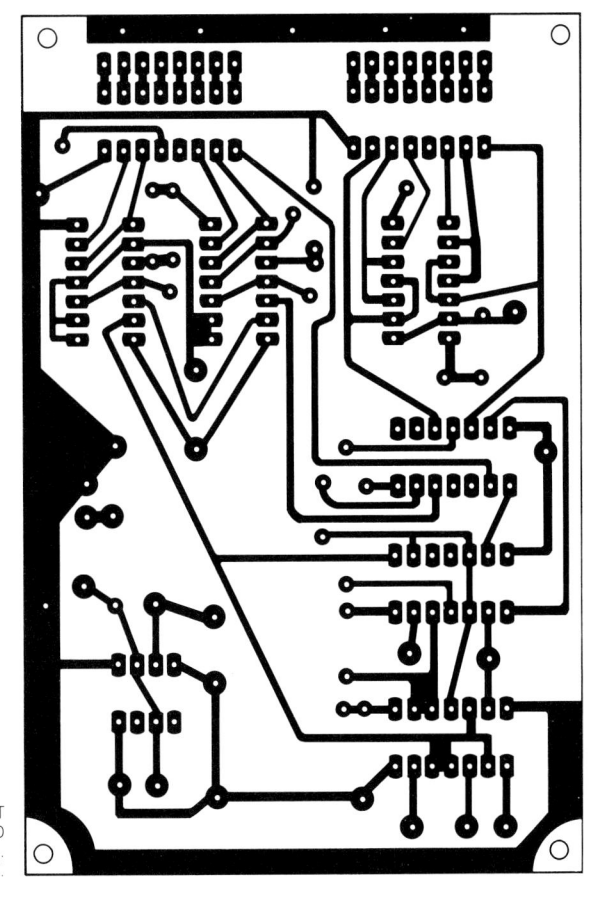

BLOCK WITH TURNOUT SIGNAL BOARD (foil side). Shown full size 3" × 4½".

BLOCK WITH TURNOUT SIGNAL BOARD. includes CdS detector and lamp driver ICs (component side). Shown full size 3" × 4½".

*Relay drive (optional)

**+9V 5 pins this row to 9V and signal lamp common leads

BT = Lamp test pins (join to GND to test lamps)

NOTES:
Join all + connectors
Join all GND connectors (supply minus)
And all similar numbers
4 of 17, 2 of 16
2 of 15, 2 of 18
2 of B
Four resistors not marked are 2.2kΩ to 4.7kΩ

FROG END SIGNALS — MAIN R G Y — DIVERGENT Y G R — POINT END SIGNALS — UPPER R G Y — R G Y LOWER

components layout but not in the schematic, are a few resistors. These are used where necessary to tie logic inputs to ground or negative. This is so that you can test boards separately: Without these resistors leakage currents inside logic switches can cause sufficient voltage that the chip thinks it has received a 1 signal. This is a requirement when a 3-aspect signal is last in a series of signals, and therefore receives no logic signal from a following block to suppress yellow when green should light: Connecting a 1-kΩ to 3.3-kΩ resistor from suppress yellow logic to ground ensures that green always comes up. However, as noted, all three board designs incorporate the required resistors where necessary.

Connections for the logic used are included in Fig. 6-9, which also shows their functions. For example, the 7427 triple three-input NOR gate is three switches, each of which gives a + output signal only when all three of its inputs are negative. You don't need to trace out these logic systems because all the relevant drawings and printed circuit boards are included.

Connections. The following codes are used in the schematics and on the printed circuit boards for input and output signal connections:

● P — From next block on point end of turnout.
● M — From next block on main route.
● D — From next block on divergent route.
● B — From block detector.
● S — From turnout; goes to logic 1 when turnout is thrown to divergent route, logic 0 for main route.
● TE — To next eastbound block.
● TW — To next westbound block.
● FE — From next eastbound block.
● FW — From next westbound block.
● FN — From next block on one-way track.
● TL — To last block on one-way track.

Note: "Signal" refers to logic signal or level, not a track signal.

Note that S is the only logic point at +, or logic 1, without external connections applied to a signal board. Therefore, if you test a circuit board and the table shows a logic 0 for S, it must be joined to negative or ground. The connections preceded by "T" transfer a relevant logic voltage to the adjacent train signal boards and those preceded by "F" receive the logic signal from adjacent boards. Put simply, the signal boards are a collection of switches that are wired and interconnected so the appropriate red, green, or yellow signal lamps operate only under preset, foolproof conditions.

Truth tables. Truth tables are shown with the schematics for the three logic signal systems and list the output operation; that is, which signals are lit for all possible combinations of input values entered as 0 (negative, or ground) or 1 (positive, approximately 5-V). This indicates the method of testing the boards simply by supplying appropriate clip leads from logic terminals to positive or minus and observing the signal lights. Note that all three logic boards are for controlling type D signals; only one red, green, or yellow light at a time.

61

Fig. 6-9 TTL ICs FOR THE LOGIC-OPERATED SIGNAL SYSTEMS

Note: Each of these ICs is made by several manufacturers, and all work well. Schottky TTL types can be mixed or matched. Use IC sockets with all ICs.

ICs FOR ONE-BLOCK, ONE-WAY TRAFFIC, FIG. 6-6

optical detector	NE555N or LM555 (276-1723)
hex inverter	SN7404, 74S04, 7404N, or 74LS04N (276-1904)
quad two-input NOR gate	SN7402, 74S02, 7402N, or 74LS02N (276-1902)
Darlington amplifier array	ULN2003A, ULN2003AN, NE5503N, or 9667PC

ICs FOR ONE-BLOCK, TWO-WAY TRAFFIC, FIG. 6-7

Same as above.

ICs FOR ONE-BLOCK, TWO-WAY TRAFFIC AND A TURNOUT, FIG. 6-8

optical detector	one NE555N or LM555 (276-1723)
hex inverter	two SN7404, 74S04, 7404N, or 74LS04N (276-1904)
quad two-input NOR gate	two SN7402, 74S02, 7402N, or 74LS02N (276-1902)
Darlington amplifier array	two ULN2003A, ULN2003AN, NE5503N, or 9667PC
triple three-input NOR gate	two SN7427N or SN74LS27N input (In the circuit of Fig. 6-8, one NOR gate in each IC is used as a two-input NOR gate by pairing gates in parallel.)

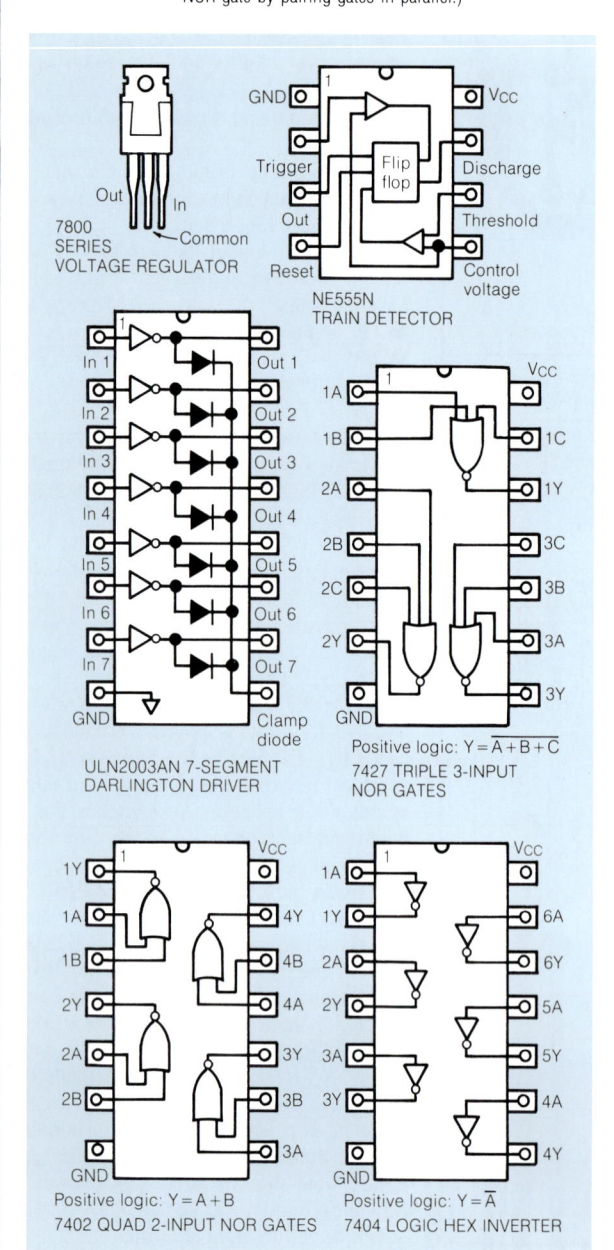

7800 SERIES VOLTAGE REGULATOR

NE555N TRAIN DETECTOR

ULN2003AN 7-SEGMENT DARLINGTON DRIVER

Positive logic: $Y = \overline{A + B + C}$
7427 TRIPLE 3-INPUT NOR GATES

Positive logic: $Y = \overline{A + B}$
7402 QUAD 2-INPUT NOR GATES

Positive logic: $Y = \overline{A}$
7404 LOGIC HEX INVERTER

Fig. 6-10 POWER SUPPLY AND LAMP DRIVER FOR THE LOGIC-OPERATED SIGNAL SYSTEMS

PARTS LIST FOR THE POWER SUPPLY

C1	2000-μF, 10-VDC electrolytic capacitor
C2	0.22-μF, 100-VDC capacitor
C3	100-μF, 6-VDC electrolytic capacitor
D1	100-PIV, 4-A bridge rectifier (276-1171)
T	6.3-VAC, 1.2-A transformer (273-050) (You may use a transformer that delivers more current, if desired.)
voltage regulator	5-VDC, 1-A voltage regulator in TO-220 case, 7805 (276-1770)
Miscellaneous	perf board or sheet of plastic to mount components, heat sink for voltage regulator (276-1363), barrier terminals, silicone sealant if parts are mounted on sheet of plastic

If your signals have LEDs, use a 0.25-W, 270-Ω or 330-Ω resistor in series with each LED.

LAMP DRIVER CIRCUIT

Each ULN2003A IC contains 7 Darlington amplifiers. Two inputs can be joined, giving the option of two separate outputs for a lamp and a relay. Relay protection diodes are built into the IC. Maximum relay current is 250 mA.

POWER SUPPLY FOR LOGIC SIGNAL CIRCUITS

Note: if using LEDs, use a 270Ω or 330Ω resistor (.25W) in series with each LED.

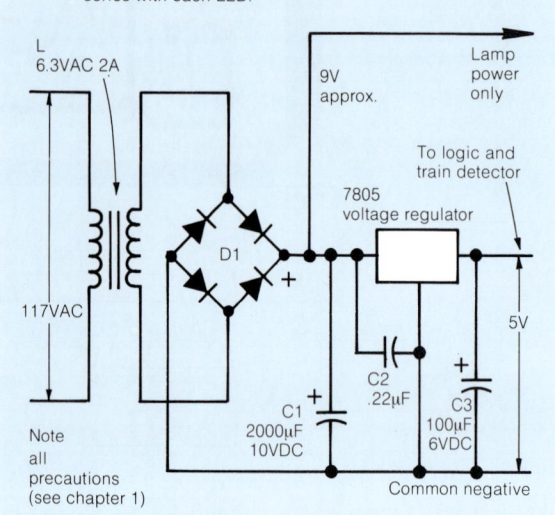

LAMP DRIVER CIRCUIT

Each ULN2003A IC contains 7 Darlington amplifiers. Two inputs can be joined giving option of two separate outputs (lamp and relay). Relay protection diodes are built into the IC. Maximum relay current is 250ma

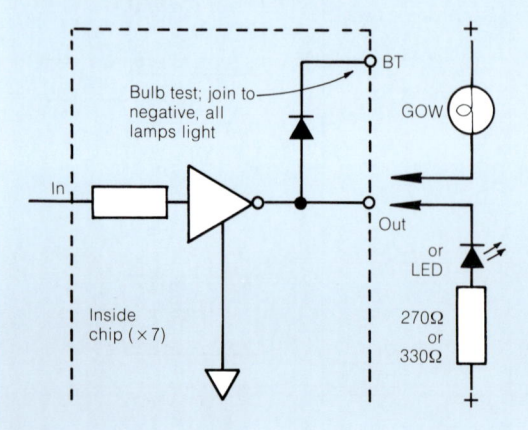

POWER SUPPLY AND LAMP/RELAY DRIVER INTERFACE FOR LOGIC SIGNAL CIRCUITS

Construction tips. You'll notice that the three boards range from fairly straightforward for one-block, one-way traffic, to fairly complex for the board which operates 12 signal lamps and is for a block containing a turnout. Figure 1-23, page 10, shows the dry-transfer photoresist patterns by Vector which are essential for these circuit boards, as well as wire-wrap pins, also by Vector, which are necessary to make board interconnections easily. (Vector's address is on page 10.) In a pinch, you can make your own pins by squeezing one end of heavy copper wire in a vise.

Interconnections. The interconnection diagrams, Fig. 6-12, use the circuits of Figs. 6-6, 6-7, and 6-8, and show ways to connect signals from one block to the next. It's easily possible to use ten of these circuits on even a small layout should you be bitten by the signal bug.

Power supply. As shown in Fig. 6-10, a 2-A supply using a 6.3-V, 2-A transformer can supply about 20 signals and modules. The module of Fig. 6-8 consumes 28 mA to 35 mA and the module of Fig. 6-6 takes 13 mA to 18 mA, in both cases including the detector. The 9-V unregulated output of the power supply gives about 40 mA for each grain-of-wheat lamp, or about 20 mA for each LED (don't forget the resistor needed for the LED!).

Only one grain-of-wheat lamp is ever lit at one time for each signal, and if you need only a dozen signals and modules, a 1-A or 1.2-A transformer (Radio Shack 273-050) will suffice. One possible problem can be caused by the TTL switches because they can draw a heavy instantaneous current and thus may produce false pulse information when they switch. If this happens, divide up your circuit among one or more extra power supplies.

Grain-of-wheat or LED? The grain-of-wheat lamp gives a brighter light output than most LEDs even when run at 9 V to ensure long life. This is particularly true when the signal is seen from the side. Most ready-made signal assemblies contain grain-of-wheat lamps. Most LEDs give good light output only from the front. Many types are described by stating the viewing angle at which their light output drops by half. This can range between ±12° to ±50°. Also,

Fig. 6-11. Two ULN2003A Darlington amplifier integrated circuits in this N. J. International Pennsylvania-type signal permit three incandescent signal lamps to burn simultaneously at constant brightness.

their light output can vary as much as 8 to 1. The following Litronix LEDs or their equivalents are good choices. All are bright, have a half angle of ±35°, and a lens diameter of 3 mm. They are:

● Red — LD30-3
● Yellow — LD36-2
● Green — LD37-3.

Smaller versions with a lens diameter of 1 mm, which are suitable for scratchbuilt N scale signals, are:

● Red — LD121-2
● Yellow — LD161-2
● Green — LD172-2.

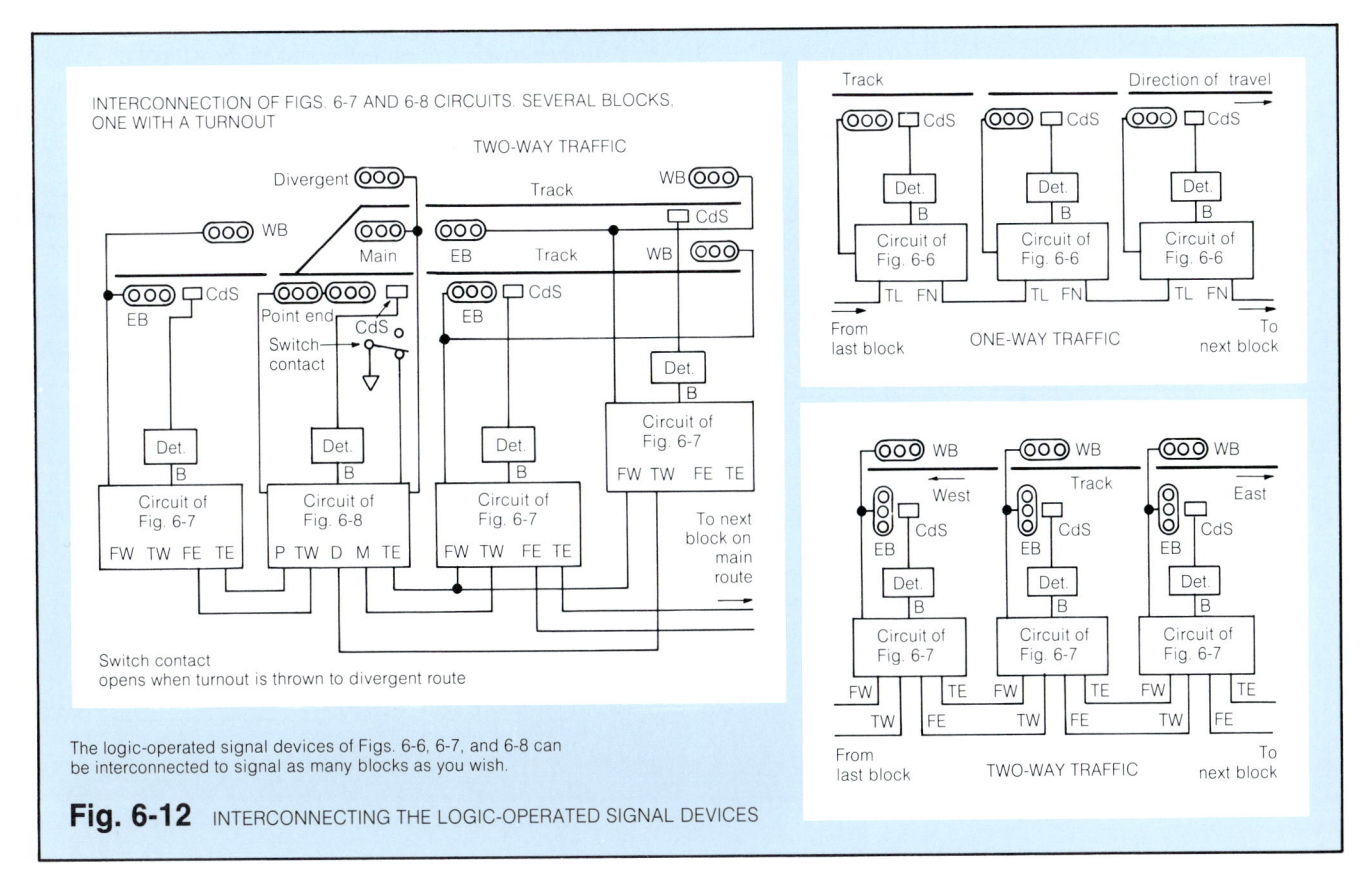

The logic-operated signal devices of Figs. 6-6, 6-7, and 6-8 can be interconnected to signal as many blocks as you wish.

Fig. 6-12 INTERCONNECTING THE LOGIC-OPERATED SIGNAL DEVICES

7 Command control

THE SIMPLEST way of operating two trains at the same time is to have separate track for each. For example, two concentric main lines, one with a yard inboard of the main line, the other with a yard outboard, will provide satisfying operation — for a time. Most of us will soon want to transfer trains from one of those two main lines to the other. At this point Linn Westcott's book HOW TO WIRE YOUR MODEL RAILROAD becomes a necessity. You need block wiring, block switches to select which block is connected to which throttle, and you need to know where to put insulated rail gaps to maintain block separation and avoid short-circuits.

Gaps and block switching cause problems for most of us; therefore, control systems which do away with most block toggle switches and rail gaps are of great interest. Electronic control systems which allow greatly simplified track wiring are termed "command control."

History of command control

Command control systems maintain a fixed power supply voltage on the rails. This may be AC or DC, and the signals which command receivers in the locomotive are multiplexed with the power supply voltage. In other words, both the power supply voltage and the command signal pass through the track, but they don't interfere with each other: Each performs only its assigned task.

Early command control systems. One of the first command control systems, Astrac, was pioneered by General Electric in 1963. General Electric discontinued Astrac soon after its introduction, and there are a very few systems still in use. Astrac employed analog, or frequency control, of up to five locomotives. Track power was a fixed 18 VAC to 20 VAC, and in essence, five control frequencies were transmitted to the rails and rode piggyback on the track power. Receivers in the locomotives, each tuned to one of the five transmitter frequencies, relayed speed and direction control for the motor through either of two small SCRs.

Digitrack was probably the first to use digital control. The Digitrack 1600 system, produced between 1972 and 1976, could control 16 or more locomotives using digital pulses sent through the track. The locomotive receivers translated the pulses into speed and direction information. Each receiver responded to a specific pulse code. A fixed 13 VDC supplied the motor power.

Contemporary command control. A revised version of the Digitrack system, now called the CTC-16, was published as a construction project in MODEL RAILROADER in a series of articles by Keith Gutierrez from December 1979 through April 1980 (with a follow-up article in December 1980). Keith sells kits that contain most parts required to build the CTC-16. Write to him at CV&P Products, P. O. Box 5772, Richardson, TX 75080 for prices and ordering information.

The CTC-16 is a digital system, as are most other contemporary command control systems. Digital systems can't go off-tune, a major problem with earlier analog systems. To be fair, though, contemporary analog, or frequency control, systems can be very good. For example, a Touch-Tone telephone key pad generates very stable crystal-controlled audio frequencies and can form the basis of an excellent control system using receivers with phase-locked loop detectors.

The British Hornby Zero 1 is yet another digital command control system. Its heart is a Texas Instruments TMS1000 microprocessor IC, and in its most complete form the system can control up to 16 locomotives and 99 accessories.

Many model railroaders have been pleased with the Dynatrol command control system from Power Systems, Inc., 56 Bellis Circle, Cambridge, MA 02140.

There are many other systems on the market, each with its own advantages and limitations, so read review articles on each in MODEL RAILROADER and other magazines before buying any system.

Command control — the disadvantages

Good as they are, command control systems aren't for everyone. First, command control is more expensive than a conventional throttle. Second, at this time the receivers have to be installed in the locos by the hobbyist — or hobby-shop owner — and may operate only on one layout. Third, compared with the best transistor throttles, some measure of fine control is lost. With most command control systems, the motors get pulse power at all times. As I mentioned earlier, this is fine for cheap motors, but it's a crude way to drive high-quality can or ironless-armature motors. Fourth, some command control systems don't allow for momentum effects. In short, command control allows great flexibility of operation and greatly simplified control wiring, but sometimes sacrifices smooth running.

Finally, good track pickup connections to

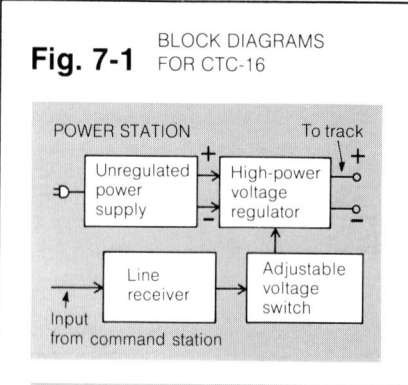

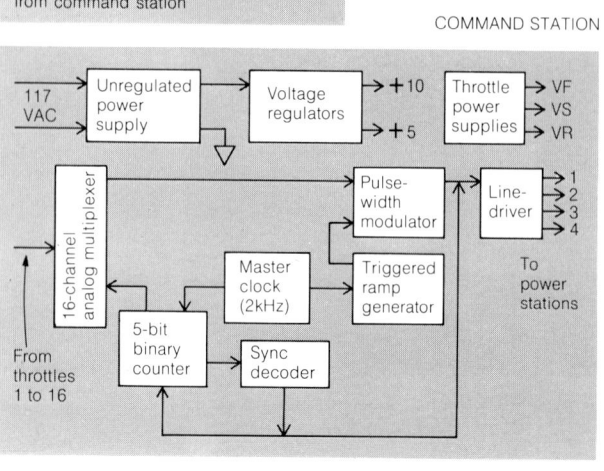

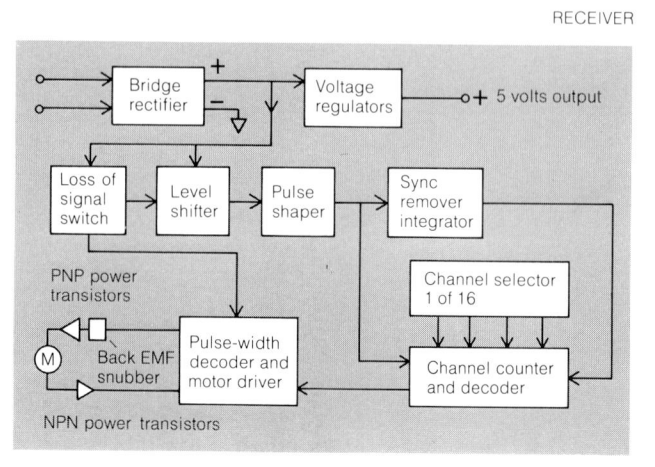

Fig. 7-1 BLOCK DIAGRAMS FOR CTC-16

Fig. 7-2 CTC-16 COMMAND CONTROL SYSTEM

MOTOR

RECEIVER — Decodes its own pulse signal for motor voltage and directional information

SUPERIMPOSED PULSES

DC VOLTAGE

THROTTLE — Controls speed and direction

COMBINED SIGNAL

COMMAND SIGNAL

COMMAND STATION — Throttle information put into pulse form

POWER STATION — Locomotive running voltage combined with pulse voltage

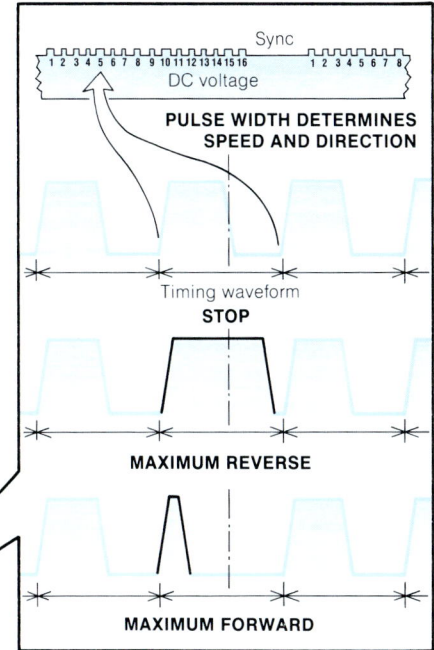

PULSE WIDTH DETERMINES SPEED AND DIRECTION

Timing waveform
STOP
MAXIMUM REVERSE
MAXIMUM FORWARD

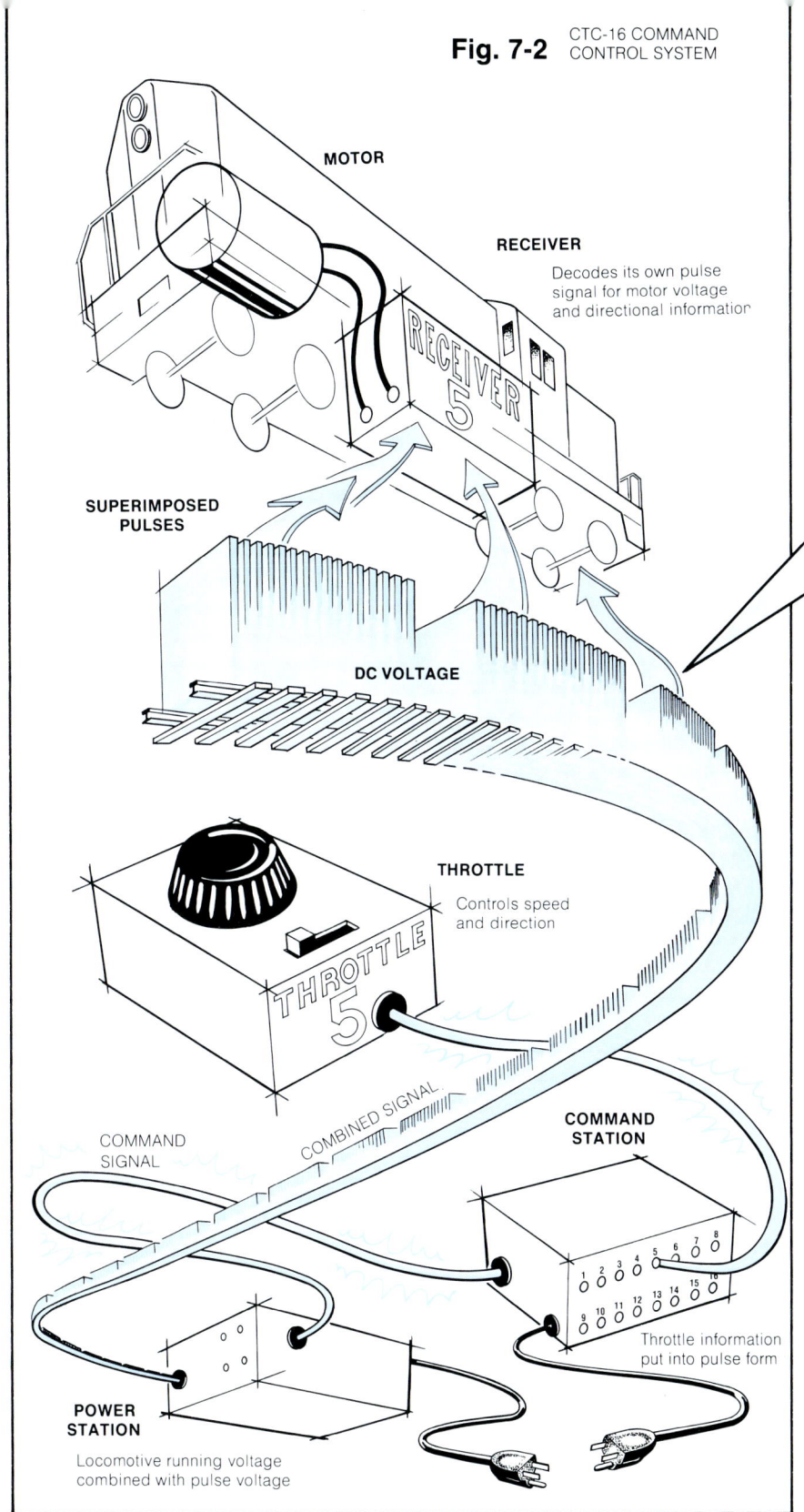

the loco are even more important than with conventional block wiring. The track must be clean because the receivers can be confused if the control signals arrive erratically.

Let's now examine two command control systems in some detail, Keith Gutierrez' CTC-16 and the Hornby Zero 1.

The CTC-16 system

The CTC-16 system has 15 VDC on the track, and works by varying the pulse width of up to 16 pulses which are superimposed on the track voltage. Each receiver can be adjusted to be controlled from one of the 16 signal pulses. Figure 7-1 shows how the CTC-16 operates and Fig. 7-2 shows the composition of:

● The power station, which supplies the fixed DC track voltage, modulated by the coded command pulses, which are injected into an adjustable voltage regulator IC.
● The command station, which generates the pulses and varies their width in response to throttle commands.
● The on-board receiver, which decodes the pulses (receivers are adjustable to respond to only one set of the available 16 pulse groups), and converts them into motor speed and direction controls. Direction is controlled by PNP and NPN power transistors in a bridge network of four devices, one pair being turned on for each direction of travel.

The greatest advantage of the CTC-16 is the simplicity of its tethered walkaround throttles: In their basic form they consist of a speed control, a direction switch, and a four-wire flexible cord. In contrast, each receiver has 36 components.

Hornby's Zero 1

The Hornby Zero 1 system is more sophisticated than the CTC-16, although these two probably represent the cream of the currently available command control systems. Hornby, a British company, is one of the oldest makers of model trains and claims to have spent more than a million dollars developing the Zero 1.

The Zero 1 is a computer system: The nerve center of the master control unit is a Texas Instruments TMS1000 4-bit microprocessor chip. This chip appears in many other devices — there are nearly 30 versions, including the chip in the "Speak and Spell" educational game.

The four units of the Zero 1. There are four units to Zero 1, Fig. 7-3. Up to three slave units can be added to the master control unit simply by snapping each to the preceding unit. Connections are by 15-contact printed circuit board edge connectors. At turn-on there can be four fully independent locomotives under control; the master control unit is automatically assigned to loco 1, and each slave to 2, 3, and 4, respectively.

The master control unit can be used to assign any of the 16 digitally controlled locomotive receivers to any of the slave units or

The tiny size of the Zero 1 receiver is made possible because it uses a triac.

Unlike the CTC-16, which is designed for walkaround control, the Hornby Zero 1 is designed to allow maximum control flexibility from a fixed central location. This is the master control unit with one slave unit; up to three slave units can be added.

The Zero 1 accessory module (shown here with its cover removed) can control up to four turnouts, signals, or anything else that can be powered by track voltage.

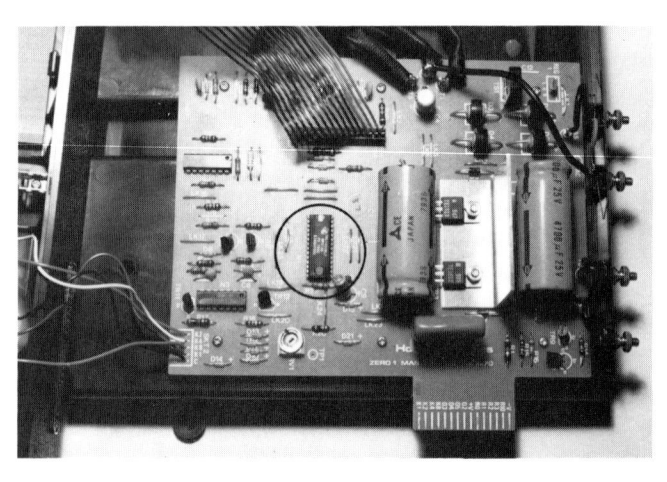

Inside view of the master control unit reveals a clean, uncluttered layout. A Texas Instruments TMS1000 4-bit microprocessor chip (circled) is the heart of the Zero 1.

Fig. 7-3 HORNBY ZERO 1 WAVEFORM DIAGRAM

even to the master control unit itself. The receiver previously assigned can be stopped, or allowed to continue on its merry way until it's reassigned back to a slave or master control unit.

The fourth component of the system is the accessory operating module. This is addressed by the master control unit. Drawing power from the track, each accessory operating module can operate up to four turnout motors or four signals, applying either bursts of power or continuous power.

The U. K. version of the Zero 1 receiver has only 14 components; its dimensions are $1\frac{1}{2}''$ x $\frac{9}{16}''$ x $\frac{1}{4}''$. The small size and simplicity are made possible, in part, because the track voltage is a + and − square wave. The receiver motor control unit is, therefore, a triac, which in effect is a bidirectional SCR, though two SCRs are used in some versions of the receiver.

No bigger than one of the four CTC-16 directional transistors, the triac does the same job — provided it is fed AC. Track power is a square wave, one form of AC, generated by a pair of power transistors in the master control unit. The triac or SCR pairs in the receiver conduct on the positive part for forward, or are synchronized by pulses to the negative part for reverse. Although track voltage swings from + 22 V to − 22 V, the average is 11 VDC, since the square wave is only on half of the time, and only half is used for either direction.

Zero 1 can dial up four different rates of momentum. So could the CTC-16 if you added a switch, a pair of capacitors, and a resistor to the throttles.

The Zero 1's control system is based upon a 32-bit code generated by the TMS1000 microprocessor, which is transmitted every third cycle of the square wave track voltage. For the 8.33-millisecond interval during which the coded information is transmitted, it replaces the track voltage, Fig. 7-3. Because the track power is turned off when the coded information is transmitted, the system is highly resistant to electronic interference. The code carries the identifying pulse for each of 16 locos and up to 99 auxiliaries.

Questions and answers about the CTC-16 and the Zero 1

● What waveforms drive the motors? Simi-

The high-frequency cab control allows independent control of two trains in the same block. Only one train is equipped with a high-frequency receiver; the other is controlled by any conventional throttle.

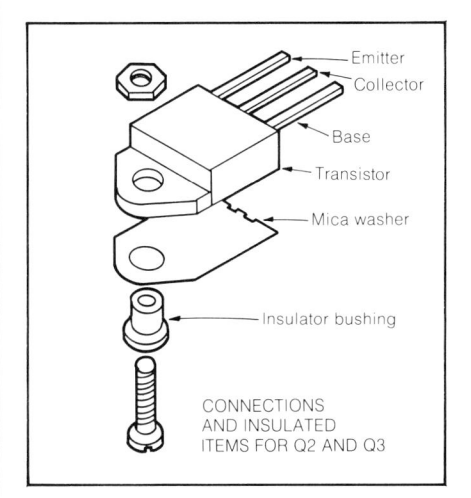

PARTS LIST FOR HIGH-FREQUENCY CAB CONTROL THROTTLE AND POWER SUPPLY

C1	2000-µF, 50-VDC electrolytic capacitor
C2, C3	0.22-µF, 200-VDC foil capacitors
C4	100-µF, 35-VDC electrolytic capacitor
C5	0.01-µF, 100-VDC foil or disk capacitor
C6	0.022-µF, 100-VDC, 10-percent polystyrene or close tolerance capacitor
C7, C8, C9, C10	4.7-µF, 35-VDC electrolytic capacitors
C11	100-µF, 35-VDC electrolytic capacitor
C12	4.7-µF, 100-VDC film capacitor (Or use two 2.2-µF film capacitors in parallel — C12 must not be an electrolytic capacitor.)
D1	200-PIV, 2-A bridge rectifier (276-1173)
D2, D3, D4	400-PIV, 1-A diodes, 1N4004 (276-1103)
D5	12-V, 0.5-A zener diode, 1N4742 (276-563)
IC1	NE555 (8-pin case) (276-1723)
Q1	5-W, 1-A NPN driver transistor in TO-220 or TO-126 case, TIP31 or equivalent (276-2017)
Q2	15-A, 40-V NPN power plastic transistor, TIP3055 or equivalent
Q3	15-A, 40-V PNP power plastic transistor, TIP2955 or equivalent
R1	1-kΩ resistor
R2	22-kΩ resistor
R3	100-kΩ resistor
R4	6.8-kΩ resistor
R5	2.2-kΩ resistor
R6	100-Ω resistor
R7, R8	560-Ω resistors
R9, R10	3.9-kΩ resistors
R11	220-Ω, 1-W resistor
R12	56-Ω, 1-W resistor
T1	20-V to 25-V, 1-A power transformer (273-1480)
Voltage regulator	24-V, 1-A voltage regulator in TO-3 case, Motorola MC7824CK, National Semiconductor LM340K-24
VR1	300-Ω to 1-kΩ linear taper potentiometer
Miscellaneous	3" × 3¼" printed circuit board, soldering pins, 4" × 7" aluminum plate for heat sink, knob, 8-pin IC socket, mounting hardware for Q2, Q3, and voltage regulator (276-1373), 1-A fuse, SPST on-off switch, SPST direction switch, SPST coarse/fine switch, plastic case (270-224)
Notes:	Install an isolation coil in series with one lead of any conventional throttle used in conjunction with this device. The coil should be about 1 millihenry and not more than 1 Ω (to avoid voltage drop to the loco). Many loudspeaker crossover network coils such as those in Radio Shack 40-1296 are suitable. Or, make your own by winding 100 to 200 turns of No. 22 enameled copper magnet wire on a 1½" length of a pencil used as a mandrel. If you use the device only as a lighting generator, omit R5 and the coarse/fine switch. Join the slider of VR1 directly to R6. If you decide to add the optional high-frequency indicator, obtain a 1-kΩ resistor, a 200-PIV, 1-A diode, and an LED.

Fig. 7-4 HIGH-FREQUENCY CAB CONTROL

The voltage regulator and transistors Q2 and Q3 are installed on an aluminum panel that serves as a heat sink. Mount Q2 and Q3 as shown in the drawing.

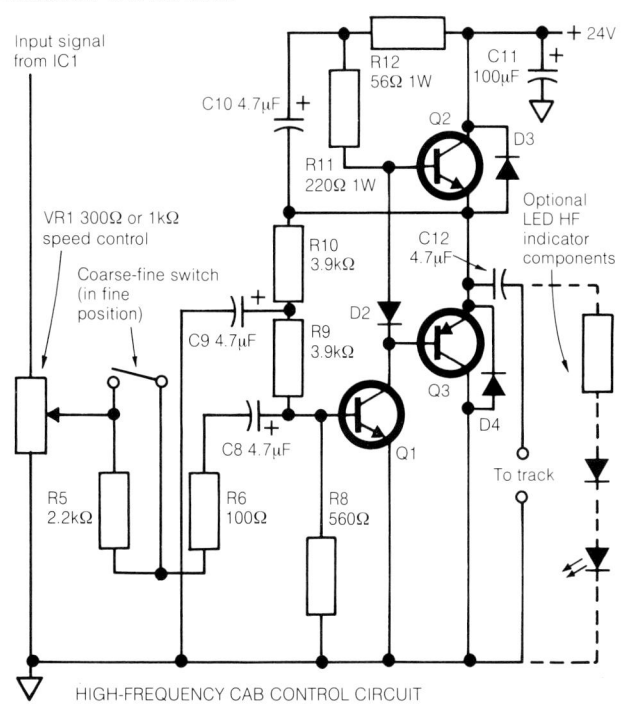

HIGH-FREQUENCY CAB CONTROL CIRCUIT

67

CAB CONTROL UNIT (component side). Shown full size 3" × 3¼".

CAB CONTROL UNIT (foil side). Shown full size 3" × 3¼".

SQUARE-WAVE SIGNAL GENERATOR

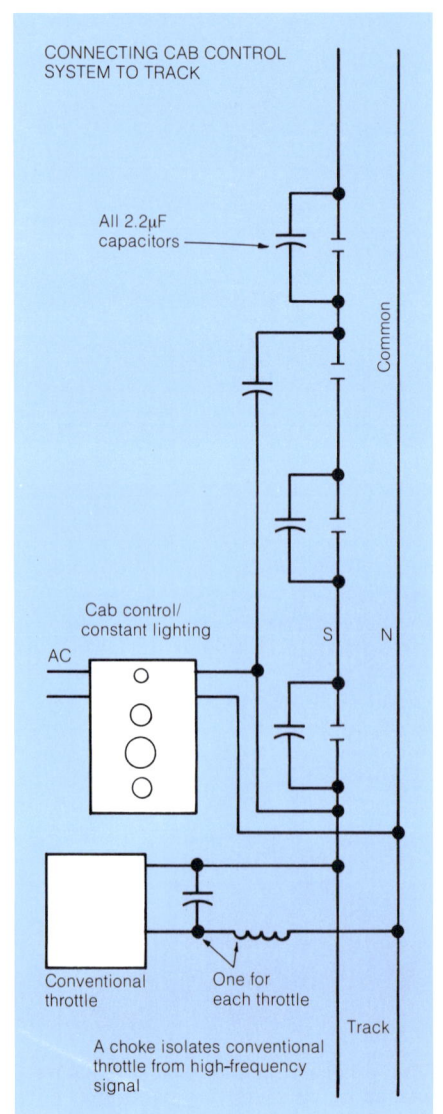

HIGH-FREQUENCY CAB CONTROL MAIN POWER SECTION

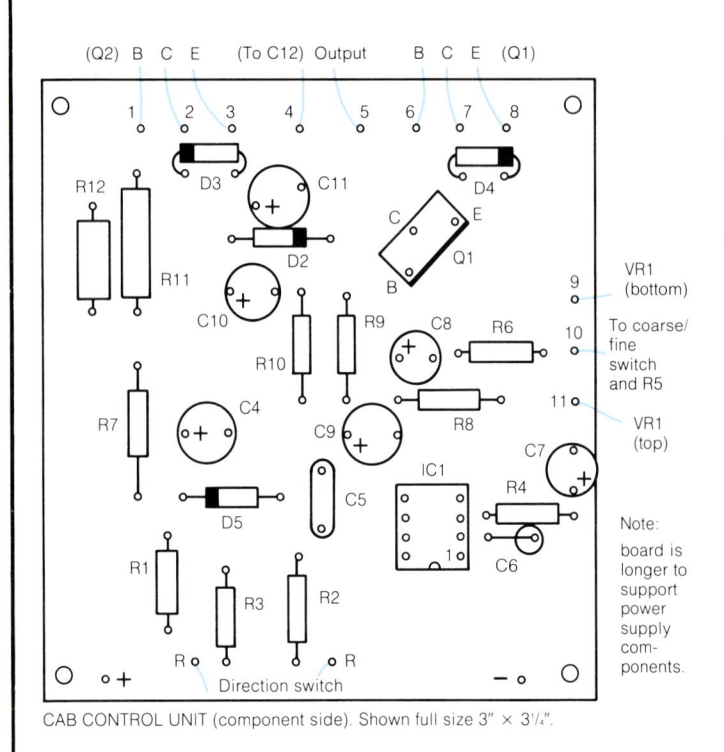

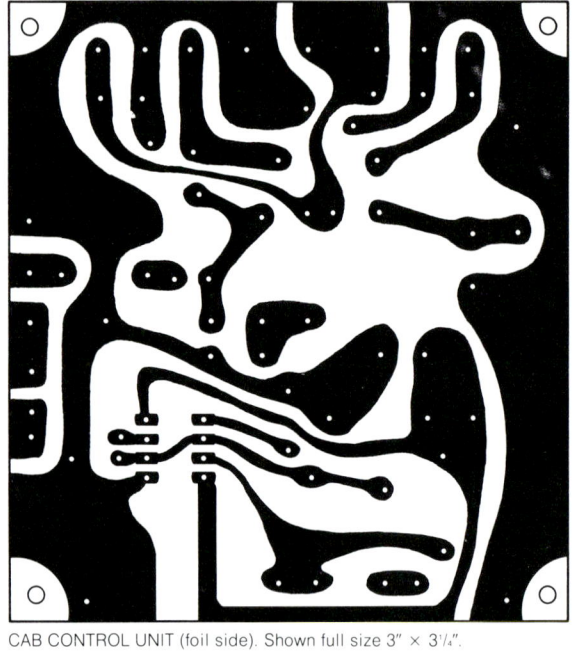

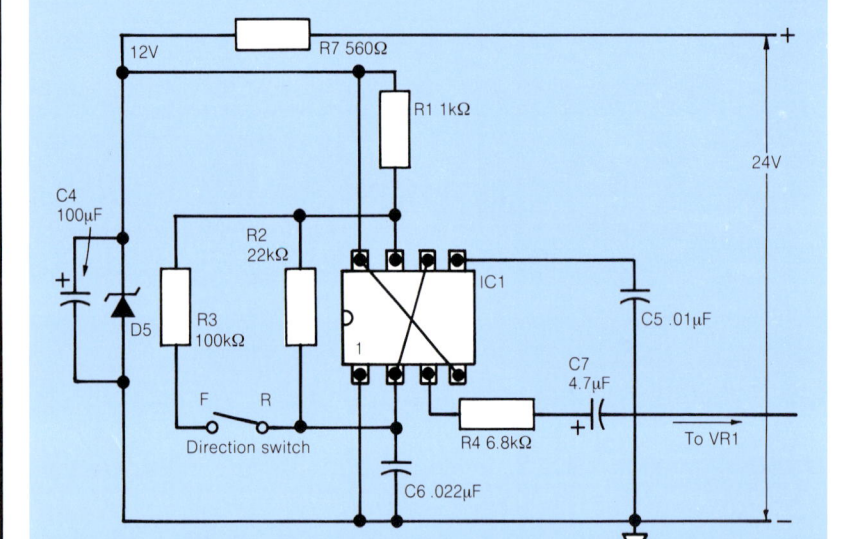

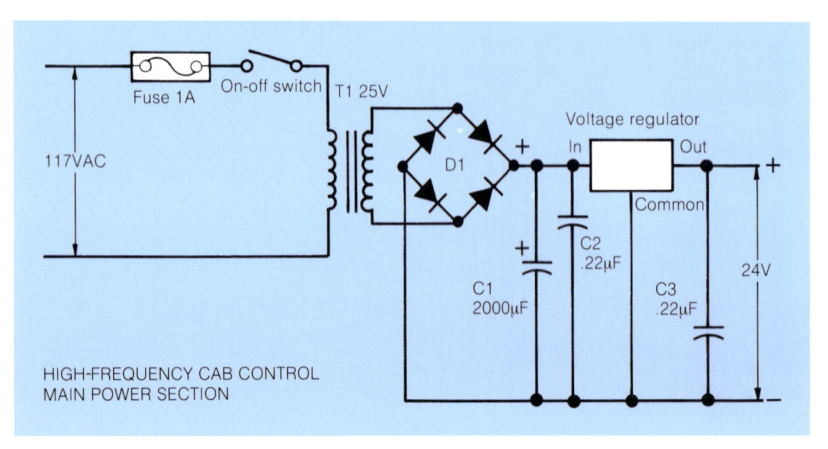

CONNECTING CAB CONTROL SYSTEM TO TRACK

A choke isolates conventional throttle from high-frequency signal

Fig. 7-4A HIGH-FREQUENCY CAB CONTROL

lar for each: a variable-pulse-width, full-amplitude rectangular DC. This makes for good slow running — but its acoustic noise may be annoying.

● Can I use walkaround control? CTC-16 is designed for just this purpose. Zero 1 may be modifiable, but it was designed for bench use. Hornby has announced that a walkaround version will soon be available.

● Which is easier to use? CTC-16, in that you can always have independent control of one, two, or even 16 locos. Zero 1 offers that same flexibility of control for up to four locos. After that the computer keyboard has to be punched. Five keystrokes are needed to transfer an assigned locomotive to one of the four slave units.

● Which gives more overall layout control? Easily the Zero 1. Punching the keyboard gives you control of up to 99 accessories, in addition to 16 locomotives. (Provided, of course, that you add the necessary modules.) However, with Zero 1, you do push a lot of buttons!

● How much motor current can be drawn? At this time both are rated for 1 A. Both can be uprated to 2 A or 3 A by changes to the motor drive devices in the receiver (two SCRs in the Zero 1 and four power transistors in the CTC-16). Neither modification is straightforward, and the required heat sinks enlarge the receivers.

● Will they operate all scales? Zero 1 receivers will fit most N scale equipment (tender or B unit installation), all HO, and all O locomotives equipped with efficient (less than 1-A) motors. The larger receiver of the CTC-16 is difficult to fit in most N scale equipment, but other comments apply as for Zero 1. The CTC-16 receiver, being kit-built, can be built in two pieces if absolutely necessary.

● Joy, oh joy, now I need no rail gaps? Wrong, you do! Rail gaps are still needed for reversing loops, wyes, and at some turnouts. In short, rail gaps are still needed to prevent short-circuits. Of course, block switches and gaps between blocks are completely eliminated.

● Speaking of shorts, how much power is in the track? Zero 1 is rated at 4 A. This includes all 16 trains (!) and accessories. CTC-16 is expandable by adding extra power stations. Each power station is also rated at 4 A. Note that 8 A to 12 A will practically melt HO code 70 track if you have a short-circuit.

● So are there any other problems? Only with lighting. Zero 1 loco lamps would get the shock of 22 V (unlike the motor, they receive both the + and the − of the track square wave). CTC-16 lamps also would receive a little higher than usual voltage. Since the track voltage in each case is fixed, both these command control systems give constant lighting. Don't forget to add the lamp load to the throttle rating. The Zero 1 voltage to each lamp can be halved by wiring a diode (1N4002) in series with each lamp. CTC-16 should have a 22-Ω, 0.5-W resistor added in series with each (12-V) lamp.

● Are repair parts available? Zero 1 has a U. S. repair center (P. O. Box 160, Goshen, KY 40026), and test procedures are established for the CTC-16. The CTC-16 uses only standard components; the Zero 1 has only two nonstandard parts, the receiver chip and the speed control switches.

A high-frequency cab control

It may be that you don't need all the features of a complex command control system like the CTC-16 or Zero 1. Here's a simpler system, Figs. 7-4 and 7-5, that will let you operate two trains on the same track without blocks or rail gaps (other than those required for 2-rail insulation).

One train operates in the normal manner, using any DC or pulse throttle and any unmodified DC motor. The other train is fitted with a receiver which blocks the conventional power and passes only high-frequency AC. The receiver rectifies the AC and passes the current to that loco's ordinary DC motor.

This system uses a special throttle that generates high-frequency AC. Both this track power and conventional DC track power are present on the track. Note that you cannot operate more than two trains at the same time, but you can have, say, three locomotives with modules, and three without. These can be operated in three pairs, one pair at a time. Also, if you already have a conventional layout with blocks, the module-fitted locomotive can be run anywhere on the layout if you couple the high-frequency signal over the rail gaps through capacitors. All DC or pulse throttles used on your system will need a blocking choke in one lead.

Two receiver board layouts are shown in Fig. 7-5. One is for O scale (motors up to 0.5 A), and will fit most tenders and even into the cab of a Rivarossi/AHM MDT diesel; the other, for motors up to 0.25 A, will fit many HO tenders, or can be placed in an unpowered diesel permanently coupled to the powered unit. Unfortunately, the standard components used can't be shrunk to N or Z scale.

How it works. The system is really a high-frequency cab unit. Although ICs are used, it's a fairly simple design and does not use digital pulses for control. An amplifier places square-wave pulses on the track, much as with the Zero 1 system. However, although the maximum amplitude of the high-frequency control pulses (24 V peak-to-peak) is similar, the frequency is much higher (20 kHz versus 60 Hz in the Zero 1). With the Zero 1, you would burn out the motor of any loco that did not contain a Zero 1 receiver. At 20 kHz, however, the inductance of the motor blocks the AC current, so the motor can't be damaged.

Consequently, this high-frequency cab control power can be placed on the track in addition to, and at the same time as, a conventional DC or pulse throttle. Two trains can run on the same track if one is adapted to run only from the high-frequency signal. This is not difficult, because the DC or pulse throttle voltage can be blocked from passing through one motor by a capacitor. The capacitor passes the high-frequency voltage, which is then rectified and supplied to that motor as filtered DC. The other motor responds only to the conventional throttle voltage.

For speed control on the high-frequency cab, the high-frequency voltage can be varied from 0 V to what is effectively 12 VDC (a 24-V peak-to-peak square wave).

Reverse. Reversing the high-frequency cab controlled motor is a problem. The track voltage is AC, even though it is high-frequency. This design uses a miniature reversing relay in the high-frequency-controlled loco. The relay is operated by a phase-locked loop IC. This chip, used in some telephone switching systems, is a switch which only turns on when a certain frequency range is applied to its input. So, all that is necessary is to slightly change the frequency to match that of the chip, at which time the relay is energized and the loco reverses. With the values shown in the parts list, the 20-kHz "forward" frequency is reduced to 17 kHz for "reverse."

The relay and chip require a power source, since they need at least 5 VDC to operate. A 9-V alkaline battery is small enough to fit in any O and many HO tenders or diesels along with the reverse detector system. The current draw is 12 mA when switched on, and rises to 100 mA for reverse only. Battery life will range from 40 hours of operation, if reverse is never used, down to 4 hours if your long-hood-forward diesel thinks it's a short-hood-forward. If the battery switch is not turned on, the high-frequency cab control will operate the train in forward only. This also happens, of course, when the battery is discharged.

Lighting generator. The maximum output of the high-frequency cab control is equivalent to 12 VDC. Lamp filaments are not particularly inductive, so they will light regardless of whether they are supplied with DC or low or high-frequency AC. Consequently, the cab control unit can be used on any conventional layout as a constant lighting generator. The "speed" control can be used to adjust brightness from zero to maximum. To prevent conventional train power from adding to the high-frequency lighting voltage, a 0.22-μF to 1-μF capacitor (not an electrolytic type) should be used in series with each lamp. When used as a lighting generator this unit will supply up to 20 or so grain-of-wheat lamps. Lamp power, when using the recommended capacitors, does not come from the conventional throttle, so its full power capacity is available for highballing your husky A-B-B-A passenger diesels over the road.

When used as a lighting generator, block connections and the transfer of the signal across blocks via capacitors are the same as when the high-frequency cab control is used to power the loco motor. The same high-frequency isolation choke must also be used to prevent the throttle from soaking up the high frequency and to prevent damage to a transistor throttle.

Assembly tips. For your convenience, the circuits are shown separately for the IC

69

SMALLER CAB CONTROL RECEIVER. Shown full size 3 5/16" × 1".   To motor   SMALLER CAB CONTROL RECEIVER. Shown full size 3 5/16" × 1".

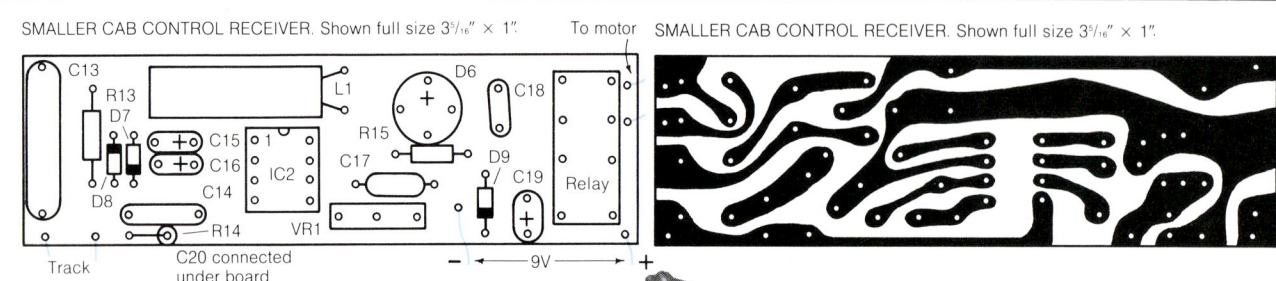

LARGER CAB CONTROL RECEIVER.

Both shown full size 2" × 2".

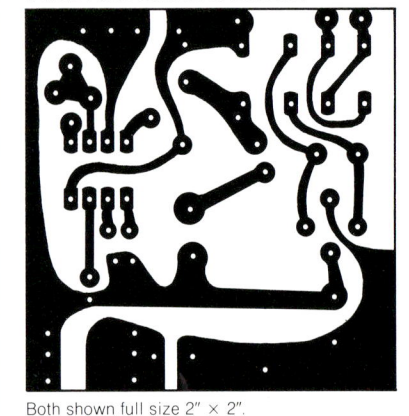

Use the smaller high-frequency receiver for motors up to 0.25 A.

The larger version is for motors up to 0.5 A; both receivers have the same circuit.

Fig. 7-5 HIGH-FREQUENCY CAB CONTROL RECEIVER

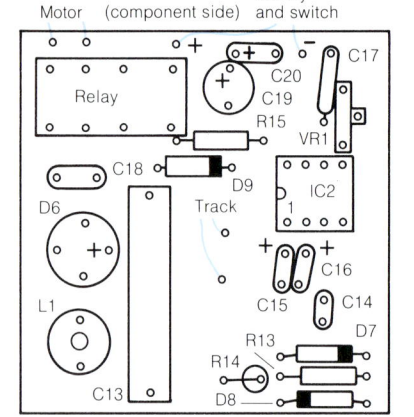

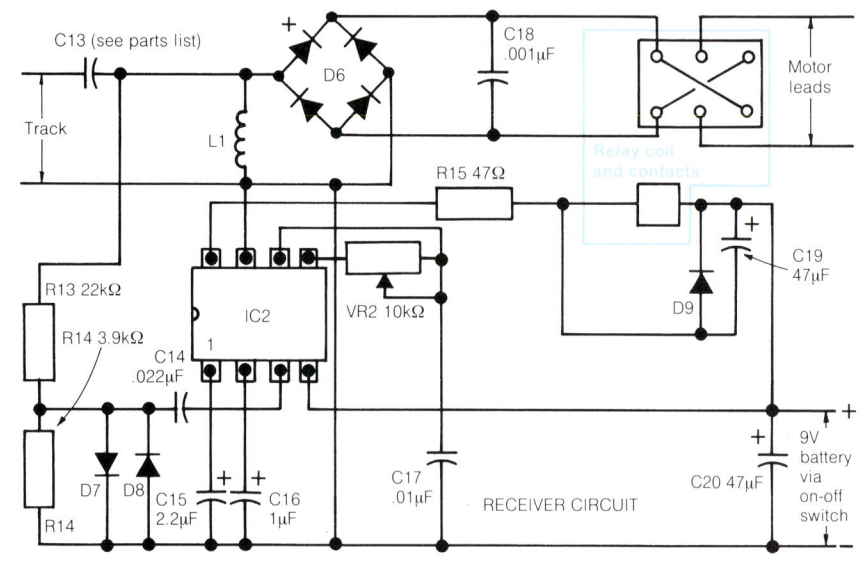

PARTS LIST FOR HIGH-FREQUENCY CAB CONTROL RECEIVER

C13	4.7-µF, 100-VDC foil capacitor for 0.5-A version (Or use two 2.2-µF foil capacitors in parallel — C13 must not be an electrolytic capacitor.) 1-µF, 100-VDC foil capacitor for 0.25-A version (272-1055)
C14	0.022-µF, 100-VDC foil or disk capacitor
C15	2.2-µF, 6-VDC electrolytic or tantalum capacitor
C16	1-µF, 6-VDC electrolytic or tantalum capacitor
C17	0.01-µF, 100-VDC, 10-percent polystyrene or close-tolerance film capacitor
C18	0.001-µF, 100-VDC disk capacitor
C19, C20	47-µF, 10-VDC electrolytic capacitors
D6	100-PIV, 4-A bridge rectifier for 0.50-A version (276-1171), 100-PIV, 1.4-A bridge rectifier for 0.25-A version (276-1152)
D7, D8, D9	200-PIV, 1-A silicon diodes, 1N4002 (276-1102)
IC2	NE567N tone decoder in 8-pin case (276-1721)
L1	coil with approximately 1-millihenry inductance at 2-Ω maximum resistance (4 Ω for 0.25-A version) (Make the coil from about 300 turns of No. 30 enameled copper magnet wire on a 1/4"-diameter mandrel. Or, modify a TV horizontal oscillator coil.)
R13	22-kΩ resistor
R14	3.9-kΩ resistor
R15	47-Ω, 0.5-W resistor (The combined resistance of R15 and the relay coil should not be less than 90 Ω.)
Relay	5-V, 50-Ω DPDT relay with 1-A contacts, IC mount type (275-215) (ITT RZ-4.5 is identical to 275-215. ITT RZ-6 can be used if R15 is reduced to 33 Ω.)
VR2	10-kΩ linear taper potentiometer, 10 mm or 14 mm vertical mount type
Miscellaneous	1" × 3 5/16" or 2" × 2" printed circuit board, miniature on-off switch or magnet and reed switch, 9-volt battery connector (270-325), soldering pins
Note:	Printed circuit board hole locations for C13, D6, relay, and VR2 may have to be changed to suit your components. Check components before drilling the board.

The larger receiver fits easily into this O scale AHM/Rivarossi MDT diesel, shown here with the roof removed.

20-kHz oscillator and the power amplifier section, although both are on one circuit board. The 555 timer IC is connected as a square wave oscillator at about 20 kHz and the direction switch places R3 in parallel with R2, which then reduces the frequency to about 17 kHz. Note that IC1 operates at 12 V and that zener diode D5 and resistor R7 are used to drop the 24-V supply to a safe limit for the chip. Voltages on IC1 should be about:
- Pin 1 — 0 V.
- Pins 4 and 8 — 12 V.
- Pins 2, 3, and 5 — 6 V.
- Pin 7 — 10 V.

The output square wave from IC1 (12-V peak-to-peak) is divided to about 0.25 V at the top end of the speed control VR1. This level is suitable for driving the amplifier (Q1, Q2, and Q3) to maximum output. The coarse-fine switch provides two levels of speed control. Use the coarse setting for motors that draw 0.5 A or more. For low-current, efficient can motors, use the fine position. For 0.25-A motors (e.g. Atlas HO diesel models), both coarse and fine can be used: The fine position gives good slow-speed control.

Voltages should be:
- E of Q2 (and E of Q3) — 12 V. (If this is more than 1 volt different, change R8 to 470 Ω or 680 Ω.)
- B of Q2 — 12.5 V.
- B of Q3 (and C of Q1) — 11.5 V.
- B of Q1 — 0.5 V.
- C of Q2 — 24 V.
- Input of voltage regulator — 35 V.
- Output of voltage regulator — 24 V.

Diodes D3 and D4 help protect Q2 and Q3 from any voltage spikes that a conventional pulse throttle may kick back through C12. Capacitor C12 couples the high-frequency power to the track. Note that D3, D4, and D5 must be installed in the correct polarity.

The voltage regulator and transistors Q2 and Q3 are mounted on a 4" x 7" aluminum plate for cooling. Each must be insulated from the plate by the appropriate mica washer and insulating bushes. Don't forget silicone grease for good thermal contact. The aluminum plate should be cool to the touch.

Transistor Q1 on the circuit board runs hot, but at about 500 mW it is well under its maximum rating.

The power transformer is mounted separately and does not appear in the illustrations. Mount the transformer as shown in Chapter 1, page 11, and observe the warnings there about working with 117 VAC.

The inclusion of a voltage regulator, and the use of extra-heavy-duty Q2 and Q3, rated at 15-A peak current, mean that repeated short-circuits give no overload voltages or currents.

In the schematic, only C13, L1, and D6 play any part in converting the 20-kHz high-frequency power to DC motor power. Coil L1 provides a DC return path for the rectified motor current. Capacitor C18 provides voltage spike suppression from the motor. If the loco motor already has a capacitor (many European models do), remove the installed capacitor.

The IC2 input signal comes from the high-frequency track voltage, divided down by R13 and R14. Diodes D7 and D8 also keep the input to the IC at less than 0.5 V. Note that IC2 turns on only when a 17-kHz signal appears. To adjust the frequency, connect the 9-V battery, turn the unit on, and very slowly turn VR2 from its maximum resistance position until the relay energizes. For this check, the receiver can be connected directly to the high-frequency cab unit: It need not be installed in a loco.

Check that the relay energizes only on reverse, and is de-energized for forward. If not, carefully adjust VR2. When the unit is calibrated, you can measure the value of VR and replace it with a couple of fixed resistors of the same value. This eliminates the possibility of vibration moving the slider of VR2.

Voltages with the relay not energized (forward position) should be:
- Pins 4 and 8 of IC2 — 9V.
- Pins 1 and 2 of IC2 — 1 V to 2 V.

Voltages with the relay energized (reverse position) should be:
- Pin 1 of IC2 — 1.5 V.
- All other voltages should be unchanged.

Coil L1 usually runs slightly warm. The bridge rectifier may get hot (because some diodes are inefficient at high frequencies) if you run motors that draw a lot of current, in which case epoxy a thin piece of aluminum to the rectifier.

If you're using efficient, low-draw motors, reduce C13 to 1 µF (D6 will then run just slightly warm). Reducing the size of C13 lets you build a receiver that will fit into many HO models. In fact, in extremely tight spaces, you can move C13 from the board and tuck it in a corner of the loco or tender.

Layout is not critical, and there is no sensitivity to spark interference from the track or the motor. There may be problems from corrosion in rail joiners: This can cause intermittent speed changes in the high-frequency cab control unit without affecting the normal DC cab control. Also, flickering lights can result when using the unit as a lighting generator. If this happens, solder a loop of wire around each rail joiner.

8 Radio control and computers

RADIO-CONTROL model cars, boats, and airplanes are common, but there have been few radio-control trains. Why? Probably because the rails provide such a good way to transmit control information along with motor power, and because through-the-rail control systems, including the command control systems we've just examined, work so well.

Also consider these facts:
● Until recently, most hobby radio-control receivers and servos were too large to fit in HO rolling stock.
● In the 49-MHz band (the most practical choice for model train control) there are only five frequencies available.
● Circuit layout is far more critical at radio frequencies than at the audio frequencies most often used for train control systems.
● Unlicensed hobbyists may not build or modify radio transmitters.

RADIO-CONTROL BLOCK DIAGRAM FOR LOCOMOTIVE USING AC TRACK VOLTAGE AS POWER SOURCE

RADIO-CONTROL BLOCK DIAGRAM FOR LOCOMOTIVE USING BATTERY PACK AS POWER SOURCE

TRANSMITTED WAVEFORM FROM LM1871N TRANSMITTER AND SIMPLIFIED EXPLANATION OF OPERATION

t_F the frame time is usually 20 ms
t_M the modulation time is fixed
t_{CH} the channel time is variable for channels 1 and 2 only

The LM1871N normally transmits channels 1, 2, and 3.

For reverse, we change the width (duration) of channel 2 from 0.5 ms to more than 1.1 ms. This is detected by the NE555 IC at the receiver.

For run and brake, either pin 5 or pin 6 of LM1871N is grounded. If pin 5 is grounded, the transmitter sends 4 channels. If pin 6 is grounded, the transmitter sends 5 channels. These extra channels are detected by the LM1872N and operate switches inside the chip.

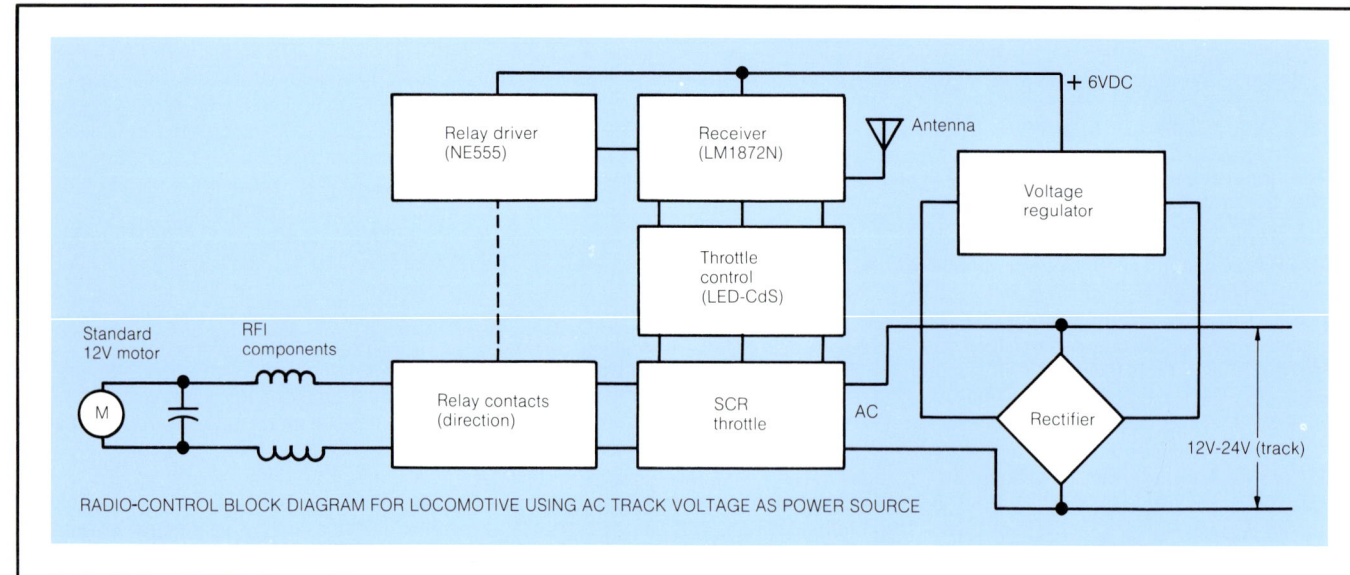

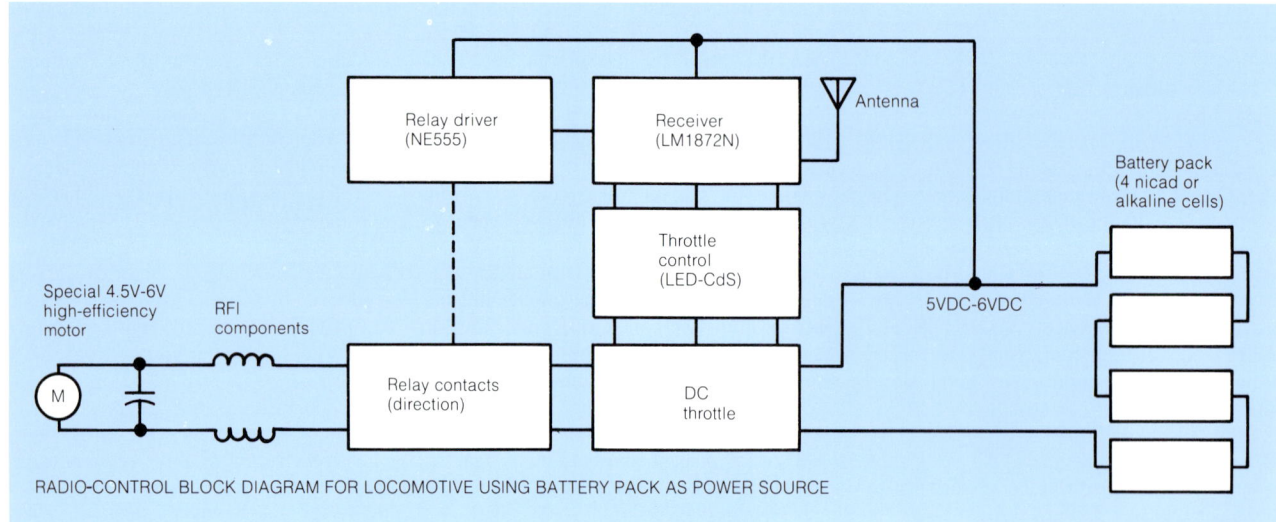

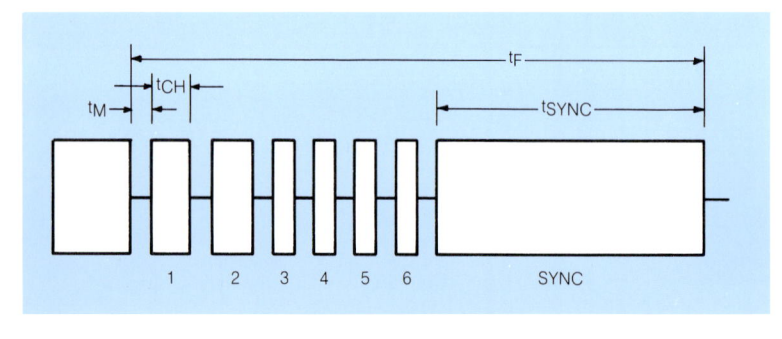

Fig. 8-1 TRAIN-MOUNTED RADIO-CONTROL THROTTLE

Still, radio control is appealing because if the train carries a receiver and other control equipment, and is powered by train-borne motor batteries, you don't have to worry about dirty track or wheels, and there's no need for reversing loops, block switches, or rail gaps.

As I've described in Chapter 2, you can use radio control to operate a trackside throttle, which does away with the need for umbilical cables, and thus offers the ultimate form of walkaround control.

If you decide to build a radio-control train or radio-control throttle, and plan to use any circuits other than those in this book (or plan to use any frequencies other than those in the 49-MHz band), first read Fred Marks' book GETTING THE MOST FROM RADIO CONTROL SYSTEMS, then obtain the appropriate license from the FCC or DOC and abide by all FCC and DOC rules. Be aware that certain of the hobby frequencies are reserved by law exclusively for model airplanes: Never use one of these for a model train. (This won't create a hardship, because there are nine frequencies that any licensed RC hobbyist can use to control any type of model.)

You'll probably want to use subminiature servos or electronic speed controls for throttle and direction control, and you'll use rechargeable nickel-cadmium (nicad) batteries for the motor. Fred's book also contains information about installing radio-control equipment in models; he's most concerned with airplanes, but the principles are the same for all types of models.

A train-mounted radio-control throttle

One radio-control option is to use constant AC or DC track voltage to power a

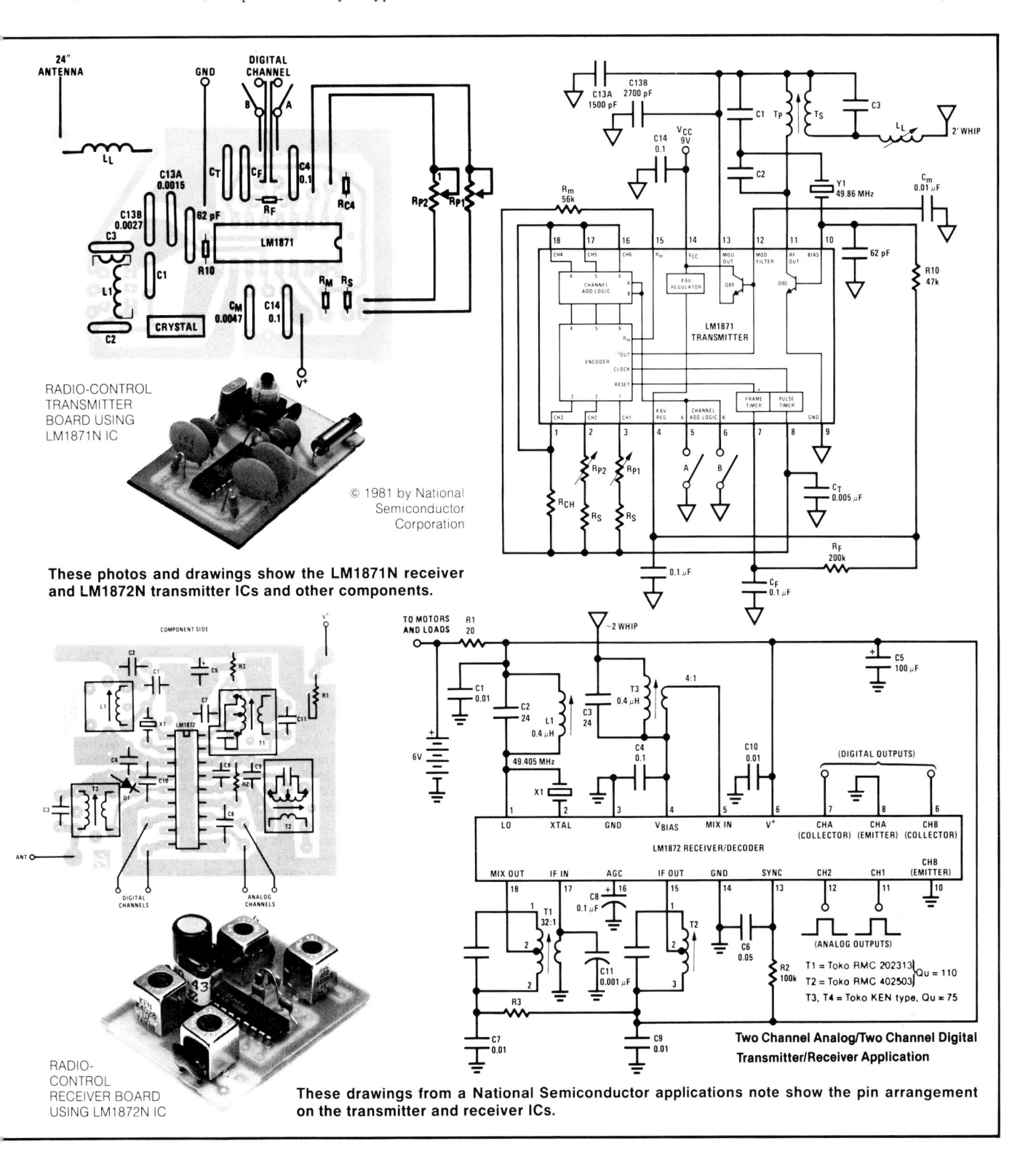

RADIO-CONTROL TRANSMITTER BOARD USING LM1871N IC

© 1981 by National Semiconductor Corporation

These photos and drawings show the LM1871N receiver and LM1872N transmitter ICs and other components.

RADIO-CONTROL RECEIVER BOARD USING LM1872N IC

These drawings from a National Semiconductor applications note show the pin arrangement on the transmitter and receiver ICs.

73

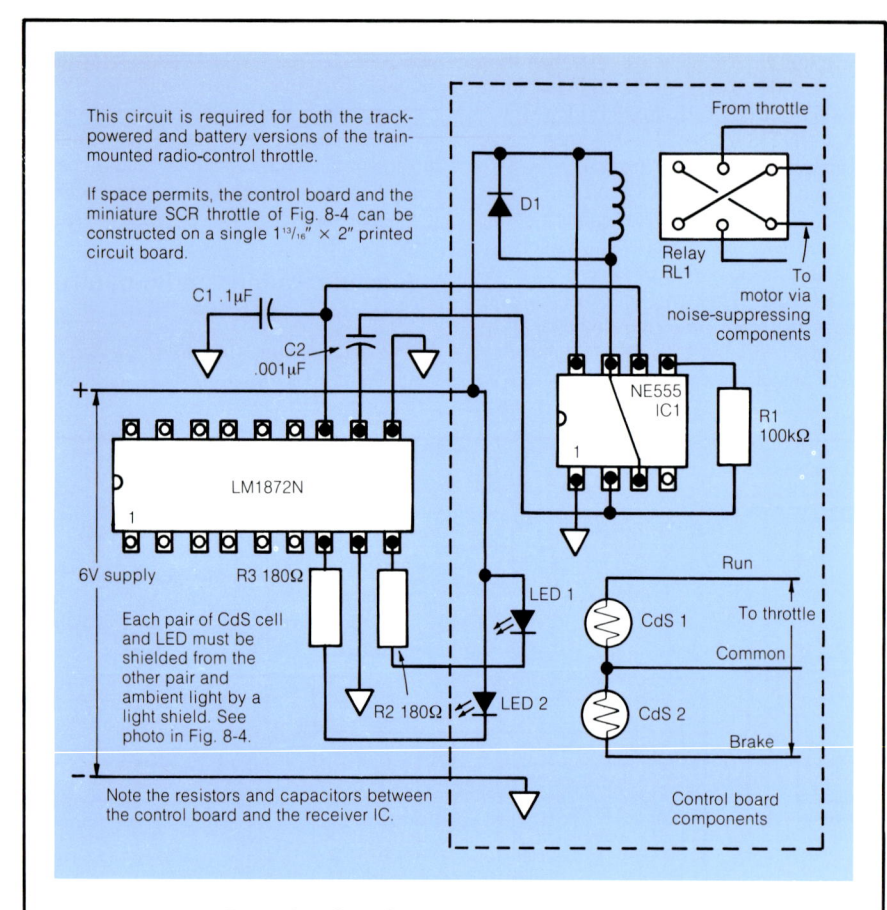

PARTS LIST FOR THE CONTROL BOARD

CdS1, CdS2	cadmium sulfide photoconductive cells with a 1-MΩ dark resistance and a lit resistance of 600 Ω or less, such as Mepco or Philips RPY58A (Radio Shack 276-116 will be a tight fit.)
D1	100-PIV, 1-A silicon diode, 1N4148, 1N4002, or similar
IC1	NE555N (8-pin case) (276-1723)
LED1, LED2	any type of green light-emitting diodes
R1	100-kΩ resistor
RL1	5-V, DPDT relay with a resistance of not less than 45 Ω (Radio Shack 272-215 or ITT RZ-4.5 or RZ-6)
Miscellaneous	13/16" × 2" printed circuit board

PARTS LIST FOR INTERCONNECTIONS BETWEEN CONTROL BOARD AND RECEIVER IC

C1	0.1-µF, 100-VDC, 10-percent film capacitor
C2	0.001-µF, 100-VDC ceramic capacitor
R2, R3	180-Ω resistors

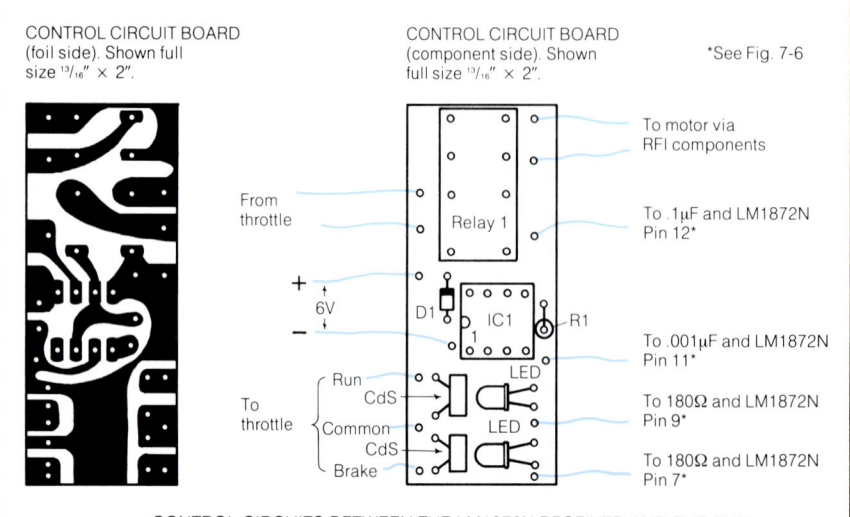

Fig. 8-2 CONTROL CIRCUITS BETWEEN THE LM1872N RECEIVER AND THE RUN AND BRAKE FUNCTIONS OF THE THROTTLE AND REVERSING RELAY

---

train equipped with a radio-control throttle and direction switch, Fig. 8-1. The transmitter and receiver are scavenged from inexpensive toys, as described in Chapter 2. Look for a toy that uses the LM1871N and LM1872N ICs. These relatively new chips incorporate respectively all the semiconductor functions of a transmitter and a superheterodyne receiver. The version used here operates on one of five frequencies in the 49-MHz band — just as the radio-control throttle described in Chapter 2, and for the reasons given there. The transmitter is low power and requires no license. You may build a receiver if you want, but you must be a licensed technician to construct a transmitter, which must then be approved by the FCC or DOC. To repeat, if you're not a licensed technician, use a toy transmitter, and make no changes to its radio frequency circuits.

Figure 8-1 also contains a simplified explanation of the pulse-width modulation technique used in this system (and other toy and hobby radio-control systems).

Receiver outputs. The receiver provides two analog and two digital outputs. I've used the digital outputs to switch on LEDs paired with photoconductive cells; one pair controls "run," another controls "brake" on the SCR throttle. A simple circuit using our old friend the NE555 converts the two analog channels to one digital switch, which operates the direction relay. I've chosen a relay-operated direction switch because the alternative is a four-transistor bridge circuit that would waste nearly 1.5 V in the transistors. The relay causes no voltage drop.

Thus, pulse, momentum, brake, and direction are controllable, and the original motor is retained with only suppressor coils and capacitors added.

Original transmitter control functions. The unmodified transmitter control functions are:

● Digital — two NO pushbuttons at pins 5 and 6 of the LM1871N. Closing these contacts makes up to 100 mA of receiver switching current available at CHA (pins 7 and 8) and CHB (pins 9 and 10) on the LM1872N. Relays could be connected here, but I've used LEDs, each of which draws about 20 mA. (Actually seeing the LEDs light when testing the receiver is a great time-saver.)

● Analog — two potentiometers at transmitter pins 2 and 3 control analog outputs on the receiver at pins 11 and 12 respectively.

Control function modifications. An LED connected to pin 7 of the receiver lights when pin 5 of the transmitter is connected to ground (minus) by a NO pushbutton. Similarly, an LED on receiver pin 9 lights when a NO pushbutton at transmitter IC pin 6 is depressed. As I said, the LEDs shine on photoconductive cells that control the run and brake functions of the SCR throttle.

On the transmitter, potentiometer Rp2 at pin 2 is replaced by a 470-kΩ fixed resistor with a shorting switch across it and pins 1 and 3 are joined. This is the direction control switch; it works by changing the transmitter pulse width from less than 1 millisecond to more than 1.5 milliseconds. (All contemporary multichannel radio-control systems use pulse-width codes similar to the coding system in the CTC-16.) This change in pulse width is detected by the NE555 IC connected to pins 11 and 12 of the receiver. The NE555 circuit energizes the direction relay only when the 470-kΩ resistor is not shorted by the direction switch at the transmitter.

Radio interference. Figure 8-1 shows the coils and capacitor which should be added in series with and across the motor leads to prevent electrical noise generated by the motor from interfering with the receiver and direction circuits. If you've installed the capacitor and coils and the direction relay still operates erratically, replace the motor brushes and clean the commutator. If this doesn't solve the problem, replace the motor.

A train-borne power supply. If you don't want to use track power, make a DC power supply for the receiver and motor by installing four or five size AA or C nicad cells (1.2 V each) or alkaline cells (1.5 V each) in one or more of the cars. The nicads cost more originally but can be recharged hundreds of times, and they weigh less than non-rechargeable alkaline cells.

You'll also need a DC throttle and an efficient 4.5-V to 6-V motor. The DC throttle shown in Fig. 8-5 works well. It can be hand-wired to fit the 1" x 2" space otherwise occupied by the SCR throttle. Be sure to use a heat sink on the transistor and allow plenty of ventilation.

The throttle wastes about 1.5 V because of voltage drop in the transistor, so the motor should be a low-draw 4.5-V to 6-V type of professional quality. One good choice is the Airpax/Philips (Cheshire, CT 06410) 9904-120-01502 motor, which draws only 150 mA loaded at 2500 rpm on 4.5 V. With this motor, a set of four AA nicads should give about 2 hours of light running. Four nicad C cells would provide about 5 hours.

If you use the battery power supply be certain to wire the NE555 reversing relay circuit so that the relay is energized only for reverse, because leaving the relay energized most of the time (as it would be if energized in forward) would decrease running time by increasing power consumption.

Devise a way to recharge the nicads without having to remove them from the train. For example, you could fit the loco with a DPDT switch that connects the battery leads to the wheels during recharging, and you could run the train onto a special electrically isolated siding track which contains power feeders for recharging.

Follow the manufacturer's suggestions when recharging nicads; in general, charge AA cells at 45 mA for 14 to 16 hours, charge C cells at 120 mA for the same time. See Fred Marks' GETTING THE MOST FROM RADIO CONTROL SYSTEMS for more information about nicads.

Installation tips. There are four small

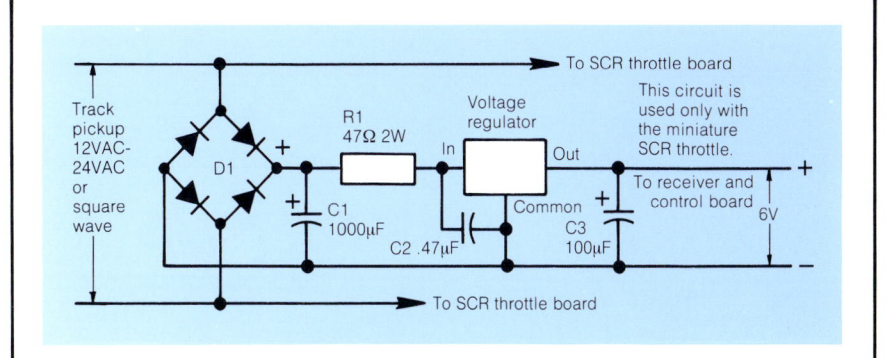

PARTS LIST FOR THE 6-VDC POWER SUPPLY

C1	1000-μF, 35-VDC electrolytic capacitor
C2	0.47-μF, 50-VDC tantalum or ceramic capacitor
C3	100-μF, 10-VDC electrolytic capacitor
D1	100-PIV, 2.5-A bridge rectifier (Radio Shack 276-1174 or General Instruments KBF-02) (Must be at least 2.5 A.)
R1	If track voltage is from 20 V to 24 V, use a 100-Ω, 2-W resistor. If track voltage is from 12 V to 20 V, use a 47-Ω or 50-Ω, 2-W resistor.
Voltage regulator	6-V, 1-A voltage regulator in TO-220 case, μA7806CU, MC7806UP, LM340T-6.0 or equivalent
Miscellaneous	7/8" x 1 7/8" printed circuit board, soldering pins

This circuit provides a regulated 6-VDC output for the receiver and control board. You may file the edges of the printed circuit board to save space. Use a heat sink (276-1363) on the voltage regulator if track voltage exceeds 12 V.

Fig. 8-3 6-VDC POWER SUPPLY FOR THE LM1872N RECEIVER AND THE CONTROL CIRCUIT BOARD

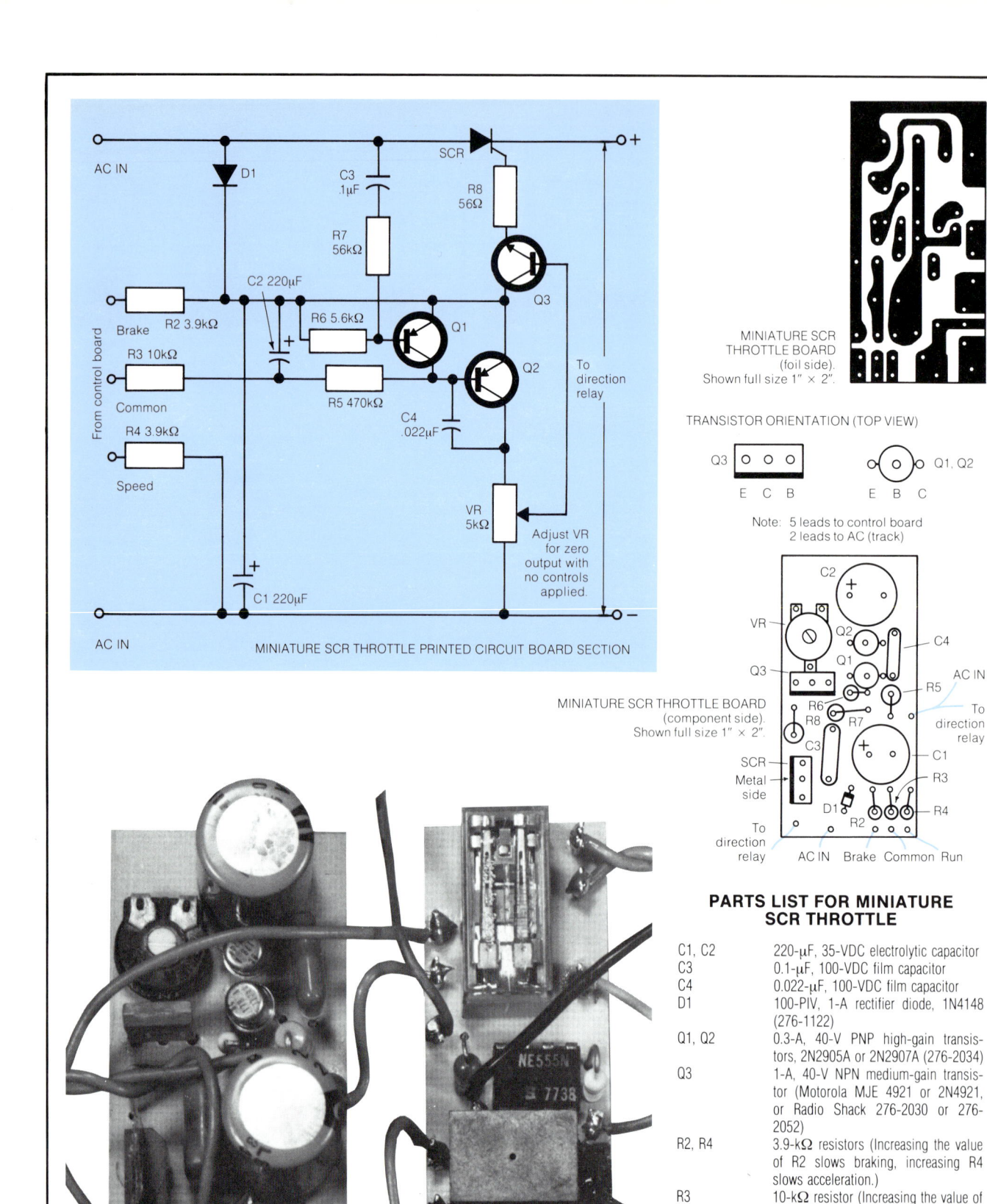

MINIATURE SCR THROTTLE BOARD (foil side). Shown full size 1" × 2".

MINIATURE SCR THROTTLE PRINTED CIRCUIT BOARD SECTION

TRANSISTOR ORIENTATION (TOP VIEW)

Q3 E C B

Q1, Q2 E B C

Note: 5 leads to control board
2 leads to AC (track)

Adjust VR for zero output with no controls applied.

MINIATURE SCR THROTTLE BOARD (component side). Shown full size 1" × 2".

PARTS LIST FOR MINIATURE SCR THROTTLE

C1, C2	220-µF, 35-VDC electrolytic capacitor
C3	0.1-µF, 100-VDC film capacitor
C4	0.022-µF, 100-VDC film capacitor
D1	100-PIV, 1-A rectifier diode, 1N4148 (276-1122)
Q1, Q2	0.3-A, 40-V PNP high-gain transistors, 2N2905A or 2N2907A (276-2034)
Q3	1-A, 40-V NPN medium-gain transistor (Motorola MJE 4921 or 2N4921, or Radio Shack 276-2030 or 276-2052)
R2, R4	3.9-kΩ resistors (Increasing the value of R2 slows braking, increasing R4 slows acceleration.)
R3	10-kΩ resistor (Increasing the value of R3 gives more momentum effect.)
R5	470-kΩ resistor
R6	5.6-kΩ resistor
R7	56-kΩ resistor
R8	56-Ω, 1-W resistor
SCR	200-PIV, 6-A silicon controlled rectifier in TO-220 case (Texas Instruments TIC106D, TIC116D, TIC116E, TIC116M, or equivalent)
VR	5-kΩ linear taper potentiometer (271-217)
Miscellaneous	1" × 2" printed circuit board, soldering pins

The throttle in the left portion of this photo is a miniature version of the SCR throttle of Chapter 2. It is shown here connected to the control board of Fig. 8-2.

Fig. 8-4 MINIATURE SCR THROTTLE

76

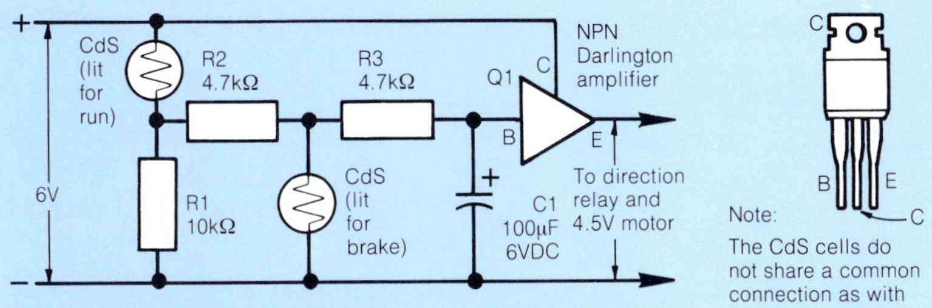

PARTS LIST FOR PURE-DC THROTTLE

C1	100-µF, 6-VDC electrolytic capacitor
Q1	4-A, 25-V NPN Darlington power amplifier in TO-220 case such as 2N6037, 2N6038, 2N6039, TIP110, TIP112, TIP120, TIP121, or TIP122 (276-2068)
R1	10-kΩ resistor
R2, R3	4-7-kΩ resistors
Miscellaneous	Heat sink for Q1 (276-1363)

Fig. 8-5 DC THROTTLE FOR USE WITH TRAIN-BORNE BATTERY PACK

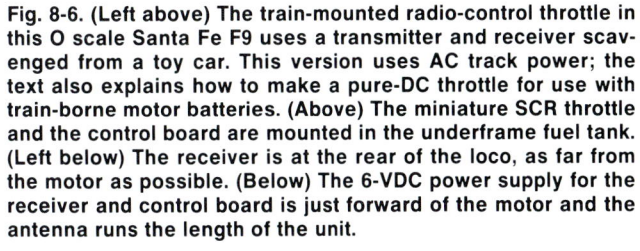

For use with a train-borne battery power supply. The LEDs and CdS cells control run and brake functions. The CdS cells mount on the control board and the remaining components can be easily hand wired.

Note: The CdS cells do not share a common connection as with SCR throttle, but are still mounted on control board.

Fig. 8-6. (Left above) The train-mounted radio-control throttle in this O scale Santa Fe F9 uses a transmitter and receiver scavenged from a toy car. This version uses AC track power; the text also explains how to make a pure-DC throttle for use with train-borne motor batteries. (Above) The miniature SCR throttle and the control board are mounted in the underframe fuel tank. (Left below) The receiver is at the rear of the loco, as far from the motor as possible. (Below) The 6-VDC power supply for the receiver and control board is just forward of the motor and the antenna runs the length of the unit.

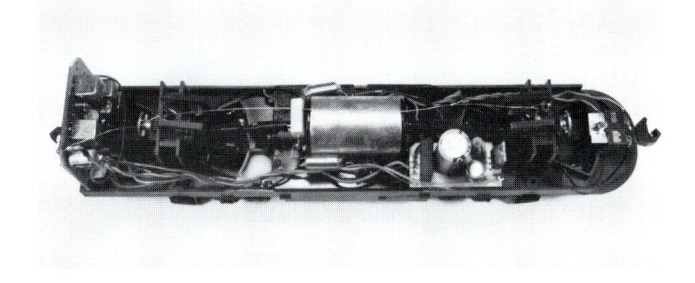

circuit boards for the track-powered version. These are:
● The receiver, scavenged from a toy, Fig. 8-1.
● The control board, driven from the receiver and operating the throttle and the direction relay, Fig. 8-2.
● The 6-VDC power supply, which supplies stable DC for the receiver and the control board, Fig. 8-3.
● The miniature SCR throttle, powered from the AC track voltage and with run and brake functions keyed from the control board, Fig. 8-4.

The battery-powered version consists of the receiver, control board, a pure-DC throttle, Fig. 8-5, and a battery pack capable of supplying about 6 V.

You should be able to fit all of the boards into an unpowered HO F-type diesel B unit. Figure 8-6 shows the boards installed in an Atlas O scale F9. The SCR throttle and the control board are fitted into the underframe fuel tank, and the iron weight that originally occupied this space has been discarded. Although the two boards in the fuel tank generate little heat, it's a good idea to drill several ventilation holes in the front and rear of the tank. As long as these holes are not too close to the edge of the tank, no one will suspect you're running on air.

The motor support board stiffeners, which project into the tank space from above, had

77

to be partly cut away to clear capacitors and other components. The motor support band was discarded and replaced with a toothpaste-size strip of silicone sealant to hold the motor. The F9 water tank was not stuffed with electronics, so if more weight had been required, I could have filled the tank with lead shot and epoxy to make up for the discarded fuel tank weight. The radio receiver board was mounted at the rear, with the LM1872N peeping through the back window. In order to reduce interference, it's always best to locate the receiver as far from the motor as possible.

The 6-V power supply can go in any convenient location. The power supply can produce up to 5 W of heat when operated from 24 VAC and the loco is in reverse, so keep the voltage regulator and the resistor well away from plastic parts. There's much less waste heat with 12-VAC to 16-VAC track supply, but nevertheless it's best to keep the regulator and resistor in the clear.

The antenna runs along the inside roof of the F9, though if a Pennsylvania version were being modeled it could be run outside. Receiver sensitivity is in part a function of antenna length. Ideally, the antenna should be about 24" long, but in practice you can control a loco from 6' to 10' away even if the antenna is a mere 3".

Testing the system. The transmitter should draw approximately 14 mA to 25 mA from its 9-V battery; the higher current occurs when a function is being transmitted. Replace the LM1871N if these currents are abnormally low or high.

If you suspect the transmitter isn't radiating, you can perform a rough-and-ready test with a shortwave receiver. Place the transmitter beside the shortwave receiver and tune to the transmitter's primary frequency or to one of its harmonics. For example, with a 49.405-MHz transmitter, tune to 49.405 MHz, 98.810 MHz, 24.703 MHz, or 12.351 MHz. You should hear noise when a function is being transmitted.

The receiver consumes 6 mA to 27 mA at 6 V depending on the function being received. Again, abnormally low or high current indicates the LM1872N chip should be replaced.

Poor reception could mean the intermediate frequency transformers are off-tune; alignment is a job for a repair shop unless you have extensive test equipment.

The control board draws 100 mA only when the relay is energized for reversing.

The LEDs make it easy to check the system and its range. They begin to flicker when the run and brake transmitter functions are pressed at maximum operating range. Don't forget to replace the light shields after the test. Similarly, at maximum range the direction relay will chatter when direction is reversed. Should relay chatter be a problem in normal operation, wire a 100-μF, 6-VDC electrolytic capacitor across the relay coil.

The SCR throttle can be checked by shorting the run and common input leads together, then shorting the brake and common leads. Test voltages are as given in Chapter 2, page 18. Note that this miniaturized SCR throttle does not have a sufficient SCR power rating to withstand short-circuited outputs, but that short-circuit protection is not required because the throttle is mounted in the loco. The SCR throttle of Chapter 2 must be able to withstand intermittent or even continuous shorts only because it can be damaged by a track short.

Some thoughts on computers

The computer scene is changing so rapidly that it's hard to make specific recommendations about computer applications to model railroading. For example, personal computers that were prohibitively expensive just a few years ago now sell for much lower prices. More and more software is available, as are detection and feedback devices. Memory capacity, once the major weakness in small computers, has expanded exponentionally.

Nevertheless, the capabilities now exist to develop a completely computer-controlled model railroad. Given sufficient detection and feedback gadgetry, you could run several trains in a more or less random fashion with all turnouts thrown automatically and all signals showing the correct aspects. In fact, many of the train detectors and signaling circuits in this book are suitable for such a computer-controlled layout. In all honesty, though, having built such a layout, how much fun would it be? So, I don't foresee wide popularity for completely automated layouts, except in special situations such as museum or store window displays.

I can see more uses for automatic train and car reporting systems, much like those used by real railroads, that will tell a dispatcher where each train and even each car is located at any time. This would be a big help to a dispatcher on a large club layout. Such a train and car reporting system would leave the dispatcher, conductors, engineers, and other operators in full control of the railroad, and would add to the fun by providing more realistic operating conditions. You'd probably need a high-quality personal computer with disk storage and a printer or video display terminal to get started with such a system.

Yet another possibility is to connect a personal computer to a command control system like the Zero 1. You could use the throttles to run several trains and the Zero 1 accessory modules to control turnouts, signals, sound systems, and whatever else you can imagine.

If you're not ready for a full-fledged computer, try using microprocessor chips from toys to control lights, sounds, and other features on a section of your layout. Many toys now use the Texas Instruments TMS1000 chip (the one that's also used in the Zero 1) and this chip can control many operations.

Finally, speech synthesizers allow you to program automatic train announcements, just as Greyhound and AT&T do now. You could even program appropriate inspirational words to spur the operating crews to greater productivity!

Postscript

I'm sure that you will enjoy the usefulness and operating fun of at least some of this book's electronic projects. I've tried to present practical designs of the type most often requested by model railroaders and I feel that along with my earlier Kalmbach book — PRACTICAL ELECTRONIC PROJECTS FOR MODEL RAILROADERS — a wide field of electronic enhancements to model railroads is covered.

Electronics develops from month to month and you can stay in touch through MODEL RAILROADER magazine, which often features electronic construction articles. The future possibilities are unlimited in technical terms, though there are problems of physical size and cost. To take a "for instance" — it is now possible to take a fan trip around your HO or O scale railroad, viewing it from the vantage point of a locomotive cab window or caboose. The trip can be displayed on a TV or video terminal, recorded on video tape with sound effects added, and mailed, perhaps to a friend across the country (or maybe to your bank manager so he can view the reason for your overdraft!

There's another point to this example: It — and others like it — demand a high standard in structures and scenery, especially when they will be scanned by the camera from just inches away. But that's yet another challenge. And, it will be fun.

Peter Thorne

North York, Ontario
April 1990

Index of projects

A

Action grade crossing with
lights and sound, 36-40
Automatic reversing loop control, 44

B

Bell ringer module, 52
Bell sound generator, 52

C

Circuit for remote turnout operation, 31, 32
Constant-brightness lighting for locomotives with can motors, 28, 29
Constant-brightness lighting with a bridge rectifier, 28
Constant 5-volt power supply, 28, 29
Current-sensitive train detectors, 34, 35, 36-40

D

Deluxe pacematic throttle, 14, 18
Deluxe sound system, 48-49
Dual-output general-purpose flasher, 32, 33

G

Gyrating headlight, 29, 30, 31

H

Hand-held walkaround control for SCR throttle, 21-23, 24
High frequency cab control throttle and power supply, 67-70

I

Improved pacematic throttle, 14, 18
Improved transistor throttle with pulse generator, 12-14

L

LED direction indicators, 26, 27
Light-sensitive train detectors, 34, 35
LMD3909 LED flasher, 29, 30
Logic-output light-sensitive train detector, 56, 58

M

Miniature SCR throttle, 76, 77, 78
Modified Twin-T train detector for positive logic, 56, 58

O

One-LED three-color logic-controlled signal, 57, 58, 62

P

Programmed turnout control, 40, 41-43, 44
Pure-DC throttle for sound through rails, 52
Pure-DC throttle for use with a train-borne battery pack, 75-77

R

Radio-control interface for the SCR throttle, 24, 25, 26-27
Relay-operated three-color signal system, 55, 56

S

SCR throttle, 18-19, 20
Simple sequential switching, 55
Simple transistor throttle, 12, 13

T

Three-light logic-operated signal systems, 58, 59, 62
Train-borne radio-control throttle, 76, 77, 78